Officers in Flight Suits

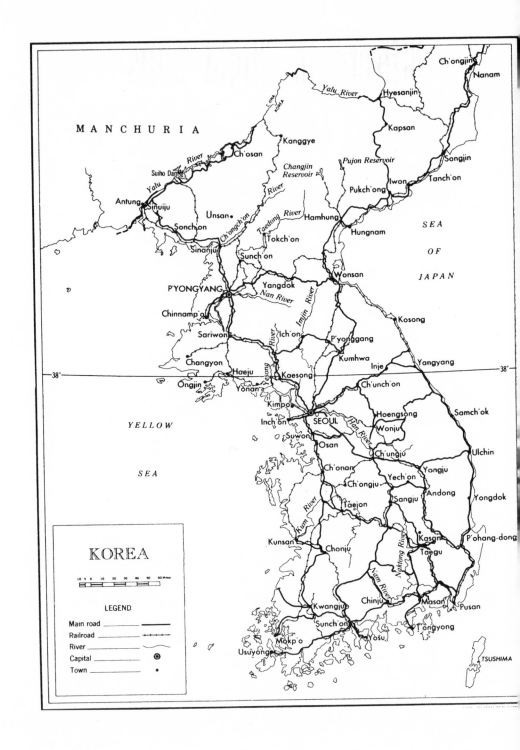

KOREA

LEGEND

Main road _____
Railroad _____
River _____
Capital _____ ◎
Town _____ •

·· Officers in ·· —

FLIGHT SUITS

The Story of American Air Force Fighter Pilots in the Korean War

John Darrell Sherwood

NEW YORK UNIVERSITY PRESS
New York and London

Library of Congress Cataloging-in-Publication Data
Sherwood, John Darrell, 1966–
Officers in flight suits : the story of American Air Force fighter
pilots in the Korean War / John Darrell Sherwood.
p.   cm.
Includes bibliographical references and index.
Contents: Introduction—An absence of ring-knockers : the social
background and education of flight suit officers—Stick and rudder
university : training and the creation of the flight suit officer—
MiG alley : air-to-air combat in Korea—Headhunters and fighting
cocks : the fighter-bomber in Korea—Thunderboxes and sabre
dancers : base life and recreation in the Korean War—Life after
Korea—Epilogue.
ISBN 0-8147-8038-5 (alk. paper)
1. Korean War, 1950–1953—Aerial operations, American.   2. Fighter
pilots—United States.   3. United States. Air Force—History.
4. Fighter planes—United States—History.   I. Title.
S920.2.U2S53   1996
951.904'2—dc20   96-10021
                    CIP

Manufactured in the United States of America

10 9 8 7 6 5 4 3 2 1

Contents

Photographs

The following photographs appear as a group after page 18:

The following photographs appear as a group after page 82:

Tables and Maps

Tables

Maps

Acknowledgments

During the Korean War, Air Force pilots received an air medal after every twenty-five combat missions flown, a Distinguished Flying Cross after a one hundred-mission war tour, and a Silver Star for heroism above and beyond the call of duty. During the course of the writing of this book, scores of individuals flew at least one combat mission in support of the campaign. Therefore, I will limit my acknowledgments to those who deserve an air medal or better for their efforts.

Special thanks to George Washington University (GWU) and the Center for Air Force History (CAFH) for research support.

The idea of a social history of Air Force pilots originated in James Horton's graduate seminar on social history at GWU. Among those who helped me fine-tune this project were William Becker, Edward McCord, and Richard Stott. Additionally, Cyndy Donnell and Michael Weeks graciously allowed me access to their computers on weekends for printing and editing purposes.

The research for this project was facilitated greatly by CAFH. During my year there as a visiting scholar, I received valuable advice from Vance Mitchell and Bernard Nalty. Special thanks to Eduard Mark and Vance Mitchell for allowing me to read and cite their unpublished manuscripts. For archival assistance, Walt Grudzinskas, Mark Ridley, and William Heimdahl were indispensable. Although heavily burdened by congressional and military requests for information, these staff members went out of their way to find obscure unit records, psychological reports, and base histories for me. They also allowed me to use their personal microfilm readers when the CAFH library readers were in use.

Other helpful archive staffs included those of the Suitland Reference Branch of the National Archives, and the Red Cross Archive in Washington, D.C. For photographs, thanks go to M. J. Bailey, Virginia Hagerstrom, and Jerry and Marty Minton.

As for libraries, the staff of the U.S. Army Library at the Pentagon allowed me to copy hundreds of pages of the *Air Force Times* for free, and Jacob Neufeld of CAFH sponsored me for a temporary Pentagon badge: a necessary prerequisite for admittance into that library. Additionally, the CAFH library and the Interlibrary Borrowing unit of GWU's Gelman Library deserve a fair share of kudos for tracking down a wide variety of dissertations, rare books, and Air Force-related fictional literature from the 1950s.

One of the highlights of this project was having the opportunity to interview actual flight suit officers. However, finding these gentlemen often proved very difficult. Fortunately, many pilot associations came to my aid. Special thanks to The Retired Officers Association and the Air Force Association for placing free advertisements in their respective magazines. Special thanks also to the Order of the Daedalions, the Mosquito Pilots Association, the F-86 Sabre Pilots Association, and the 58th Fighter Association for their assistance in tracking down Korean War pilots. Finally, a "Distinguished Flying Cross" should be awarded to every pilot who donated an afternoon or a morning to be interviewed. In particular, special thanks to M. J. Bailey, George Berke, Earl Brown, Hank Buttleman, Woodrow Crockett, Perrin Gower, James Hagerstrom, Howard Heiner, E. R. James, Kenneth Koon, Howard Leaf, Roy Lottinger, Jerry Minton, Robert Pomeroy, Robinson Risner, Curley Satterlee, Dewey Sturgeon, Frank Tomlinson, and Paul Turner.

Special recognition and a "Silver Star" are reserved for the people who freely donated substantial amounts of their time to this book. Yvonne Kinkaid, chief librarian of CAFH and the wife of an F-105 fighter pilot, obtained a beautiful office for me in which to conduct interviews, and she helped me find a host of documents. At the same time, she taught me many valuable lessons about Air Force etiquette and granted me access to her extensive military and government network for the sake of tracking down pilots. Without Ms. Kinkaid, my oral history project would never have gotten off the ground. Daniel Mortensen, a historian with the Air Staff History Office, and George Berke, a former F-84 pilot and English professor at the Air Force Academy, read through my entire manuscript and offered a wide range of suggestions. Dan

Mortensen and George Berke, in particular, helped boost my morale during the difficult writing stage of the book.

Shirley Turner, a technical editor at Sandia National Laboratory, provided technical editing support for this project. Ronald Spector read through several drafts and assisted me in every way imaginable. His guidance enabled me to strike a careful balance between new and traditional military history. Randy Papadopoulos, military history colleague and swimming partner, listened to my research and writing problems every day between laps and came up with some very useful suggestions to improve my work. Timothy Bartlett, on a reconnaissance mission to Washington from his base at New York University Press, discovered this manuscript thanks to a little forward air control from the chairman of the history department, Ed Berkowitz. Bartlett has been a tireless supporter ever since.

Thanks go to my parents for encouraging me at every step. Finally, a word of thanks to my friend, history colleague, and wingperson, Aimee Turner. Not only did she read and critique every word I wrote, she also steered me away from numerous flak traps and stuck with me—even when I decided to cross the Yalu.

1

Introduction

The Essential Factor

At 0600 on 10 October 1952, Major Robinson "Robbie" Risner, a fighter pilot stationed at Kimpo Air Field, South Korea, opened his eyes and surveyed his quarters. He noted the drafty windows, the ammunition crate furniture, and the pot-bellied stove. Excited about the day's flight, Risner jumped out of bed, snatched a flight suit, and headed out into the forty-degree air. A quick shower followed by a bland breakfast of powdered eggs, weak coffee, and cold toast was in order.[1]

After breakfast, Risner proceeded to the operations hut for the intelligence and weather briefings. The intelligence officer went over the standard escape and evasion routes. The men privately scoffed at the notion of escape and evasion: any American shot down over the Yalu River would inevitably end up in a POW camp.[2] Next, the weather officer reported clear skies over the Yalu. The pilots welcomed this good flying weather, so too did 4th Group leader Royal Baker—a fighter pilot as "thirsty for kills" as the young lieutenants he was briefing. On this particular day, Colonel Baker informed the men that the code word to turn off the identification-friend-or-foe signal (IFF) was "pussy willow." Without being explicit, Baker had just given the group tacit permission to disregard the standard rules of engagement, and cross the Yalu into China. It was MiG hunting time. Risner smiled. With the IFF disengaged, the American radar operators would not be able to spot him if he chased a MiG into China.

After the hour-long briefing, Risner followed the other pilots to the squadron operations room and put on his survival gear: a rubber suit, a "Mae West" inflatable life preserver, and a Colt-45 pistol. He had to keep reminding himself not to get too excited, too quickly. There was still much work to be done before he could strap on the F-86 and barrel down the runway. He needed to confer with the crew chief to make sure all was in order with plane number 824, "Robbie's Hobby." He also had to take a 360-degree inspection walk around the plane. During the inspection, he noted with pleasure the five red stars stenciled underneath the plane's name. Today Risner hoped to add a sixth.

At 0900 Risner and his wingman, Joe Logan, taxied down the Kimpo runway. The other two pilots followed in quick succession. This flight, code-named "John Red," made its way to the Yalu, some thirty minutes from Kimpo.[3] The flight's mission was to protect a squadron of USAF fighter-bombers that was scheduled to attack a chemical plant at the mouth of the river. When the flight arrived at "MiG Alley,"[4] Risner immediately gave the "pussy willow" command and took the flight on a sweep along the Chinese side of the Yalu. This preemptive maneuver would give the fighter-bombers maximum protection against any potential MiG attacks.

The initial sweep yielded no MiG sightings. On the second sweep, however, Risner saw a glint of sunlight at his twelve o'clock low. As if by instinct, he knew that this sparkle meant MiGs. He ordered his flight to drop their wing fuel tanks. The four MiGs did the same as they made a 180-degree turn and retreated back toward their base at Antung. These MiGs were hungry for the lower performance F-84 fighter-bombers, and had no intention of tangling with the top-of-the-line F-86s. But Risner had other plans. He aligned his pipper on the tail-end Charlie and gave his six M-3 .50 caliber guns a squeeze.[5] The incendiaries shattered the MiG's canopy.

In an effort to escape, the MiG pilot descended at maximum speed. At one point the MiG did a half-roll and flew upside down for fifty seconds as Risner pounded him with short bursts from his machine guns. The MiG then entered into a split-S,[6] and Risner thought to himself, "This is going to be the easiest kill of my career." Risner, convinced that the MiG would not be able to pull out of the S in time to avoid hitting the ground, made an angling split-S and braced himself for the impending explosion. Nothing happened.

The MiG did not crash as Risner had so smugly predicted. Instead, it pulled out of the dive just in time, creating a billowing cloud of dust and pebbles over a dry riverbed. The MiG, now flying five feet over the deck, was too low to hit with the F-86's guns, which fired slightly upward. But Risner had too much drive to cut off the chase. He was not about to let all those practice dogfights flown in the F-51 over the Oklahoma skies go to waste. Finally, he had met his match—a pilot who would force him to draw on every skill he had ever learned. Risner was about to embark on the ultimate dogfight.

At this point, Risner could not kill the MiG but at least he could take a good look at his foe. He maneuvered his F-86 alongside the MiG-15. As they coasted wingtip to wingtip, Risner peered into the now open cockpit. He could see the eyes of the pilot and the stitching of his leather helmet. Risner noticed that the pilot's oxygen mask was gone: it had been sucked off when he shot away the canopy. The MiG pilot returned Risner's gaze and raised his fist in defiance.[7]

The MiG then throttled back in an attempt to catch Risner off guard. He hoped to slip behind Risner and pound him with his 20- and 37-millimeter cannons. But Risner had too much situational awareness to fall for such a trap; he did a high G-force roll over the top of the MiG and came down behind it. Simultaneously, the MiG broke right, pulling all the G's it could. But Risner stayed behind the MiG. He later commented, "I never thought about what I was doing, it was all reflex."

After several minutes of hard maneuvers, both planes exited the dry riverbed and began to climb a heavily wooded hill. To Risner's surprise, the MiG executed one of the craziest maneuvers he had ever seen. In an effort to gain a small speed advantage, the MiG did an inverted roll and flew upside down over the hill. His open cockpit was just a few feet from the treetops. Risner's wingman, Joe Logan, who had been flying high and to the right the entire time, screamed into the headset: "Hit him lead. Pound him!"[8] But Risner could not. He was doing all he could just to stay behind him.

The planes rounded the hill at .8 Mach, then all of a sudden the MiG cut his throttle and Risner rolled over the top of him. Wingtip to wingtip now, the MiG pilot again raised his fist at Risner. Next, the MiG made an abrupt, full-throttle, 90-degree turn to the left. Risner knew that this was his last chance to blow this guy out of the sky. He let his pipper creep toward the MiG's tailpipe, and just as he was about to fire, Risner heard Logan's voice: "Lead, they're shooting at us." The two planes were now directly over the Chinese air base at Tak Tung Kau.

Despite this warning, Risner continued the chase: he was too close to let the MiG slip away. The MiG pilot erroneously assumed that the flak from the airfield would scare him off. It did not. Risner chased the MiG in between two hangars. When the MiG attempted to land on the dusty runway, Risner hammered him hard. He blew four feet off the left wing.

As the wing burned, the MiG pilot desperately sought out the grassy side of the runway for an emergency landing. Risner still had no intention of letting the plane land; he fired all of his remaining ammunition into its tailpipe. The MiG would not give up: it leveled off and attempted a "belly landing." At this point, his luck ran out. The MiG burst apart in a tremendous explosion, and pieces of flaming aircraft flew all over the airfield, igniting the parked aircraft nearby. "Red lead," Logan yelled ecstatically, "you just destroyed the whole Communist air force." Risner chuckled but he was more intent on getting his wingman and himself safely back to base than reveling in his victory. Risner and Logan threw the coal to their engines and made a steep climb away from the base.

As the F-86s climbed out, they passed over some 250 anti-aircraft guns which lined the perimeters of both Tak Tung Kau and Antung air bases. Flak exploded all around them as the pilots "jinked" to avoid it.[9] Just before Risner and Logan crossed the Yalu back into North Korea, Logan radioed Risner, "Lead, my fuel gauge is down." Risner flew around Logan's F-86 to make sure that the fuel tank had not been hit. It had. Fuel and hydraulic fluid were streaming out of Logan's belly. Risner radioed Logan, "It looks like you've been hit."

Fearing that his wingman would not have enough fuel and fluid to make it back to Kimpo, Risner decided on a bold course of action. He ordered Logan to open the throttle up: "Might as well use it before you lose it, Red 2." As soon as Logan ran out of fuel, Risner would position his nose behind Logan's stricken aircraft and gently push it periodically until they reached the friendly island of Chodo, where Logan could safely bail out.[10] Risner figured that enough air would be flowing through Logan's tailpipe and the gap below Risner's tailpipe to prevent Risner's F-86 from stalling, but the move was still risky. While executing this maneuver, Risner realized that he placed his own aircraft in danger. If he sucked in any damaged engine parts from Logan's plane, his own engine might quit, or worse yet, explode. To the pilots' utter amazement, the emergency maneuver worked.

Risner successfully pushed Logan's plane to a point ten miles off the coast of Chodo. At this point, Logan radioed Risner, "OK, I am going to bail out. I'll see you in a little while as soon as they pick me up." Risner watched Logan bail out and then turned and headed for home. For a while, Risner could hear the rescue operation unfolding on the emergency channel. The last thing he heard before he lost the signal was the rescue pilot saying, "He's in trouble, I am going to put a man in the water for him."

As Risner flew back to Kimpo, the adrenaline began to wear off and a warm feeling of satisfaction enveloped him. He had just fought the most challenging dogfight of his career and saved his wingman to boot. While on approach, Risner considered doing his customary low victory roll past the air traffic control tower but decided against it. After his thirty-five-mile jaunt into China, he did not have enough fuel. Risner just wanted to land, take a hot shower, and go over the mission with Logan at the officers' club when he arrived.

Two hours later, Risner went down to the runway to meet the SA-16 seaplane from Chodo. The doors opened and a rescued pilot emerged. It was not Logan. Joe Logan, former all-American swimmer, had drowned when his parachute cord became tangled around his neck. Risner went home and recited Psalm 23, then he went to bed.[11] The previous feelings of victory and triumph had vanished. Two days later, Major Robinson Risner shot down another MiG.

Flight Suit Attitude

In 1987, the Air Force Historical Foundation sought to identify twelve officers who helped mold the institutional culture of the United States Air Force. Predictably, most of the men in the resulting study, "The Makers of the United States Air Force," were chosen for their role in shaping Air Force strategy and transforming the service from a small branch of the Army to a fully independent air arm. One officer, however, was picked not based on his bureaucratic achievements, but because of his warrior spirit; that man was Brigadier General Robbie Risner. According to the study's editors, he reawakened a "keener appreciation of our fundamental purpose as a service." That purpose is to fly and fight.[12] By choosing Risner, the Air Force Historical Foundation held this pilot up as a model for others to emulate.

In this book, the warrior spirit of fighter pilots like Risner will be defined as "flight suit attitude." Risner had that "indispensable ingredient" which enabled him to take risks others would not dream of taking.[13] James Hagerstrom, a fellow ace from the Korean War, put it in simpler terms: "Robbie Risner had *it!*"

Flight suit attitude, in its basic form, was a sense of self-confidence and pride that verged on arrogance. For a flight suit officer, the aircraft of preference was the high-performance, single-seat fighter, although one could find him in almost any model. This culture placed a premium on cockiness and informality. A flight suit officer spent more time in a flight suit than in a uniform. In his world, status was based upon flying ability, not degrees, rank, or "officer" skills. This world, not surprisingly, was overwhelmingly male.

When flight suit officers did associate with women, the women generally fell into two categories: officers' wives and bar-room sluts.[14] A flight suit officer was more comfortable flying at close to Mach 1 with the guys than he was at a formal dinner sponsored by the Air Force Officers' Wives Association. In short, he yearned for a completely operational environment devoid of wives, where women entered the picture only as prostitutes.

During the 1950s, a critical mass of flight suit officers could be found in Korea fighting the air war. This book will examine these men and their conquests, both in the skies and in the "hotsy" baths outside of Tokyo. It also will explore the entire context of the flight suit officer's life in an attempt to unearth the origins and meaning of flight suit attitude. Questions which will be considered are as follows:

- From what social backgrounds did flight suit officers come? How did their education and economic status contribute to their development as pilots? Did pilots with college or military academy degrees perform better than those who entered into pilot training with only two years of college?
- How did aviation training help to transform them into flight suit officers? To what degree did they enter the air service with flight suit attitude, and how much of it was instilled in them by their flight instructors and classmates in training?
- What was the relationship between flight suit culture and combat effectiveness? Did the culture produce superior fighter-interceptor pilots? What about fighter-bomber pilots? How did flight suit officers perform as wartime leaders?
- How did their off-duty activities effect their mission performance? Did flight suit culture tend to produce antisocial and misogynist officers, or were the off-hours antics of these pilots a harmless way for them to escape from the pressures of war and flying?

The study concludes with a brief survey of the post-Korean War careers of the principal pilots highlighted in the earlier chapters of the book, and explores how their flight suit experiences in Korea influenced their later military and civilian careers.

Why Korea?

Korea was chosen as the centerpiece of this study for several reasons. First, I was anxious to fill a significant gap in the historiography of American air power. Robert Futrell and Richard Hallion have each written very thorough operational histories of Air Force and Navy aviation during the Korean War;[15] however, there are no social or cultural histories of the air war similar to Ronald Schaffer's or Michael Sherry's works on strategic bombing in World War II.[16] Despite the limited literature on the topic, the air war in Korea remains a very significant chapter in the history of American air power. During the conflict, the Soviet Union challenged American air supremacy with its most advanced fighter of the time—the MiG-15. In battles over MiG Alley, American fighter pilots would defeat the "MiG menace" in some of the most celebrated aerial battles of the Cold War. In addition to the MiG battles, the U.S. Air Force burned down virtually every major town and city in North Korea, demolished its entire crop irrigation system, and killed close to one million civilians.[17] In the words of Korean War historian Bruce Cumings, it was "one of the most appalling, unrestrained, genocidal air campaigns in our genocidal twentieth century."[18] Yet, the story of the men who participated in these campaigns is largely untold.

In addition to elucidating historiographical concerns, Korea, in many respects, is a perfect laboratory in which to study the flight suit attitude of fighter pilots. While a certain pilot cockiness has existed since the dawn of flight, it became institutionalized in Korea. Korea was the first war where the Air Force fought as a truly independent service. Pilots, for the first time, could cultivate a flight suit attitude free from the Army's "Prussian" bureaucracy and legal system. Not surprisingly, many Air Force types fondly refer to 1947 as the year of "emancipation."[19]

More significantly, Korea was a fighter pilot's war in a way that World War II was not. Unlike the Second World War, where the efforts of fighter pilots were often eclipsed by the massive, strategic bombing raids of the Eighth and Twentieth Air Forces, fighter pilots in Korea commanded center stage. Not only was strategic bombing severely limited (it was only employed at the very beginning and end of the Korean War), but fighters proved less vulnerable than bombers to enemy groundfire and MiG attacks. As a result, fighters were used for every type of mission imaginable: they formed the key component in the Far Eastern Air Forces' air order of battle. In June 1952, for example, the Far East Air Force possessed 507 fighter aircraft, compared to only 197 multiengine bombers.[20] As George Berke, a Korean War pilot, put it, "The fighter was what the Air Force really did the job with."

A Note on Sources

As anyone who has worked in the field of air power history will confirm, the Air Force is very guarded with its records: thousands of cubic feet of documents from the Korean War are still marked "Top Secret," "Secret," or "For Official Use Only." One can't help but wonder if these documents contain information vital to the national security of the nation or if the Air Force simply wants to control access to its history. Consequently, my creative abilities became a significant factor in this endeavor to write a social history of fighter pilots.[21] To fill the gap in sources, I relied heavily on memoirs, diaries, unit records, letters, and personal papers. I also came across two novels about the war which were of particular value: *The Hunters* (New York: Harper, 1956) by James Salter (originally known as James Horowitz), and *Troubling of a Star* (New York: Lippincott, 1952) by Walt Sheldon. *The Hunters*, based on Salter's own experience as a fighter pilot with the 4th Fighter Interceptor Wing, is, in essence, a primary source on air-to-air combat: Salter graduated from West Point, spent twelve years in the Air Force as a fighter pilot, and earned one MiG kill in Korea.[22] Similarly, Sheldon's book on fighter-bomber pilots is based on his extensive experience as an Army Air Force captain in World War II, and as an Air Force combat correspondent in Korea. During Korea, Sheldon flew twenty-five combat missions in various aircraft and received an Air Force Air Medal for his service.[23]

Far and away my best sources of information on the war, however, were the actual living participants. These men could convey emotions and attitudes not found in the bureaucratic language of official sources. They also responded immediately to almost every question I bombarded them with. Overall, approximately fifty flight suit officers granted me interviews, but I chose to focus mainly on eleven central figures whose experiences were representative of the group. Some of the interviews took place at Bolling Air Force Base in Washington, D.C., but many were held in the homes of the pilots. It was not unusual for a pilot to spread out an old flight map on his coffee table and show me the exact flight path of a former mission. As I sat down to write the manuscript, I would often telephone the central characters of the story to clarify a point or gather additional information. In essence, they functioned as living archives.

An Absence of Ring-Knockers:
The Social Background
and Education of
Flight Suit Officers

At the onset of the Korean War, the Air Force was only three years old. As a result, its social composition resembled that of the U.S. Army, the service from which it had recently detached itself. Like the Army officer corps, the Air Force officers came from a predominantly white, Protestant, rural background. The Air Force officer corps, however, differed from the ground service in one important aspect: education.

Unlike his peers in the Army and Navy, the average Air Force officer in the 1950s did not possess a four-year college degree. While 75.4 percent of the Navy's regular officers and 62.8 percent of the Army's had baccalaureate degrees in 1948, the Air Force could claim only 37.05 percent, a figure well above the 13 percent national educational average for men over the age of twenty-five at the time, but devastating to a new service working to establish an "elite" image during a period of intense interservice rivalry.[1] In all, between July 1946 and December 1947, 77 percent of the 14,000 regular commissions handed out went to officers without a four-year degree.[2]

This educational deficit was partly the result of a rapid expansion of the Air Force between 1940 and 1947. During this period, its officer corps grew from 10,000 to 40,000.[3] The Air Force pilot training system, though, is also partly to blame. Its Aviation Cadet program, the largest Air Force commissioning vehicle (about 2,000 annually in 1948 and 1949), washed out an average of 50 percent of its cadets; therefore, educational levels had to be kept very low in order to ensure an adequate flow of pilots.[4] When the Aviation Cadet program reopened after a postwar hiatus in 1947, a cadet had to pass only a two-year college equivalency test and a physical to be admitted. Eventually, in 1949, two years of college became mandatory; nevertheless, educational levels remained low: only 2 percent of the program's graduates in 1948 and 1949 had a four-year college degree.[5]

In addition to having fewer college-educated officers, the Air Force also had fewer service academy graduates. Sociologist Morris Janowitz, in his landmark study of military officers during this period, found that only 48 percent of the Air Force generals in 1950 were military academy graduates, compared to 97 percent of the admirals.[6] The Army had a similar percentage of academy graduates in its flag officer grades as the Air Force in 1950, but the percentage of academy graduates in company and field grades was significantly greater. Between 1947 (the year the Air Force became an independent service) and 1955 (the year the Air Force Academy was founded), only 28.8 percent of West Point graduates and fewer than 7 percent of Annapolis graduates opted to accept Air Force commissions.[7]

Culturally, the Air Force's dearth of academy graduates had profound implications. Military academies, above all else, serve as indoctrination centers for officers: they are the wellspring of shared values and traditions. As Janowitz states, they "set the standards for behavior for the whole military profession" and are a "pervasive source of like-mindedness" and conformity.[8] The hazing, the endless routines, and the core curriculum of the academy create direct links among graduates, links which in turn are continually strengthened throughout an officer's career. The best description of this process can be found in the introduction to Stephen Ambrose's laudatory history of West Point, *Duty, Honor, Country:*

The long gray line goes by constantly. The cadet sees the veterans who have gone before him and the new plebes who will follow. He realizes that the whole is greater than its parts, that it embodies both past traditions and new wars, and he sees what it takes to be a soldier. Academy graduates continually renew their contacts with the school; they often marry in the chapel, serve on the faculty as instructors or tactical officers, attend class reunions, and finally are buried in the cemetery. The constant funerals of the old graduates, with the flag over Trophy Point at half-mast, help the cadet visualize the long gray line. When a graduate of 1925 meets a graduate of 1955 in some Far Eastern outpost, the discussion can center around the same curriculum, subject material, traditions, and often teachers. The two graduates probably share the same feelings about their alma mater, and even some of the slang they use may be identical.[9]

In some cases, such indoctrination merely creates a strong fraternal bond and sense of shared mission among fellow academy graduates. In others, though, it instills a sense of intellectual and moral superiority that can influence decision-making and create caste-like barriers to promotion within a service. The influence of a West Point degree in the Army, for example, is epitomized by a practice called "ring knocking." Ring knockers tap their class rings on furniture to subtly identify themselves as academy graduates. They often assume that such a display of status will guarantee them favorable treatment.

The Air Force did not yet have a "long gray line" in the 1950s. One did not need a West Point or even a college degree to gain promotions in the Air Force. If an officer could fly well and was fortunate enough to see combat in Korea, there was no limit to how far he could rise. Although this situation would change once the Air Force established its own military academy in 1955, during the Korean War the major requirement for high rank was a set of silver wings and a flight suit. Not surprisingly, this service became a haven for middle- and working-class youth anxious to start a military career but too poor to pay for four years of college, and unprepared to meet the service academies' admissions requirements. In a survey of 115 Air Force generals and colonels from the 1950s period, sociologist Irving Casey discovered that 13.5 percent of the generals and 35 percent of the colonels came from blue-collar backgrounds.[10] By comparison, a similar survey of the Army and

Navy by Morris Janowitz found that only 5 percent of its leadership in 1950 came from a working-class background.[11]

A few representative biographies of Korean War fighter pilots follow. These bios will reveal a group of relatively shy individualists who, for the most part, came from middle- and working-class backgrounds. As children, these men were captivated by the image of the pilot as seen in films such as *Dawn Patrol* with Errol Flynn, or in World War II news reels about fighter pilots. As young adults, they joined the Air Force because they could not afford college and wanted to avoid being drafted as enlisted men. In short, they joined because they wanted to transform obligatory military service into a glamorous adventure.

Robinson Risner

Born on 16 January 1925, Robinson Risner[12] grew up in the geographic heart of the rural depression of the 1930s: Tulsa, Oklahoma. His father struggled to provide for a family of ten children by working first as a sharecropper, then as a day laborer with the Works Progress Administration.

To mitigate the hard effects of rural poverty, Robbie worked during most of his childhood. He started out as a newspaper delivery boy, then ran errands for the local drugstore, and finally ended up as a soda jerk. Risner also spent a great deal of his time with a youth group run by the Assemblies of God. This experience inculcated him with a strong belief in God and helped him get over his youthful shyness and insecurity. Sports were also a refuge for Robbie: he wrestled both in junior high and high school. His favorite activities, however, were horses, motorcycles, and airplanes. He bought a motorcycle during his senior year of high school, and began flying light aircraft soon after his graduation in 1942. Flying became such an addiction that when he turned eighteen in 1943, he decided to enlist in the Army Air Forces (AAF). This was a period when the AAF was admitting pilots without college degrees. All Risner had to do to be accepted into the Aviation Cadets program was pass a two-year college equivalency test and a physical.

Risner desperately wanted to fly fighters in World War II, but was instead assigned to Panama.[13] Initially, he flew P-40s and P-39s out of a small jungle airstrip at Aguadulce, near the Colombian border. For Risner, the 30th Fighter Squadron at Aguadulce was the epitome of a flight suit outfit. The pilots lived in tarpaper shacks, flew every day, and had very few other duties. This lack of responsibility combined with loose supervision allowed nineteen-year-old pilots like Risner to go completely wild. "We never passed a sailboat or a kayak or anything without turning it over," recalled Risner. "We also tangled fishing nets and blew roofs off of village huts." When his outfit transferred to Howard Air Base, they broke all of the glasses in the officers' club during their first month there, and were barred from the club for the remainder of their tours.

When Risner was not flying, he was driving his motorcycle at breakneck speeds on the narrow dirt roads of Panama. One day, a friend insisted on driving Risner to town on the bike himself. As luck would have it, this friend drove the motorcycle like it was a P-40. On a steep mountain turn, he decided to pass a bus and ended up laying the bike down in the process. Risner was thrown stomach first on the ground and shattered his wrist; his friend did not suffer even a scratch. This story, however, had a happy ending. At the hospital, Risner met his future wife: "A cute, blonde Army nurse named Kathleen Shaw from Ware Shoals, South Carolina." Female companionship, though, did not slow this young flight suit officer down a bit. Instead, Kathleen became his sidekick, and the two lovers spent their off-hours flying DDT spraying missions or riding through the countryside on Risner's motorcycle. Upon completion of their tours, a friend of Risner's who was a general's aide arranged for Kathleen and Robbie to travel home on the same troopship. Risner claimed that "lying on the deck under the moonlight with the breeze blowing across our bodies did it."[14] The two lovers became engaged on ship and were married in September 1946, after both were discharged.

Following Panama, Risner spent the next five years working at a variety of dead-end civilian jobs. Initially, he went to trade school to learn how to be a front-end alignment mechanic. He then tried running a gas station for a year, and finally ended up running a four-story parking and service garage. Fulfillment did not come from work: it came from flying P-51s on the weekends and during vacations with the Oklahoma Air National Guard. The highlight of Risner's Guard career was an unauthorized flight made to Brownsville, Texas, to pick up shrimp for the annual "Wing Ding" party. Risner, who lacked experience flying with instruments, got lost in heavy overcast and was forced to make an emergency landing on a dry lake bed in Mexico. He ended up spending the night in his cockpit while a hurricane bombarded the Mexican coast, and if that was not enough, a bull nearly gored him the next day. When he finally reached the comparative safety of Tampico, local banditos attempted to rob him. Through it all, Risner maintained a high degree of humor, even when the U.S. Embassy berated him for flying an armed fighter in Mexico and warned him to "keep a low profile."

When he returned to the states, Risner continued to train hard with the Air Guard until 1950, when the Korean War broke out. After learning that his Guard unit would not be sent over, he volunteered for service with the 118th Tactical Reconnaissance Squadron. To meet the jet time requirements for this position, Risner flew every day for the next twenty-five days in F-80 Shooting Stars.

On Risner's last day in Oklahoma, his family got together for a farewell picnic at the family farm. During the reunion, his brother brought out a beautiful, unbroken mare and challenged Risner to ride it. Although his father pleaded with him not to get on the horse, Risner's stubborn flight suit nature kept him from backing down. He got on the horse and took one of the worst spills in his equestrian career, breaking his hand and wrist. But this was hardly going to stop Risner from fulfilling his dream of seeing aerial combat in the skies over Korea. At his point of embarkation in San Francisco, Risner threw a raincoat over his cast and walked right onto the transport. Once in Korea, though, he had to pass a physical before he could be flight certified. According to Risner, he told the doctor that the cast had been on for months and convinced him to replace it with a leather cover even though the bones had not even begun to heal. The next day, Risner slipped his wrist out of its sling, put on a flight suit, and flew his first combat mission of the war.

Earl Brown

Earl Brown's[15] life could have easily taken a very different turn if it had not been for the generosity of his uncle and aunt. Earl, actually William Earl, was born in the Bronx on 5 December 1927 at Lincoln Hospital, but soon after his birth his natural parents split up and his mother moved to South Carolina. Rather than have Earl live with his mother in the South, Earl's uncle, a letter carrier from Englewood, New Jersey, and his aunt, a housekeeper, offered to take him in. His natural father also chose to live in the same town, where he worked as a chauffeur and later as the manager of a small sewing factory.

Englewood was a middle-class bedroom community of New York City, complete with tree-lined streets, parks, and two-story brick houses. Although his ward, the 4th, was primarily black, as was Earl's family, Earl's house was located on a racially integrated block and had a two-car garage. The people in his neighborhood ranged from professionals to tradesmen, but all considered themselves to be middle class.

What was remarkable about Earl's childhood was its stability. His uncle had a secure civil servant position during a period of great economic uncertainty. Earl could walk to school, to the park, to town, or to church. His doctor, the only black physician in town, lived across the street, and the community house, where he attended scout meetings, was only a block away. In short, his entire childhood world was self-contained and ordered. On weekdays, Earl attended school and played in the local park; on Sundays, he went to church. To earn money, Earl helped his aunt clean houses—a job which gave him the opportunity to borrow books from the personal libraries of the town's wealthy citizens. Earl also delivered two major black weeklies: *The Amsterdam News* and *The African American*. During World War II, these papers contained many stories on blacks in the military, especially Benjamin Davis, Jr., and the Tuskegee airmen. "Their training at Tuskegee, their missions oversees, and their individual stories," Earl recalls, "provided me with a whole series of role models who were doing something that I never dreamed a black man would be allowed to do." Another man who inspired Earl was Charles Lindbergh. Lindbergh married a young girl from Englewood named Anne Morrow; he also parked his airplane at nearby Teterboro Airport before his nonstop flight to Mexico City in 1927.

During high school, Earl became a star pole-vaulter and even set a number of state records. This experience placed him in the athletic clique, and also made him eligible for college athletic scholarships. Although his uncle graduated from the prestigious Hampton college, a black institution, an alumnus of Penn State who had seen Brown on the track team convinced him to go to Penn State instead. Thus, Earl would continue to remain in an integrated, middle-class environment.

At Penn State, Earl took pre-med courses because his natural father wanted him to be a doctor. Unfortunately, he did not do well in chemistry and theoretical physics; consequently, when he applied to medical schools in 1949 he was rejected across the board. Brown blames his poor academic performance on an overextended college schedule. In addition to spending four years on the track team, Brown worked as a maintenance person in fraternity houses and was a member of the Penn State ROTC unit for two years.

Track participation was a condition of his athletic scholarship; two years of ROTC was a university requirement; and work was necessary to supplement his income and pay for his room and board. Brown, in short, was very active in college, but primarily for financial reasons. In fact, his only activity which did not fulfill some requirement was his membership in the all-black fraternity, Omega Si Phi. But he was too busy to enjoy fraternity life and, moreover, "never considered himself to be a joiner or a fraternity type of guy."

Considering that Brown eventually rose to the rank of three-star general in the Air Force, it is somewhat ironic that he did not continue his ROTC training. He was turned away from a military career early on by a former B-17 pilot in his boardinghouse named Smitty. Smitty had witnessed the high loss rates of the Eighth Air Force in Europe and had become very anti-military as a result. At the boardinghouse he advised all the young students to "stay away from the ROTC!" Brown heeded this advice, and in the end, it cost him two years in grade.

Rather than flying airplanes after college, Brown ended up driving an

While training demanded that aviation cadets wear clean, pressed uniforms, pilots, once in the field, would quickly jettison this regulation look. (Courtesy United States Air Force)

A chorus line on the flight line? These aviation cadets walk hand in hand down the flight line of Hondo Air Force Base, Texas, in 1952. Training initiated young pilots into the brotherhood of the flight suit. (Courtesy Far East Air Forces)

Four Headhunters of the 80th Fighter-Bomber Squadron eat their powdered eggs before another mission up north. The tension of the moment is evident in the expressions on the pilots' faces and the lack of conversation at the table. (Courtesy Far East Air Forces)

Flight leader Captain John S. Stoer briefs an F-94 crew prior to an alert mission, August 1953. Note the laid-back atmosphere of this briefing room: wicker easy chairs and feet on the table. (Courtesy Far East Air Forces)

With the briefing over and the equipment checked and ready for takeoff, these pilots read while on standby alert. Note the baseball cap worn by the pilot on the left. These hats were an important part of unit pride and flight suit élan: each squadron in Korea had its own baseball caps custom made in Japan. (Courtesy Far East Air Forces)

With the eerie confidence that comes from having flown thirty-one fighter-bomber missions, Lieutenant Louis A. Dupont, an F-84 pilot with the 27th Wing, calmly eats a carton of ice cream as a he waits for "start engine time." (Courtesy Far East Air Forces)

Four flight suit officers of the 4th Fighter-Interceptor Wing walk back to their alert shack after pulling a two-minute alert on the flight pad at Kimpo field, December 1953. From left to right: Second Lieutenant Charles L. Jones, First Lieutenant Ken Soloman, Second Lieutenant D. N. Mooney, and Second Lieutenant Don Harryman. (Courtesy Far East Air Forces)

A formation of checker-tail F-86 Sabre jets from the 51st Fighter-Interceptor Wing turn over MiG Alley, October 1952. The F-86 was the Air Force's top-of-the-line fighter-interceptor during the Korean War. Although its chief rival, the MiG-15, could out-accelerate, out-climb, and out-zoom the F-86 at any altitude and enjoyed an estimated minimum 5,000-foot top ceiling advantage, the Sabre pilots generally defeated their Communist counterparts over the skies of MiG Alley. This was mainly due to superior pilot training and skills; however, certain technological advantages also contributed to the plane's legendary success. Although clearly slower, the Sabre could out-turn the MiG in level or diving turns below 30,000 feet, and could out-dive it in sustained dives. The Sabre also had a more sophisticated, radar-ranging gun sight, heavy armor plate, bulletproof glass, and adequate cockpit pressurization and temperature controls. It was truly the Cadillac of fighter aircraft during the Korean War. (Courtesy Far East Air Forces)

FACING PAGE: *Air Force F-84 Thunderjets of the 447th Fighter-Bomber Wing set out on a bombing run against targets in North Korea. The Republic F-84 was the Air Force's workhorse fighter-bomber. Although much too slow to challenge the MiG-15, it developed the reputation of being the best ground-support fighter in the theater. By the end of the war, a total of 335 of these aircraft were lost, and more than 50 percent of these losses were due to ground fire. (Courtesy Far East Air Forces)*

Pictured here is a MiG-15 which was flown to Kimpo Air Force outside of Seoul on 21 September 1953 by a North Korean defector. Air Force markings were painted on the plane so it could be safely flown to Japan. (Courtesy Far East Air Force)

Suspected troop concentration point or innocent civilian village? The fire at the top of this picture reveals the destructive power of napalm. These bombs, made from jellied gasoline, were a staple weapon in the air war against North Korea. January 1951. (Courtesy Far East Air Forces)

An Air Force H-19 helicopter of the 3rd Air Rescue Group is seen hoisting this unidentified airman from Far East waters. This airman was lucky. Pilots who bailed out over the North Korean peninsula were generally captured. (Courtesy Far East Air Forces)

Lieutenant Donald P. Streich inspects a basketball-size hole blown in the wing of his F-80 Shooting Star during a Fifth Air Force close air support mission in March 1951. Note Lieutenant Streich's "Mae West"-style life jacket, his large survival knife, and flight suit hairstyle—long, unwashed, and uncombed. (Courtesy Far East Air Forces)

Pilot James Hagerstrom's 100th mission photograph. (Courtesy Virginia Hagerstrom)

Pilot M. J. Bailey stands in front of his F-80, Pat's Pot. The name refers to his wife Pat, who was pregnant when he left for Korea. (Courtesy Jim Bailey)

ambulance for Harlem Hospital on the graveyard shift—a tough job which involved wearing a white suit and picking up diabetics, drunks, and the homeless at all hours of the night. His plan was to drive an ambulance until he could get into medical school. "Instead, the Korean War broke out that summer," recalls Brown, "and I applied for the Aviation Cadet program to avoid the draft." The Air Force, in short, was not part of his original career plans. Brown was not atypical. Only one pilot in the study intended to make the Air Force a career from the very start, and he was a West Pointer.

Woodrow Crockett

While Earl Brown enjoyed a comfortable, middle-class childhood, Woodrow (Woody) Crockett's[16] vacillated between lower middle class and poor. Crockett spent his early childhood in the impoverished share-cropper community of Homan, Arkansas, about eight miles from Texarkana, and thirty-five miles from Hope. Later on in high school he would travel to Little Rock, but through it all, his exposure to rural, black poverty at a formative age would leave an indelible impression. Woody knew that he had to succeed at all costs to avoid a life as a plantation laborer.

Fortunately, Crockett had a mother who was just as devoted to his success as he was. She ran a two-room elementary school for black children and taught the first through fourth grades. Because most other professional occupations were denied to African Americans, teaching, like postal work, was a very prestigious profession for blacks in the early twentieth century. (It is interesting that the mother of Chappie James, the first four-star black general in the Air Force, also ran a school for black children.) Not surprisingly, Crockett's mother was a pillar of her community. Besides teaching, she also attended teacher training sessions at Pine Bluff on weekends, taught Sunday school, and ran a molasses mill to supplement the family income. Many years later at the age of sixty, she received her B.A. from Texas College. She died one year later.

If his mother provided the positive incentives for Woody to succeed, his physical surroundings left much to be desired. Crockett, the fifth child in a six-child family, grew up in a three-room house which consisted of a kitchen, two bedrooms, and a hallway in between. Except for a small wood stove, this house had no amenities—no central heating, no telephone, no insulation, no bathroom, no plumbing, and no electricity. Woody shared a bed with two older brothers and was forced to sleep in the middle. To get to school, he relied on a horse-drawn buggy. Woody's material conditions, though, were far superior to the average sharecroppers, who lived in true shacks.

Because opportunities in Homan were so bleak for African Americans, Crockett's parents decided to send him to a new black high school in Little Rock called Paul Lawrence Dunbar High. Fortunately for Woody, his basic living expenses while in Little Rock would be provided for by his sister, a nurse at the county hospital who earned an income of sixty dollars a month. However, soon after he started school, his sister was laid off, and things became very difficult. Woody and his sister moved into a $1.23-a-week boardinghouse and were forced to starve themselves in order to meet the rent payments. "I remember only having ten cents a day for dinner," recalls Woody, "and so we bought five cents' worth of pork and five cents' worth of beans and that was dinner day after day after day." Although beans, pork, and corn bread curbed his hunger during these lean years, clothing needs became a more difficult problem to solve. After he got down to one pair of trousers, Crockett was so ashamed that he couldn't face his classmates, and began to avoid school—a difficult crisis for this straight-A student.

Life improved somewhat for Woody toward the end of high school when his sister got a job as a housekeeper for the Webster family. Mr. Webster was an engineer for the Rock Island Railroad, and he paid Crockett's sister a small salary of five dollars a month and allowed her and Woody to live in a one-room apartment over the garage. Woody cut grass in the neighborhood for twenty-five cents a lawn and performed other housekeeping duties. He also worked as a mess attendant for the National Guard at Fort Robinson. "Manual labor and plantation life," claims Woody, "were prime motivators to work hard in school."

Woody worked so hard that his sister agreed to pay for part of his college education. Because Dunbar High had a junior college, Crockett stayed there and taught integral calculus to help defray his college costs: his goal was "to become a Ph.D. in math at age twenty-five." However, he felt guilty about "taking money from his sister," and so he worked twelve-hour days as a dishwasher at a local cafe in a desperate attempt to pay for college. When this attempt failed, Crockett looked to the U.S. Army as an economic solution: "My plan was to save money for three years and come back and finish my education, but the Pearl Harbor attack occurred during that period and I never could get back."

Crockett, on 18 August 1940, was assigned to the 349th Field Artillery Regiment at Fort Sill, Oklahoma. The 349th was the first black field artillery regiment in the regular Army. It was activated two days before Crockett arrived, and was equipped with the twenty-four-model 1918 French 155-millimeter guns, one of the largest single-load guns in the army inventory at the time. These guns weighed more than 28,000 pounds and could fire a ninety-five-pound shell 18,000 yards. A ten-ton International Harvester tractor was procured to move these massive weapons.[17] Needless to say, an assignment to this elite unit was prestigious, and Crockett excelled as a soldier. His math skills and personal discipline helped him rise quickly to the rank of sergeant by October 1941, and also earned him the Model Soldier of the Regiment award in 1942. His commander, Lieutenant Colonel Charles Boyle, wrote the following about Crockett in his commendation order: "This Model Soldier has high technical skill and has exhibited soldierly qualities of leadership, loyalty and initiative. Sergeant Crockett has no disciplinary action against him and has lost no time under the 107th Article of War. His service and character set a standard for men of this regiment to attain."[18] With this award, Crockett also received a recommendation to attend Officers' Candidate School (OCS). Crockett would have entered the standard Army OCS if it had not been for an Army Air Forces poster in his orderly room that encouraged men to join the AAF pilot corps and earn $245 a month. That captured Crockett's attention because second lieutenants in the regular army were earning only $125, and privates, $21. "If you had to be in the service," figured Crockett, "why not go for the best and most exciting job." Crockett, like Brown, was not motivated to join the Air Force for a career; it was simply the best option available for someone anxious to fulfill his military obligation in a prestigious manner and earn money for school in the process.

Frank Tomlinson

As emphasized earlier, the young Air Force, on balance, was not officered by men from elite backgrounds. However, there were exceptions, and Frank Tomlinson[19] was one of them. Not only did he come from a long line of Southern plantation owners, but his family were Episcopalians and he could point to relatives who had fought in every major American war. Ironically, despite this background, Tomlinson joined the Air Force for the same basic reasons as Crockett and Brown—to avoid the draft and fulfill his military obligation under the best of circumstances.

Tomlinson was born in Pine Bluff, Arkansas, in 1929. His father was a civil engineer-turned cotton broker, and his mother was an active member of Arkansas society. The Tomlinson family could trace its roots back to 1620, when the first Tomlinson came over as an indentured servant. John Knox, George Washington's chief of artillery, was a distant relative, and Tomlinson's great-grandfather Jenkins was a cavalry commander in the Texas cavalry under General John Hood, the Confederate general who unsuccessfully defended Atlanta against Sherman's assaults. After the Civil War, Tomlinson's family managed to hold onto its position as part of the Arkansas elite by retaining three plantations. Tomlinson's aunt even designed the Arkansas state seal.

However, with the Great Depression, the Tomlinsons' social standing began to decline. The family lost two of its plantations, and Frank's father lost his job as a civil engineer. While the senior Tomlinson was "devastated over having to become a mere mortal," the Depression did not bother the son too much. The family still managed to live in a big house with forty acres and two black sharecropper families. Food was never a problem because much of it was grown or hunted on the family land. "Frankly, life was kind of fun," he recalled, "I spent a lot of time in the woods, hunting and fishing, and sort of grew up by myself."

In high school, Tomlinson kept to himself and quietly pursued his studies; at home, most of the family attention focused on his sister, a debutante who was "the darling of society" in Pine Bluff. Because she had the biggest house in town, Tomlinson's mother hosted weekly parties for debutantes and Aviation Cadets from nearby Greenville Field. A cadet (later a B-29 pilot) named Les Helmes eventually married Frank's sister; however, according to Frank, he had "no influence whatsoever" on his decision to join the Air Force.

Upon graduation, Tomlinson's mother wanted him to pursue a banking career and make money; obediently, Tomlinson became a finance major at the University of Oklahoma in 1947. Oklahoma was cheap (about three hundred dollars a semester total) and had a good football team. "I also got the heck away from my mother and the society that I didn't feel a great part of anyway," recalled Tomlinson. "It was a good choice. I enjoyed it."

Unfortunately for Tomlinson, college life was cut short after two years due to a lack of money, and Frank left school to work as a bank clerk in Pine Bluff. A year later in 1950, Tomlinson discovered he was number one on the local draft. He quickly applied to the Aviation Cadets. Not only did the Air Force solve his draft problem, but it also got him "the heck out of Arkansas." It enabled him to leave a dead-end job and domineering mother for an opportunity to fly one of the fastest fighter aircraft of the period—the F-86 Sabre.

He took all the tests in July 1950, was accepted, and then was told by the local recruiter to go home and wait for orders. Frank waited and waited until his deferment ended around January 1951. He then returned to the recruiter who told him the following: "Well, we can't find your paperwork, we know they're going to draft you, and so we'll send you to become an enlisted man, and then we'll find your paperwork." And that is how Tomlinson entered the eight-week basic training course at Lackland Air Force Base in San Antonio, Texas.

At Lackland as a one-striper, Tomlinson dreamed of one day making buck sergeant. To him, it was all a "grand adventure." It was the first time he had ever been on a train, seen tall buildings, and watched television. 40,000 men lived at Lackland, some in tents, and most had signed up with the Air Force to avoid the draft. Tomlinson remembered the routine as follows:

> Initially, everybody got up at five in the morning, and you would shave, shower, clean up, make your bunk, get ready for inspection; then you would fall out, usually about 6 o'clock. Have inspection, get inspected, march to the dining hall, eat, come back, have a few minutes to finish getting the barracks ready, and then you would be out for, uh, either calisthenics or a specific course: hygiene, medicine, all the basic things that they assume nobody knows, which is probably right so I can't complain about anything. And then you learned about chemical warfare, and then you went to the rifle range and did all the basic stuff that people had to know about.

After basic, he was assigned to Perrin AFB, in Sherman, Texas, as a one-striper until his cadet class began in November 1951. "I never did make buck sergeant," he laments. "I guess my initial career was a failure."

Robert Pomeroy

Like Tomlinson, Robert Pomeroy[20] also came from an elite background. Because he is the only West Pointer in this study, his experiences, like Tomlinson's, provide an interesting contrast to the others.

Pomeroy grew up in Dalton, Massachusetts, a small mill town in the western portion of the state. His father ran the Bay State Mill for Crane Paper Company, a company famous for making fine stationary and currency paper for U.S. dollar bills, stocks, and bonds. He also was the superintendent of company housing and the chairman of the town finance committee. Although Dalton was run by a board of selectmen, "most people considered him to be the unofficial mayor" because of his various titles and because "he had the ear of the Crane family." Like many other mill towns, corporate paternalism prevailed in Dalton: the Crane company paid for a portion of the school budget, provided college scholarships for youth, paved the roads, and owned most of the real estate in town. As the chief Crane executive in the town, Mr. Pomeroy had considerable influence. However, because he retired from the company when Robert was in high school, his influence waned during Robert's adolescent years.

As would be expected for a prominent family, the Pomeroys lived in the nicest part of town, in this case, an elevated area away from the mills. Robert grew up playing the clarinet, building model airplanes, and playing sports. Although he was never a great player, basketball was his passion, and he considered himself to be an integral member of the high school basketball clique. Robert also played clarinet for the high school band. He eventually started a swing band which toured the environs of western Massachusetts, including such spots as the North Adams Polish American Club and the Grange Hall.

Unlike most of the other pilots in this study, Pomeroy decided on a military career early in life. As a young man, he gained early military exposure from a scoutmaster who ran the Dalton troop "like a battalion." During World War II, he served as the high school air raid warden, a spotter, and a courier for the Dalton civil defense organization. More influential, though, was his brother, an air-minded young man who built model airplanes and later became a B-24 pilot with the 480th Anti-Submarine Warfare Command. One of Pomeroy's greatest memories from childhood was watching his brother and other young men flying gas-powered model airplanes: "Before radio control, people would load a plane up with gas and have cars chase it for up to five miles."

Another person who opened Robert's mind to the potential of aviation was Alexander de Seversky. Seversky's book, *Victory through Air Power,* "was the first book on theory I had ever read," recalled Pomeroy. "It made air power accessible to the lay person."

Although aviation was his dream, a practical desire to earn a college degree convinced Pomeroy to seek admission to the U.S. Military Academy at West Point. But the road to West Point was impeded by a variety of course prerequisites that could not be met through an ordinary high school curriculum. Consequently, Pomeroy had to attend a special, private preparatory school to take the special courses needed for admission.

Fortunately for him, money was not a great problem and his father chose to send him to Peekskill Military Academy (PMA) in Peekskill,

New York. Coincidentally, Peekskill's main square is graced with a statue of Robert's distant relative, General Seth Pomeroy, a Revolutionary War general who fought at the battle of Bunker Hill. Pomeroy left his best friends, his girlfriend, and an opportunity to play with the Dalton baseball team in the state championships at Fenway Park (Dalton lost) in order to attend PMA for his senior year. What Pomeroy discovered when he got there was an elitist school with no blacks, a place where Puerto Ricans and Mexican Americans were called "spics," and Jews, "kikes." While at PMA, Pomeroy met his future wife at a local dance and met a gay man for the first time, an English teacher who wore his necktie over his shoulder. PMA, in short, opened Pomeroy's eyes to the real world.

At PMA, Robert also joined the basketball and football teams, but was very much a "middling athlete." On the first day of football practice, he was first-string varsity; a week later, he was second-string junior varsity. Sports, however, would always be a part of his life: later in his career, Pomeroy coached an intramural team at the Air Force Academy, and a championship team at the Royal Air Force College at Cranwell, England.

After a year at PMA, Pomeroy passed the entrance examination and was made a principal alternate to attend the U.S. Military Academy at West Point. At his academy interview in New York City, the interviewing officer asked him if he had ever had a "homosexual experience," to which he replied: "Homosexual experience? I never had a sexual experience!"

Pomeroy's military academy years were typical.[21] As he admits himself, "You had to be crazy to enjoy life at a service academy, but you stick to it because of the rewards at the end—career, knowledge, and good officership." Besides, if it had not been for West Point, Pomeroy "might have ended up as a glider pilot." In the end, he graduated 139th in a class of 301, and like 111 of his classmates, pursued aviation as a military career. The class of '48 was the last class to send more than 25 percent of its graduates to the Air Force.

Paul Turner

Paul Turner[22] applied to a military academy (the U.S. Naval Academy), but he did not get in. Unlike Pomeroy, he never had the opportunity to attend prep school or play basketball, nor was his father an important figure in local politics. Instead, Paul worked his way through junior high school, high school, and junior college. Turner, in short, lived a working-class existence during childhood—an experience more common among pilots than Pomeroy's privileged background.

Turner was born in Sacramento, California, in 1929. His mother, a nurse, had immigrated from Liverpool, England, when she was fifteen, and settled on the West Coast. In California, she met her husband, a switchman who "boomed" around the country with the railroads. He also was an official with the SNAKES, the Switchman's Union of North America. This combination of labor activism and railroad work meant that Paul's father was rarely home. At one point, the father even got into dispute with Samuel Gompers and was forced to go into hiding for two years. When his father was home, he would allow laid-off workers to live in the garage of their small two-bedroom ranch. "He didn't see them as hobos, he saw them as men down on their luck," recalled Turner.

Paul gained exposure to working-class life not only through his father, he also experienced it personally as a railroad callboy. His job was to go around town at odd hours of night and round up train crews. Later in high school, he left the railroads to become a printer's "devil"—a messy job which involved making mattes for advertisements and putting all the type in the printing plates. Work was necessary because money was extremely tight. Dad would scrounge for potatoes in railroad cars, and the Turners would observe meatless days on countless occasions. Through it all, Paul developed a profound respect for the plight of the worker and workers' movements—a respect that would later save his life during interrogation sessions near Pyoktong Number 2 POW camp in North Korea.

Although life was certainly hard for Paul as a child, there were a few bright spots. His father's position in the railroads allowed Paul to travel free to local California ski spots. He would get up at two in the morning, travel to Sugarbowl in the Sierras, work the ski lifts in the morning, and then ski all afternoon. Skiing, in turn, became a lifelong passion. "Skiing is much like flying," Paul believes. "You are all alone up there and when things get mixed up, it's all up to you." Through skiing, Paul met many Army Air Force pilots. Because AAF pilot salaries were relatively high in the 1940s, these men had plenty of spending money. Seeing these men in their smart uniforms and hearing their stories on the long lift rides inspired Paul: he dreamed of becoming a pilot himself.

One non-pilot who influenced Paul was Dick Buick, the ski racer whose story is depicted in the film *The Other Side of the Mountain*.[23] Dick helped Paul become a proficient enough racer to earn a ski scholarship to attend Colorado College. Unfortunately even with the scholarship, expenses were too high at this elite, private college, and Turner instead lived at home and attended Sacramento City College (now Sacramento State). Years later, Dick would tell Paul that he would gladly have given up his racing career just to have flown the F-86.

In addition to skiing, Paul also had a keen interest in aviation. One of his earliest memories was hearing a plane in the air and wondering what it was. As a child, Turner built models and grew up on movies like *Dawn Patrol*. To him, aviation represented "the chance to do your own thing without limits." In high school, he "followed World War II in great detail, and enjoyed every minute of it." Later as a college student, Paul worked as an aviation mechanic at McClellan AFB in Sacramento installing communications equipment in B-29s.

Eventually, work and school became too difficult to balance, and Paul left Sacramento City College with an associate's degree to work full time as an aviation mechanic. The year was 1950, and soon America was embroiled in the Korean War. As a young man with no deferment, the draft appeared inevitable to Paul, and so, like Tomlinson, Crockett, and Brown, he said "to hell with this," and applied for the Aviation Cadets.

M. J. Bailey

Like Turner, M. J. Bailey[24] came from a humble background, worked as an aircraft mechanic, and joined the Air Force primarily to avoid being drafted into the Army.

Bailey was born in Winona, Wisconsin, on 22 September 1922, but was raised in Huntington Park, California, where his father worked as a barber. He attended Bell High School and enjoyed science. As a future flight suit officer, it is not surprising that his favorite hobby was driving hot rods (Model A Fords equipped with V-8 engines) on dry lake beds, places where he would later fly F-80s as a test pilot.

After graduating from high school, Bailey took a civil service test in aircraft mechanics and then went to work at McClellan Field as a civil service P-38 mechanic.

In 1942, Bailey enlisted in the Aviation Cadet program at Mather Field near Sacramento, California, and graduated in class 44G in August 1944 as a P-40 fighter pilot. For the remainder of World War II, Bailey flew ground support missions in P-40s for the 6th Fighter Squadron, 1st Air Commando Group in Assansal, India. The 1st Air Commando, under Phil Cochran, was a composite group consisting of fighters, bombers, transports, and liaison aircraft. Most of its work was in Burma in support of General Joseph Stillwell's operations.

After the war, Bailey flew P-80s and Bell P-59 jets as a test pilot at Mather Field and later with the 412th and then the 445th Squadron. When the Korean War erupted, Bailey was a reserve officer who had just been cut from the force and awaiting discharge at Sheppard Air Force Base in Wichita Falls, Texas. In early July 1950, Bailey was scheduled to go before a pilot evaluation board and was expecting to lose his wings and be discharged because the Air Force was "getting rid of surplus reserve officers at the time." Instead, on the morning of 4 July 1950, Bailey was awakened at 0700 and told to report to Nellis AFB, near Las Vegas, Nevada. He was going to gunnery school. Korea, in short, gave Bailey a new "lease on life." Rather than having to leave the service and face the civilian job market without a college degree, Korea gave Bailey the opportunity to fly F-80s with the 7th Squadron, 49th Group.

George Berke

Most of the pilots in this study have fond childhood memories of aviation, but few joined the Air Force solely to become a pilot—draft avoidance, salary, and status were equally important aspects of their decision-making calculus. But for George Berke,[25] flying was the only goal, and the Air Force was a natural way to achieve it.

Born in Plainfield, New Jersey, on 8 June 1927, Berke grew up as a "nonobservant Jew" in the middle-class "WASP" town of Westfield. His father ran a gas station, and George worked there part-time "to keep up with his wealthier friends." Like Turner, George paid close attention to World War II—especially the air war. All of his friends' brothers were in the AAF at the time, and the high point of his days in high school was watching them buzz the school in fighters and bombers. "Everyone would run out and gawk," recalled George. "The principal would then call out the name of the plane and identify the pilot by the tail markings: 'Its a B-24; it must be Malcolm!' "

So inspired was George by these incidents that he took flying lessons with money he saved from his gas station job and earned his pilot's license at sixteen. From that point on, his nickname was "Ace." "I would fly around the town in a Piper Cub," George declared, "and drop notes asking various girls for dates." Flying, in short, was a defining event for George: as he himself admitted, "I couldn't join the country club because of anti-Semitism, but flying was something I could do; it was a great equalizer."

When George turned seventeen in late 1944, he immediately sought and gained parental permission to join the AAF as an Aviation Cadet (at that time, no college credit was necessary). Unfortunately for him, time was not on his side. In 1945, Berke entered the AAF as a private and attended basic at Keesler AFB, Biloxi, Mississippi; while there, the war ended. Berke remembered the day vividly because his bunkmate and many others slotted for pilot training broke down and cried. Berke did not give up; instead, he signed up for crew training at Scott AFB, near Belleville, Illinois. When he arrived at Scott, however, the first thing he saw was a bulletin board with rows of names—everyone whose name began with an A, B, or C was scheduled to be "RIFed" (short for reduction in force). Berke still didn't give up! When he got to the out-processing center, he volunteered to be a medic there.

As a medic, Berke's first assignment was as venereal disease inspector. He would sit behind a table and ask the GIs to "take it out and milk it down." Later, he graduated to urinalysis, and finally, to serology—giving laboratory tests for syphilis. In between, he did everything from drawing blood to checking pulses. "The whole process," according to Berke, "was a complete disaster." Three hundred and fifty men had to be out-processed per day, and rarely was a doctor available to supervise the site: "We made everything up as we went along." They filed their own fingernails to check pulses, sharpened their own needles, and came up with a relief system for drawing blood: after so many misses, you were yanked out of the line as a blood sample collector. By the end of the day, everyone was drenched with blood, but this did not bother George. He prided himself on his work, and to this day insists on drawing his own blood at the doctor's office. The Army as an institution, though, troubled him greatly: "People were dying in military hospitals for lack of proper care and disorganization and chaos ruled the day."

After Berke was honorably discharged, he entered Rutgers University on the GI bill in 1947. Time away from school had left him academically unprepared, but with the help of an understanding English professor, Berke managed to do quite well. After he flunked several English assignments, this professor, who was an expert in Persian poetry, pulled him aside and said: "George, I will make a deal with you—If you get an A for the final, I will give you an A for the course." This kind of academic motivation not only enabled him to get through Rutgers, but also helped him secure a teaching post at the Air Force Academy toward the middle of his career, then an M.A. in English and a Ph.D. in education.[26] Rutgers, then, transformed a fun-loving flyer and closet intellectual into a self-proclaimed "iconoclastic officer."

While he was in college, though, flying still had a tremendous appeal and when the Korean War began, Berke did not hesitate to reenlist and make a second go of it. As he put it, "Flying just sucked me up."

Howard Heiner

Howard Heiner[27] was born in Sandpoint, Idaho, on 22 July 1929, and came from what he describes as a blue-collar background. His father was a farmer and later the town water supervisor, and his mother ran a sewing shop. As a child, Heiner was "deeply religious and attended church every Sunday." During World War II, his father, the son of German immigrants, quit his job and moved to Spokane. This was very hard on Heiner—so hard, in fact, that he chose to stay in Sand Point and live at the local fire department. While attending high school, Heiner joined the forest service, fought fires, and drove mules to fire spotters in remote locations. This work earned him enough money to attend the University of Idaho, and made him very "independent and stubborn."

In college, Heiner majored in forestry, edited the college forestry magazine, and became very active in intramural sports. He also drank beer with World War II veterans and listened intently to their stories. Heiner was twelve years old when America had entered World War II and was "proud of the country for entering." He was also proud that his two brothers-in-law had served in the Army and Navy during the war. Hence, when the Korean War began, he joined the Air Force Reserve Officers Training Corps (AROTC) because he "felt [he] needed to do [his] patriotic duty." As he put it, "I signed up to fight in Korea out of the patriotism of World War II."

Having heard about flying, Heiner was interested in the Air Force even though he had never flown. He took the Aviation Cadet test and passed. The cadet program, however, would not allow him to marry his college sweetheart until after receiving his commission. AROTC, on the other hand, promised to give him a commission after only a year, and allowed him to marry before aviation training. As a result, he graduated from college, received his commission, and got married—all in one weekend.

Raymond "Dewey" Sturgeon

Like Heiner, "Dewey" Sturgeon[28] came from humble roots in rural America. He grew up in Templeton, Indiana, on a farm: "It was just Dad and I and two tractors." Sturgeon attended high school in Oxford, Indiana, and graduated in 1942. Because he worked on a farm, he was deferred from the draft, but he felt "so guilty about it that he decided to go anyway in 1944." Sturgeon joined the Marines because they "had such nice uniforms." Unfortunately, the week before he was supposed to enlist, Sturgeon's combine got choked with soybeans, and his legs were sucked in trying to unclog it. Even though both legs were broken, he was able to pull the pin on the combine, clamber into his tractor, and slowly make his way home. Sturgeon ended up in the hospital for eight days and in leg casts for six months.

Although World War II was over by the time Sturgeon fully recovered, he decided to enlist in the Air Force in 1946. Although flying seemed completely "out of reach," he loved the idea of being around aircraft and did not want to be an infantryman with bad legs.

As an enlisted man, Sturgeon went to engine mechanic school—a program he claims "helped him get through the technical aspects of cadet training." To graduate, you had to assemble an engine "from scratch." After graduation, he was assigned to Chanute Field, near Rantoul, Illinois, to teach mechanics to other students. As an instructor, Sturgeon impressed not only his students, but many of his sergeants as well. These senior NCOs, in turn, coached him for the pilot exam and the two-year college equivalency test. Sturgeon claimed, "Until that point, I never thought being a pilot was in my reach but lady luck was smiling on me," and he passed.

Sturgeon was sent to primary training at Goodfellow AFB, in San Angelo, Texas, and then to multi-engine school at Barksdale AFB, near Bossier City, Louisiana. However, in early 1950, a year after graduation, he was cut from the Air Force in a RIF. "Getting cut after a year was one of my biggest blows," he recalled. "I thought I was done and would never see a plane again." Although he wanted to get into crop dusting, his parents convinced him to come back home and work on the farm for a hundred dollars a month: "I was planting corn and beans and when I saw a plane fly over I said 'Boy, that is where I am supposed to be.' " So in December 1951, when the Air Force Reserve asked him if he wanted to be recalled voluntarily, there was no hesitation: "I knew when I was recalled that I would make a career of the Air Force." He also knew he wanted to transfer to jets. However, the Air Force Reserves told him that if he wanted to fly jets, he would have to go to Korea. In typical flight suit manner, Sturgeon said, "Fine, I want to go—it's right up my alley."

James Hagerstrom

James Hagerstrom[29] was born on 21 January 1921 into a Midwestern, working-class family. His father was an electrician with the Iowa Public Service Company and the son of Swedish immigrants. He grew up in a three-bedroom wooden house in Waterloo, Iowa, and first became interested in aviation in 1934, when he paid fifty cents for a ride in a Ford Tri-Motor.

During high school, Hagerstrom, like many future pilots, was too small to play football, and so he wrestled and swam instead as an "adrenaline release." He was also an avid model airplane builder.

In 1941, Hagerstrom attended the University of Iowa and participated in Army ROTC. A year later, he transferred to Iowa State Teacher's College in Cedar Falls and helped to establish an aero club there. By Thanksgiving of his sophomore year, he joined the Aviation Cadets and was sworn in on 15 January 1942. Next came primary training at Bakersfield in California, where he wore coveralls and a civilian suit because the school had no uniforms. He graduated from flying training in July 1942, and was sent to the Pacific to fly P-40s with the 8th Fighter Squadron, 49th Fighter Group in New Guinea. "New Guinea," remembered Hagerstrom, was a "terrible place": "I slept in a tent with dirt floors, washed in the river, and contracted malaria." In spite of these hardships, Hagerstrom managed to shoot down six Japanese fighter planes. One mission was particularly emblematic of the aggressive attitude of the ace. Hagerstrom and another pilot took on fifteen Japanese fighters in an attempt to rescue two P-38s. During this mission, Hagerstrom shot down four planes, establishing himself as a young ace (a pilot achieves ace status after five kills).

After 170 combat missions, Hagerstrom was transferred to the States, and in June 1945 he was discharged from the Army Air Forces. The next day, a Sunday, he drove to Iowa State Teacher's College and did what any flight suit officer would do: he knocked on the president's door and told him he wanted to finish school. The president personally opened the registrar's office and enrolled him on the spot.

After receiving a degree in economics in 1948, Hagerstrom entered the municipal bonds market in Texas. He also joined the Texas National Guard—a unit he described as "the bottom of the heap." Bottom of the heap or not, the unit (which eventually named a hangar after him) kept him in "the flying business" until the Korean War. Once the war started, Hagerstrom secured a recall to fly F-86s with the 4th Wing—"the assignment I had spent my life preparing for."

Although some of the pilots surveyed came from well-off families, as a group their backgrounds were hardly elite. None came from families listed in the social registers of New York, Baltimore, San Francisco, Chicago, Philadelphia, Boston, or Washington. Nor did any attend an elite four-year boarding school such as Choate, St. Mark's, St. Paul's, Andover, or Exeter. Finally, none attended an Ivy League college. In short, none can be classified as what sociologist C. Wright Mills defined as the "Metropolitan 400": "the solid core of wealthy families" which together represent a nationally recognizable upper class in the United States.[30]

Instead, most came from middle- and lower-middle-class families, families that emphasized upward mobility but rarely had the means to provide their sons with access to the traditional mobility elevators— elite private schools and colleges. None of the pilots in this group attended a private college, and only one attended a private prep school (Pomeroy). Furthermore, of the four who did earn a baccalaureate before entering the Air Force, the degrees of two were paid for by the military.[31] In every other case, there was not even enough family money available to get these men through state schools such as the University of Oklahoma, Louisiana State University, and Sacramento City College. In other words, if this latter group were to rise in society, they had to find an alternative to education.

The Air Force became that alternative. It got them out of dead-end jobs—be it driving an ambulance in Harlem, working as a railroad machinist, or clerking in a small-town bank—and onto a professional career path. In the socially competitive, white-collar world of the 1950s, the Air Force offered them tangible status symbols: gold lieutenant's bars, silver wings, and a state-of-the-art fighter with their name painted right on the fuselage. "The reward of the Air Force," according to Berke, "was not a large office and all that bureaucratic stuff, but your own airplane; that's what people want: a plane with your name on it so wherever you go people know who you are!" For Berke and others like him, therefore, flying offered status and freedom unobtainable in the increasingly bureaucratic marketplace of the 1950s.

A final theme worth considering is Michael Sherry's "entrepreneurial model of service." According to Sherry: "The status, rewards, and duties of combat airmen moved them toward an entrepreneurial or occupational model of service. Self-interest was defined as distinct from the war-winning purpose of the organization; rewards were defined by and carried over into the civilian marketplace; the rituals of military life were subordinated to the attainment of skills and status useful in a larger world." [32] Sherry is accurate in emphasizing the link between status and the air service. To a man, the pilots in this study joined the Air Force because it was a "first-class" way to perform a military obligation. Contrary to the Sherry thesis, though, they did not seek skills which they could then "market in the outside world" once their enlistments were up; rather, for these men, the Air Force would become an end unto itself. Although only one of the pilots entered the Air Force to become a career officer, all but one would choose an Air Force career after the Korean War ended.

— ·· 3 ·· —

Stick and Rudder University:
Training and the Creation
of the Flight Suit Officer

Some people sat down when the Air Force became a new service and decided that hey, we are the Air Force. We are not the Army's airborne cavalry, we do not have centuries and centuries of traditions to hamper our progress, we're going to do things our way. And they deliberately set out at Nellis to produce the best-trained, best-equipped fighter pilots in the world. And they did! —Frank Tomlinson [1]

The Air Force's emphasis in the 1950s on the singular skill of piloting distinguished it from the other services. During the Korean War, over 50 percent of the Air Force Officer Corps had silver pilot's wings, and almost all commanders were pilots: 200 of the 207 Air Force general officers in 1950 were pilots.[2] Furthermore, unlike the Army and the Navy, where most officers received their commission from ROTC or the military academies, two-thirds of Air Force officers received their commission directly through the Aviation Cadets—a program that combined officer candidate school with pilot school. Pilot training, in short, was the primary military initiation for the majority of Air Force officers. Even if you were a West Point graduate, your first substantive experience with the Air Force, inevitably, was pilot training. Pilot training defined

37

the Air Force officer and presented him with skills and values necessary to flourish within the Air Force environment. In both a physical and psychological sense, it lifted him from the ground and transformed him into an "air-minded" individual and a member of the Air Force's "flying elite."

At the same time, training was also a grueling initiation process complete with hazing, washouts, accidents, and even death. An average of only 61.6 percent of those who entered the training program earned their wings.[3] Furthermore, a majority of the washouts were due to "flying deficiencies" rather than academic or disciplinary problems.[4] So difficult was the process of learning to fly military aircraft that the Air Force Training Command, despite its dual mission to create officers and flyers, actually emphasized the latter more so than the former. Half of each training day was spent on the flight line or in the air, one-on-one, with instructors who were often civilian contractors with no prior military experience.[5] While on the line, students wore flight suits and were told not to salute officers or worry about standard military discipline: flying and all that goes with it, they were told, were to be their only concerns.[6]

The end result of this intensive, flight-oriented program was a more casual officer than the average Army second lieutenant or Navy ensign. "The impression of the Air Force that I had in the late '40s and early '50s," recalls Robert Pomeroy, "was a guy with a crushed hat and a cavalier attitude. In those days, flying was riskier than it is now: we learned to eat, drink, and be merry because tomorrow you may die."[7] In short, to survive flight training, one had to be "cockpit-minded": technique had to take precedence over military discipline, leadership, and hierarchy. A flight suit attitude was not simply an expression of machismo, it was a means of psychological survival in a danger-filled environment.

Pilot training defined the young Air Force officer of the 1940s and 1950s and created the flight suit persona. As much an initiation ritual for these men as a place to develop practical skills, pilot training was a critical indoctrination period for the young officer. If a trainee could overcome the various barriers to becoming a pilot (washouts, accidents,

fear of flying, and the possibility of death), he could enter the brotherhood of the flight suit. Ancestry, education, and prior military training
or military academy experience had very little to do with one's status in
the Air Force: wings, the flight suit, and eventually, the one hundred-
mission Distinguished Flying Cross was what truly defined one as "elite"
in this service. Training tested a young man's skill and courage; it also
taught him that he would "sink or swim" in the Air Force based on his
ability to fly, and that life outside the "flight suit" was secondary.

Selection and Testing

The process of choosing pilots was hardly a science in the 1950s, but it
was not as random as it had been in earlier years. During World War I,
applicants were "spun in a spin chair to test their equilibrium," and men
"who could ride well, sail a fast boat, and handle a motorcycle were
considered good prospects."[8] It was not until 1941 that the Army
decided to implement a more "scientific" test, known as the "Standard
Nine," or "stanine" for short. Because this test dictated who would
become a pilot in an organization dominated by pilots, it played a
crucial role in shaping the entire nature of the Air Force officer corps
during its early history.

The "stanine," which changed little from World War II to the Korean
War, tested a pilot on a broad range of intellectual and physical skills.
But because flying was considered a mechanical skill, above all else, the
test emphasized hand-eye coordination, excellent vision, and sound motor skills more than any other abilities.[9] Those who passed tended to be
athletic, but not necessarily intelligent in the traditional academic sense.
Training Command studies suggested that "other than perhaps increasing self-confidence, education and academic attainment could not . . .
improve [a pilot's] chances of finishing training." Consequently, the
humanities and social sciences sections of the test were "rated next-to-
last, just ahead of vocational skills."[10] A pilot could be deficient in both
of those areas and still pass. When this factor is combined with the low
educational requirements for aviation training (i.e., two years of college),
it becomes clear that the Air Force had the least-educated officer corps

in the 1950s. This was a serious problem for a service that took pride in its ability to field some of the most technologically advanced weapons in the military.

At the heart of the problem was the fact that demand for pilots was outstripping the supply. When the Aviation Cadet program reopened in 1947 after a postwar hiatus, it had to train only 3,000 pilots annually; in 1950, this number had increased to 4,000; and by 1952, with demands brought on by the Korean War, the Air Force needed 7,200 pilots a year.[11] To meet these large production goals, the Air Force sent twelve traveling Aviation Cadet selection teams around the country in an attempt to recruit college students. Local Air Force bases also arranged base tours for high school seniors and college students. Recruitment letters were even sent out to all acquaintances of cadets, officers, and instructors.[12] These efforts were not enough: between 38 percent and 50 percent of those accepted into the program in the early 1950s were washing out.[13] The Air Force needed more pilot recruits. One of the major problems with college recruitment was that initially college students used the Aviation Cadet program as a loophole to avoid the draft. Before 1951, the Air Force granted immunity from further military service to all aviation washouts in an attempt to make pilot training more attractive to civilian recruits. This policy encouraged many young men to sign up for Aviation Cadets, and then resign after the first week or two of training. Between 1949 and 1950, for example, 18 percent of Aviation Cadets resigned during this initial period. Although this number might reflect the initial shock cadets felt upon entering a rigorous training program, the Air Force suspected draft avoidance as the primary cause.[14] Consequently, General Disosway, the Air Staff Director of Training, "ordered all civilian Aviation Cadet applicants enlisted as privates, USAF, for a period of four years."[15] Cadets who resigned after February 1951 would serve out the rest of their military time as Air Force privates.

Despite the efforts of Disosway and others, cadet shortages persisted during the Korean War. Table 1 describes the efforts of the Air Force to rectify the problem.[16] Clearly, the knee-jerk reaction of the Air Force to cadet shortages was to lower the entrance requirements—a solution which served to further water down the intellectual caliber of its officers.

TABLE 1.
Responses to the Aviation Cadet Shortage, August 1951–May 1952

September	—Men with prior service who were eliminated from training excused from further service. —Minimum qualifying air crew battery (stanine) test score reduced from six (out of nine) to five.
November	—Requirement that enlisted men serve eighteen months before applying for flight training waived.
December	—Applicants with two or more years of college obligated to only two years of enlisted service if eliminated from training.
January	—Time between testing and notification of the applicant of test results was streamlined and reduced. —Flight training applicants given priority handling. —Minimum educational level for enlisted applicants *reduced to high school diploma.*
February	—Minimum age for applicants lowered from twenty to nineteen.
April	—Number of Aviation Cadet selection teams increased. —Minimum qualifying stanine score reduced to three.[16]

Another deficiency which the Air Force had difficulty addressing in the selection process was its lack of black pilots. When it integrated in 1949, 7.2 percent of the enlisted personnel were black, but the percentage of black officers was far lower: only 368 of 25,523, or 0.6 percent. In flight training, the numbers were equally low: only 11 of 1,356 (0.8 percent) ROTC student officers and 22 of 2,085 (1.1 percent) Aviation Cadets were black in 1949.[17]

These numbers did not improve much as educational standards were lowered for the program. By the end of 1952, blacks still represented only 1 percent of the Air Force officer corps.[18] Of the 93 cadets and student officers in pilot George Berke's class 53-E at Hondo AFB, only one student (an Aviation Cadet) was black and all the instructors were white; at Williams AFB, his basic school, 2 of the 106 students were black, as were 4 of 64 instructors.[19]

Clearly, the Air Force was not working hard enough to recruit blacks during this period. When it became a separate service in 1947, only 247 (.4 percent) of its 49,529 officers were black.[20] By 1950, that number increased to 411, but black officers still represented only .6 percent of a total Air Force officer corps of 69,901.[21] In fact, black officers did not reach the 1 percent mark until 1953, and remained under 2 percent of the officer corps even as late as 1972.[22]

A 1948 study by the Industrial College of the Armed Forces (ICAF), entitled "Training and Utilization of Manpower," theorized that this racial disparity stemmed from the lower educational and health levels of blacks—factors it blamed on discrimination. It went on to argue that it was not the military's responsibility to promote racial justice: "Only as society changed could the military employ more blacks." Furthermore, "a division into white and Negro units was not the answer," nor was placing blacks in service and mess units.[23] In the end, the ICAF report recommended that nothing more should be done except additional studies.[24]

Although educational deficiencies may have barred blacks from many high-skill military jobs, pilot training should not have been greatly affected given that the stanine ranked academic achievement in its second lowest category. A far more plausible reason for the deficiency is the Air Training Command's quota system. In a move designed to decrease racial tensions at its many southern training facilities during the 1949 Air Force integration, the ATC "on its own instituted a 10 percent quota to prevent bases from becoming overpopulated with blacks." The ATC attempted to further appease white civilian contractors and the white communities surrounding these bases by only sending them blacks of the "highest caliber" to "ease the shock of integration."[25] According to the ATC history: "A nucleus of high type, well trained and properly oriented Negro airmen would serve as a forerunner in establishing the confidence necessary to facilitate increased assimilation of Negro personnel."[26]

Preflight

The basic curriculum of flight training changed little between the end of World War II and the Korean War. Aviation Cadets were given four weeks of "Preflight" officer training at Lackland AFB and then sent to one of ten "Primary" schools, where they were joined by ROTC and military academy graduates.[27] Primary lasted eighteen weeks and consisted of ground courses in basic navigation and instruments plus 120 hours of elementary flying. After Primary, students attended an eighteen-week "Basic" course which consisted of jet transition for fighter pilots and two-engine transition for bomber pilots. Pilots were also introduced to the dangerous but crucial art of formation flying and given advanced instruction in instruments and navigation. The final stage of prerated training was "Advanced," a twelve-week course that trained the pilot in his specialty area—fighter tactics, gunnery, rocketry, bombing, and so forth.[28]

Of all these stages, Primary was the greatest hurdle: the pressures of learning to fly for the first time strained even the best students. Eighty-six percent of those who washed out in training did so in Primary.[29] "It was a common sight after a hard day of training to return to the barracks and find another cadet packing his bags," remembered Paul Turner. "It was murder."[30] Paradoxically, rather than assigning its top military instructors to these schools, the Air Force chose to staff nine out of ten with civilian contractors.[31] Originally, the contractor schools were set up during World War II as a means of conserving military pilots for war duty. However, when the Aviation Cadet program reopened in 1947, the Air Force reinstated many of these schools as a cost-cutting measure.[32] Hence, civilians not only became significant "gatekeepers" in the pilot training program, but also played a very important role in shaping the values and ideas of the young pilot. Not surprisingly, these values tended to relate more to the art of flying than to the profession of arms. A report written by the Air Training Command summarized the situation well:

> Contractors are too prone to emphasize the flying phase and minimize the importance of the others [i.e., the military and academic phases] to the extreme of being uncooperative and unsympathetic to the problems of the military and academic training organization. Many of these men do not actively support and respect the individual objectives of all of the phases of training [and] are not really cognizant of their jobs at the Primary schools.[33]

As civilians, though, how could these men be expected to impart cadets and student officers with military values and officer skills? Most had neither the training nor the interest to accomplish such a mission. As professional pilots, their only concern was with flying and all that went with it.

Initially, the Air Force attempted to cope with the problem by setting up a Preflight program at Lackland AFB in 1949 for Aviation Cadets.[34] Actually, preflight training dates back to November 1940, when the Air Corps established four-week boot camps for pilot trainees at reception centers at Maxwell Field, Alabama; Kelly Field, Texas; and Santa Ana Field, California. These programs, however, were eliminated along with Aviation Cadets in 1946, and *did not* resume in 1947 when Aviation Cadets reopened. Apparently the Air Force, in its initial haste to build up its Cold War-rated force, did not consider military indoctrination to be a priority for pilots. It set up a "stopgap" four-week program in 1949 only after two separate panels recommended an extensive program.[35]

For the four-week Preflight program, the Aviation Cadet did not fly or even take classes on flying. Instead, he was processed into military life and taught all the basic military skills: "Drills, Ceremonies, and Inspection, Physical Training, and Effective Expression."[36] It was here that the cadet began to learn about the many rituals of military life. He was told to address his classmates not by their first names but by "Mister" followed by their last name. He was also instructed to maintain an impeccable appearance at all times or face demerits: shoes and buttons, for example, had to be shined before each breakfast formation. Finally, he was subjected to a host of stringent rules. The following are a sample:

- Cadets, upon leaving the barracks to go anywhere except to a scheduled formation or to meals, will sign the sign-out book with the exact time of departure and the exact time of return to the barracks, no matter where the destination.
- Cadets will not read or loiter in the latrines.
- Cadets will not proceed through the barracks in the nude or be in the latrine nude unless taking a shower.
- Cadets will not hang pictures on the walls, make any changes or additions to their rooms or barracks.
- Cadets will not create a disturbance or make unnecessary noise at any time.
- Cadets will not short-stop food being passed to another Aviation Cadet, without that Aviation Cadet's specific permission.[37]

The Aviation Cadet also had to adhere to a strict honor code. Under the code, anyone caught "cheating, stealing, or lying" was tried by the Honor Council, a collection of officers and generally at least one cadet. The code also stipulated that "anyone who withholds the knowledge of any honor code violations . . . will receive the same penalty as the person who actually committed the offense"—generally dismissal from the program.[38] The same honor code also applied to cadets and student officers in the Primary, Basic, and Advanced schools.[39]

Overall, the honor code, the other regulations, and the general military discipline of Preflight were supposed to "provide cadets with the fundamental knowledge required for their later development as Air Force officers," and "eliminate those students at once who were mentally, physically, or emotionally unsuited" to be Air Force officers.[40] In practice, preflight training was too short to do either. Most of the pilots I spoke with either did not attend or did not remember this phase of the training. To a man, the pilots considered Primary to be the most memorable initiation experience. As Tomlinson pointed out, "It was where the rubber met the road."[41]

It was in Primary where cadets were first exposed to the discipline and hazing of "upperclassmen," a far more incorrigible group than the drill instructors at Preflight. More important, Primary blended the rigors of military initiation with those of flight initiation. In Primary, cadets and student officers learned all the basics of flight: how to take off, land, and fly simple maneuvers. It was there that they first discovered the joy and fear of flying.

Primary

The metaphor which Pomeroy used to describe the social composition of Primary is a three-cornered hat: on one corner were the military academy graduates, on another, the ROTC officers, and on the third, the Aviation Cadets. Flying officers (the ROTC and military academy graduates) represented about a third of the Primary class. They lived and ate separately from the Aviation Cadets, earned about ninety dollars extra a month, were allowed to drink alcohol at the local officers' clubs, and were not "required to spend so much time in drills, ceremonies, and inspections as were the cadets."[42] Furthermore, if a student officer washed out, he would still be an officer, but if the same occurred for the Aviation Cadet, his Air Force career was essentially finished: before 1951, he would be discharged; after that date, he would be compelled to serve out his term as an enlisted man. Not surprisingly, the relationship between Aviation Cadets and student officers tended to be tense at first. However, as time went by and the men got to know each other, a more casual flight suit relationship developed. While on the flight line, military rank distinctions and discipline were minimized: saluting was forbidden and hazing was an absolute "no-no." As fellow students, Aviation Cadets and student officers needed all the support and camaraderie they could muster from on another; they could ill-afford to jeopardize the relationship with traditional military rigmarole. "You shared successes and failures," claims Pomeroy, "and after a while some cadets and officers even began referring to each other by their first names."[43] The fear, the challenges, and dangers of learning to fly, in the end, would enable these men to transcend distinctions in military status and become a unified band of brothers. Symbolizing this unity were the silver wings each man would receive at the end of Advanced training.[44]

In spite of the casual nature of the flight line, the Aviation Cadet still had to undergo a certain amount of traditional military initiation in Primary. Some of it consisted of drills and formations described in the Preflight section, but another part of it was the hazing they inevitably received from upper-class Aviation Cadets in the barracks and the mess halls. The most common form of hazing was the "brace," an exaggerated and highly uncomfortable form of attention which junior cadets were forced to assume for a long period of time. Crockett, a Tuskegee airman, remembers how upperclassmen would often turn on the lights in the middle of the night and brace the junior cadets or make them run in place. He also recalled how one upperclassman, Price D. Rice, "called him into his room and made him sit on an imaginary stool with his arms out against the wall, like wings, while he studied navigation." As Crockett's examples reveal, hazing was actually quite mild in Primary. In fact, the most pernicious form of hazing was the "square meal"—a practice whereby a cadet was forced to eat his meal at attention in a rigidly prescribed format. However, when it became so severe that cadets were unable to eat and were constantly seen rummaging for food during their spare time, ATC eliminated it in September 1950, along with excessive bracing.[45]

Perhaps more serious than standard hazing was the abuse some students received due to their religion, sexual preference, or race. "Nobody wanted to be ethnic in the military," claimed Berke, a Jewish American who even went to Christian chapel in an attempt to fit in. Nevertheless, he was still "made fun of a lot." Part of the problem was that as the senior student officer, Berke had to march other student officers, including some West Point and Annapolis men, to class, but he also believes that his religion was partly to blame. "The guys in my class set up a washout pool, and were betting that I would wash out first."[46]

Like religion, racial differences could also pose problems for the young cadet. At many of the contract fields in the South, blacks simply could not leave base due to fears of being attacked by the local white population. Tomlinson remembers that black pilots were told to stay on base at his civilian contractor school at Bainbridge, Georgia, because it was "cracker country" back then.[47] Crockett, for instance, never left the Tuskegee training base during his entire training period in the early 1940s.[48] Even as late as the 1960s, at nearby Maxwell AFB in Montgomery, Alabama, home of the Air Command and Staff School and the Air War College, black students were officially discouraged from socializing in white homes: "Students who still desired to entertain or study with Negro classmates were told to inform their neighbors that a fellow student, a Negro, was coming to call, and were advised to be sure that whites knew just who he is and why he is coming."[49] Abuse, incidentally, was not confined to the off-base activities of black trainees. At Tuskegee, Crockett remembers one civilian instructor who would not pass a single black student for six months. White instructors at Tuskegee also refused to eat in the same dining room with blacks.[50] Even after integration in 1949, there were still noncommissioned officers' clubs, officers' clubs, and other facilities where blacks were not welcome.[51] According to historian Alan Gropman, "The practice was introduced to establish branch clubs on the same base and it was tacitly understood that one club was for whites and the other for blacks. Such arrangements have persisted to 1985." [52]

Although students of different racial and religious backgrounds often suffered from various forms of harassment while on and off base, their presence in training was officially tolerated—but such was not the case for gay men. Homosexuality was banned by the Uniform Code of Military Conduct, but enforcement was not always standard or uniform. When a gay man made an advance to another cadet in Turner's class, vigilante justice prevailed: cadets forcefully removed the suspected gay man from the barracks in the middle of the night while he was sleeping. None of the cadets were punished for their behavior and the gay man was quietly kicked out of the program. [53]

Hazing and other forms of emotional and psychological harassment could indeed be excessive in certain cases, but for most pilots, it was a minor aspect of the overall training experience. If one could survive the rigors of flight training, one could certainly endure a bit of hazing and military discipline. In fact, as Berke recalls: "You simply didn't have time to worry about that kind of stuff. In training, you were always under the gun, and there was always an instructor in the flight. You were interested in mechanical types of things, and you were always being evaluated on that. They didn't teach you management or officer skills, they were only interested in turning out cannon fodder for the war." [54]

The basic trainer in Primary was the North American AT-6 Texan, "a single-engine, propeller-driven, two-place trainer" with a top speed of 210 mph. [55] When Tomlinson first sat in the cockpit, what struck him was how many dials and switches there were in this "relatively simple aircraft." He did not have too much time to think about it because his instructor then got in the back seat, and the next thing he knew he was up in the air. "Gee, this is absolutely marvelous," he recalled. "This is the funnest thing I've ever done in my life. I always thought it was gonna be fun, and you bet, it was fun." [56] For others, like Earl Brown, flying took some getting used to:

> After looking forward to my first flight for so long, I was devastated when I got airsick. Fortunately, we had been warned by the upperclassmen, so I had an empty potato chip bag in my pocket into which I deposited my

breakfast. After the second time I got sick, my instructor pilot (IP) said, "Brown, it's that damn bag you carry. You expect to get sick and so you do. Leave that bag behind and you won't get sick." So I left the bag behind and on the next flight, I had to throw up in my hat.[57]

Brown, in the end, conquered his sickness problem and became a very proficient fighter pilot, but he was fortunate to have had a sympathetic instructor, an Air Force officer named Philip Plotkin. Captain Plotkin volunteered to take four of the six black pilots in class 51-H because he was "a little guy and had some idea what these guys were going through." Despite Plotkin's best efforts, though, Brown was the only black pilot to graduate in class 51-H.[58]

Although many pilots had fond memories of their instructors, not all did. For Berke, "The instructor was not your friend: every ride was a check ride, and they were trying to wash you out the entire time." Pomeroy's second instructor was an extremely overbearing person who would yell at a cadet over the intercom for the entire flying lesson: "If you did something right, it was just luck." This instructor washed out five students, and Pomeroy claims he would have been one of them if it had not been for West Point: "You had to have rocks in your head to enjoy the academy, but it did give you an emotional reserve and teach you how to let verbal abuse roll off your back!"[59] On one memorable training flight, Pomeroy was placed under a hood and told to fly with instruments only, a standard but very stressful exercise. As the flight progressed, his instructor got increasingly riled at him over a series of small errors, and in the end the instructor forgot to put down the landing gear, forcing Pomeroy to make an unplanned belly landing. Fortunately, this incident was an instructor error, and Pomeroy was not washed out. In retrospect, recalled Pomeroy, it was "a nice learning experience."[60] Pomeroy was lucky, but others were often not.

Because the Air Force wanted to eliminate people early to save time and money, it granted its Primary instructors tremendous latitude to wash out candidates. In 1952, for instance, the Training Command planned to wash out a total of 29 percent of the pilots, 25 percent in Primary. In the end, it washed out 36.5 percent, 30.8 percent in Primary.[61] Given the candidate shortages for aviation training, washing out large numbers of cadets appears to be a somewhat contradictory policy.

The "washout," however, was a fundamental barrier to entry into the rated Air Force and very much a part of the practical Social Darwinism which defined pilot training.

The majority (approximately 57 percent) of all washouts in Primary were for flying deficiencies. Only an average of 1.5 percent washed out for academic reasons, and it was believed that these pilots failed the ridiculously simple academic tests on purpose.[62] Inevitably, flying proved to be the greatest hurdle. But flying was also the hardest skill to judge—evaluation standards tended to be capricious at best and arbitrary at worst.[63] Instructors could fail a pilot for everything from very straightforward criteria like not knowing procedures to very subjective ones such as "how well you control the aircraft or the aircraft controls you."[64] Gaining the proper "feel" for the aircraft made all the difference, as one cadet explained:

> As the plane climbed, he [the instructor] explained about coordinating rudder and aileron pressures in turns, about the "feel" of the airplane, about how too much rudder without aileron control made the airplane skid to the outside of the turn and too much aileron control without rudder made it slip to the inside. Demonstrating, he told me how to feel it in the seat of my pants when we slipped or skidded, and to note how the wind came through the side of the cockpit when a turn was uncoordinated. Hanging on grimly, with increasing queasiness, I tried to feel what I should.[65]

During the first phase of the eighteen-week Primary program, a pilot learned how to "shoot" normal and forced landings, how to turn, and how to recover from stalls and spins. In the second phase, he learned figure eights and "chandelles, or abrupt climbing turns."[66] The third phase, or "accuracy phase," emphasized precision, power on, power off, and short-field landings, and the last phase, "the diversified stage," stressed "loops, turns, and rolls."[67] The flying curriculum was forever being refined by the Training Command headquarters in Waco, Texas, but no matter how much headquarters attempted to micromanage the course, it was the individual instructor in the end who had the most control over standards. He was the one who decided whether your performance on various maneuvers was "above average, average, below average, or failing." [68] These grades, in turn, went into a folder which followed a pilot for his entire career, and in many cases, determined his entire future as an Air Force officer. According to Tomlinson, "If in later life you decide you want to fly such and such a plane, they go back and look at your basic grades to see if you had trouble with any of the characteristics deemed necessary for that plane." [69]

Getting a bad grade was one thing but a "washout" was tantamount to complete and utter failure. As one airman put it, "It sounded as though you turned colorless and just faded away, like a guilty spirit." Another explained the process in Social Darwinist terms: "If you were a flier, you passed; if you weren't, you washed out—fell out of the air, and became a lower order of being." [70] Pomeroy remembers vividly the day when one of the cadets in his group of four washed out: "When he got out of the cockpit that day, he looked completely beaten." Like a pariah, anyone washed out was immediately isolated from the group and transferred to another base. [71] Berke explained that "if you could fly, we accepted you, and if you couldn't, out!!! We didn't want you around."

Clearly, washing out was an emasculation of sorts, but who tended to wash out? Tomlinson speculated that some "either couldn't hack it or found that they didn't really have that initial desire." [72] A World War II pilot divided washouts into two groups: "First, there were those who had previous civilian flight training, who evidently had trouble flying the Army way." The second group were the ROTC and West Point graduates who "did not seem as motivated as were Aviation Cadets." [73] Berke, who fell squarely into the first group, in some respects fits this former characterization. "Everything to me was unfair and chicken shit; I considered myself a superior pilot from the word go, and as far as the niceties went, I let it all slide." Slide or not, Berke not only made it through the program, but graduated second in his class. If anything, prior flying experience appeared to improve a cadet's chances of making it through the program. However, when the Air Force set up a course in light plane training in late 1952 to provide cadets with some flying experience before Primary, attrition rates still hovered around 38.4 percent, a much higher figure than the planned 29 percent. The Air Force, in the end, blamed the continued high attrition on the lower stanine score of its applicants.[74]

A better example of a group which may have benefited from prior flight training was service academy graduates. An Air Training Command analysis of class 53-E found that while 149 out of 773 Aviation Cadets (19.3 percent) were eliminated, only 9 out of 109 Naval Academy students (8.3 percent), and 13 out 111 West Pointer cadets (11.7 percent) washed out.[75] Pomeroy, who bitterly rejected the contention that West Point graduates were not as motivated as Aviation Cadets, claimed that service academy graduates performed better because they had already "been through a pressure-filled indoctrination."[76] When other officer groups accustomed to military life are examined, however, Pomeroy's argument appears specious. The same study of 53-E found that 23.5 percent (19 out of 81) of ROTC and Officer Candidate School officers in the class washed out, compared to 19.3 percent of the Aviation Cadets.[77] A more plausible explanation for the better performance of the academy types was the flying indoctrination program which all Air Force-bound West Point and Naval Academy cadets attended during the summer of their junior year. During this introductory course, cadets not only received academic instruction on flying, but were also given actual flying time on T-6 and T-33 (jet) aircraft.[78] Pomeroy received ten hours of T-6 training during his tour and even dropped dummy bombs from an AT-8 into the Quaban Reservoir—Massachusetts's chief freshwater source![79]

All other factors being equal, additional flight training may have marginally improved some pilot's chances of graduating from Primary, but in the end, as the Air Force's experience with the stanine test suggests, one's ability to succeed, more than any other factors, rested on individual motor skills and a capacity to cope with the stress of flying. The stress of flying, in particular, was a rude awakening for many a young Aviation Cadet. Occasionally, those who began to fear climbing into the cockpit would approach their commanders and declare "lack of motivation" as their reason for resigning. Paul Turner's brother washed himself out in just such a manner. One day, he simply went to the base commander and told him: "I don't enjoy going down to the flight line, and I don't enjoy flying planes." More often, though, flying anxiety manifested itself in a rather bizarre condition known as fear of flying or FOF. Air Training Command analyses of classes 52-E, F, and G reveals that an average of 7.5 percent of those eliminated were washed out due to FOF. More significantly, these same studies reveal that FOF was the third greatest cause of eliminations after flying deficiencies and physical deficiencies.[80]

FOF was not a new psychological condition in the 1950s; in fact, documented cases can be found as early as World War I. H. G. Anderson, a World War I Royal Air Force flight surgeon, was one of the first physicians to study the phenomenon extensively. He defined FOF, or "aeroneurosis" as he labeled it, as "unhappiness in the air, introspection, and morbid thoughts." Aeroneurosis, he claimed, could be caused by the stress of flight training, the shock of an aviation accident, or the anxiety of combat flying. Through his experiences in treating patients at a British flight training center, he concluded that "experienced pilots were the most likely to overcome aeroneurosis."[81]

During World War II, more investigations of FOF were undertaken, but general definitions remained vague. Douglas C. Bond, a psychiatrist with the Eighth Air Force in Europe, posited that FOF patients fell into three distinct groups:

> 1) fliers with childhood predispositions to phobic behavior that resulted from unresolved oedipal conflicts—their phobic symptoms grew and (if untreated) eventually rendered them unable to perform their duties; 2) fliers who exhibited a more restricted phobic pattern—noting that one could find a neurotic pattern in anyone if one looked deeply enough, he said the reluctance of his second group to fly was precipitated by more personal and intense circumstances than the first group; and 3) fliers who were simply physically exhausted, and treatable with a week's rest.[82]

P. F. Eggerston, disputing Bond's claims about unresolved oedipal conflicts, argued that FOF related to a propensity for suicide in pilots, or a "suicidal dynamic."[83] Finally, R. R. Grinker and J. P. Spiegel, two doctors who worked with AAF fliers during the North African campaign, described the phenomenon as "the anticipation of danger, experienced by the ego, which led the flier to behave as if formerly experienced dangers were present." They also drew a distinction between pilots suffering from simple exhaustion and those suffering from the FOF neurosis.[84]

During the Korean War, Dr. Lucio Gatto conducted what would become a widely cited study of FOF. He identified two forms of FOF: "Basic Universal," and "Fear of Flying Syndrome." Basic Universal FOF, he believed, was the "inherent fear of being maimed, mutilated, or killed by falling through space and hitting the ground with great force." By comparison, FOF Syndrome was "a complex reaction occurring among previously adjusted flying personnel, and characterized by various defensive and maladaptive behavioral processes which express anxiety over various external and internal conflicts, frustrations, insecurities, and dangers."[85] FOF Syndrome, in other words, was a form of anxiety that manifested itself as FOF but was not necessarily linked to any particular aspect of it. Flyers who developed FOF later on in their careers generally suffered from FOF Syndrome, whereas those who developed FOF during their first training flights in all likelihood suffered from Basic Universal FOF.

While Gatto's definition of FOF is somewhat vague, his understanding of FOF's symptoms is much clearer.[86] They included sleeplessness, nervousness, agitation, somatic complaints, nightmares, passive and or aggressive reactions, claustrophobia, alcoholism, and phobic responses to planes.[87] In short, they included symptoms which directly interfered with a pilot's ability to operate aircraft. The Air Force hierarchy, however, tended to treat FOF as a personnel problem rather than a medical condition.[88]

At the beginning of the war, officers or those who expressed a fear of flying were immediately grounded and compelled to face a review board, consisting of their squadron commander, their base commander, and other officers at their local base or training facility. Although a discharge from flying duties was practically guaranteed, the board, to discourage others from using FOF as a means to avoid flying, would subject the officer to a series of humiliating questions relating to the individual's patriotism and self-worth before reassigning him to a nonrated job.[89]

In order to ensure impartiality, decisions of local boards were then reviewed "all the way up the chain of command with the final decision made by Headquarters, USAF. Higher officers tended to be even less sympathetic than the local boards. SAC commander Curtis LeMay's reaction to FOF, in many respects, typified the attitude of the Air Force leadership. He had no use for pilots who could not "cut the mustard," and believed anyone professing FOF was a "contaminating influence" who should immediately be court-martialed and dismissed from the service.[90] Air Force Chief of Staff Hoyt Vandenberg similarly favored some form of punishment, and believed that FOF represented a desertion from a "sworn duty." Vandenberg's views began to soften somewhat as more and more experienced pilots, including combat veterans, began to complain of FOF. It was one thing to court-martial Aviation Cadets, but quite another to try an officer who had already served his country honorably in a war.[91]

When Vandenberg finally issued a policy directive in April 1952, he rejected LeMay's draconian suggestions and opted instead for a new two-category FOF policy. A flier declaring FOF would receive a medical examination, and "if diagnosed as having a psychoneurosis that manifested itself as FOF, he would be treated as a patient, grounded, and given proper psychiatric care."[92] Interestingly, the treatment would focus on specific symptoms of FOF because the policy did not recognize FOF as a medical condition.[93]

On the other hand, if a flight surgeon found that the flier did not have a "disabling psychoneurosis," the entire matter would be handled administratively. Trainees and pilots with less than ten years of service were automatically given a general discharge "for the convenience of the government": a "general" discharge was "neither honorable or dishonorable."[94] For those with more than ten years of service, exceptions to this discharge policy could be made, but "only in unusual instances and where the individual possessed a critically needed non-rated skill."[95]

It is hard to know the exact number of trainees who opted out of flying by professing FOF. What is clear is that between June 1950 and November 1952, over 880 cases were reported.[96] Of this number, only a small group of 134 lieutenants and captains was thoroughly analyzed by the Air Training Command. One hundred and thirty-one were recalled reservists, three were regulars, and none were "green" Aviation Cadets. Most of the men (101) were "observers undergoing training for assignments to the Strategic Air Command and crew duties in the B-29," and at least eighty-one had flown combat missions in World War II. Finally, a majority had wives and children.[97] Clearly, these veteran airmen understood war and its many dangers. As Vance Mitchell writes in *Personnel Policy History of the Air Force Officer Corps, 1944–1974,* "Now older, more settled, and faced with the prospect of combat in an unpopular war, they had neither the emotional reserves nor the will to face again the threat of violent death."[98] Gatto, similarly, discovered that about 50 percent of the FOF patients he treated in Korea were World War II veterans, and most "were married men with definite home responsibilities."[99] His belief was that these men felt a degree of conflict over their combat duties and were therefore highly susceptible to stress reactions.[100]

Despite the considerable numbers of cases of FOF in Primary and Basic training (approximately twenty-one per class in 1952), however, neither Gatto nor the ATC attempted systematically to analyze FOF cases at this level.[101] Part of the problem, according to a 1952 ATC Conference report, was that flight surgeons found "it hard to evaluate fear of flying at this stage of the game, particularly if the individual has never flown before." Another problem was that the ATC believed that FOF was simply a "made-to-order" excuse for men wishing to reduce their tour from four years to two. Finally, Aviation Cadets and student officers could resign from aviation training at any point in their program with very few questions asked; consequently, the Air Force was not compelled to investigate or review them in a systematic way—they were simply cast out into a nonrated or an enlisted job and forgotten about.[102] In all likelihood, therefore, the number of FOF cases in training was larger than ATC records suggest. However, insufficient follow-up investigation makes it difficult to characterize the type of individual who might have been particularly susceptible.[103]

What we do know is that FOF is the clearest manifestation of the stress from which every cadet and student officer suffered. Primary's emphasis on solo flying guaranteed that each aviation student, at some point, would have to confront all of his innermost fears and insecurities. Alone in a small airplane, he would have to take off, land, and perform a myriad of technical functions, all without losing his nerve—one small mistake could result in washout or even death. Not surprisingly, many men did not make it: Turner's brother "didn't see flying as worth the risk." Another friend of Turner's took drugs to help him get through, but eventually smashed his aircraft into a mountain at Nellis AFB. Those pilot trainees who did make it, though, could loosen up a bit and begin to assume the swaggering ways of a USAF pilot. After all, they had conquered the discipline of Primary, its host of often hostile instructors, and, most important, flying itself. Although silver wings were for the future, the Primary graduate knew in his heart he could fly an airplane.

Basic

In one respect Basic was very similar to Primary: fundamental flying maneuvers and techniques were still emphasized. However, Basic differed in several significant respects. First, the elimination rate dropped precipitously. The average attrition rate for class 52-E, F, G, and H in Primary was 26.75 percent, but in Basic, it was only 8.08 percent. Similarly, 27.5 percent of classes 53-A, B, C, D washed out in Primary, compared to only 11.38 percent in Basic.[104] Second, the accident rate increased: during the first six months of 1952, seven pilots were killed in Primary, compared to thirty-two in Basic.[105] Very few pilots went through Basic without seeing at least one colleague killed. It was a place where young men just beginning to cope with the exhilaration of flying began to understand its many dangers.

At the heart of the "accident problem" were the jet aircraft. For most of these pilots, Basic was their first initiation to jets. Although some pilots destined for the Korean War attended multi-engine Basic schools to learn the rudiments of bomber flying, the majority attended jet transition Basic schools. In September 1952, for instance, the Air Force had 2,392 students enrolled in jet transition schools, and only 987 in multi-engine schools.[106] The difficulty with jets in the 1950s was that they were neither easy to fly nor particularly safe. For the young student aviator, they were also alien. "Prop planes," remembered Berke, "had all the good smells and were familiar . . . [but] jets were uncomfortable, and smelled lousy." They were also famous for killing pilots who did not pay close attention to what they were doing.[107]

The aircraft used in the transition of students from propeller-driven planes to jets was the Lockheed T-33, a two-seat version of the Lockheed F-80 Shooting Star (famous for killing six test pilots, including America's number-one World War II ace, Richard Bong).[108] The T-33, or T-Bird as it was called, was powered by a General Motors Allison engine and could fly 600 miles per hour, about 150 miles per hour faster than top-rated prop planes like the F-51.[109] Besides being somewhat unstable in level flight, the T-33 could not fly straight up and had an extremely tricky throttle. Unlike a T-6 or an F-51, where one could "move the throttle rapidly from idle to full power" and get a decent response, recalls Brown, "this engine had to be carefully and *slowly* coaxed to full-power level, [and] if the pilot advanced the throttle too quickly, the sudden addition of fuel would cause the engine temperature to rise above limits" and explode.[110] Sudden throttle movement, in flight, could also cause a compressor stall—a dangerous situation which often required the pilot to bail out if he could not restart the engine or if he was simply too close to the ground. Brown described the "bailout" as follows:

[The bailout] presented the pilot with an array of possibilities. Ejection seats were a necessary feature because the speeds at which jets flew made manual bailouts *extremely* risky. Ejection seat bailouts were only . . . risky. For taller pilots, ejection raised the hazard of knees hitting on the windshield rail while leaving the plane, which would really smart. Pilots could wear two types of parachutes in the T-33; either the back pack, which fit between the pilot's back and the back of the seat, or the seat pack, on which the pilot would sit, leaving more room to push back in the seat. The length of the pilot's thigh was measured, and if it went beyond a certain length, he had to wear the seat pack. This gave him a few extra inches to keep them from striking his knees as he ejected. But in the early days, I never knew a fighter pilot to turn down a chance to fly simply because the right parachute was not available. Some guys were so big that even with the seat chute, there was no room for a safe ejection.[111]

In addition to confronting the T-33's mechanical idiosyncrasies, a student flying it for the first time also had to adjust to much higher G forces than in the T-6. Six G's were routine in combat maneuvers—a state which made "your ten-pound head weigh sixty pounds."[112] Pilots had to wear inflatable G suits to prevent "blood from pooling in the lower part of the body and make it easier for your heart to work."[113] Nevertheless, a pilot unaccustomed to the strain of constant G's could easily lose his orientation in the air, as did one of Brown's classmates. It was toward the end of the day and the sun was visible at altitude, but not at ground level. In an effort to conserve fuel, Brown's flight was letting down at a horrendously fast rate. Everyone was becoming disoriented from the G forces and changing light conditions, but one pilot became so disoriented that he flew his plane right into the ground. According to Brown, "This put a damper on things for a while, but we were soon back at training with added motivation to learn all we could to prevent something like this from happening to us."[114] The Air Force did not give pilots an opportunity to grieve: "You were thrown from one lesson to the next without much reflection, and never given time to work out problems."[115]

Partly responsible for the frenetic state of affairs that Brown describes were the instructors. Basic instructors insisted on pushing students to their limits. "The whole philosophy of flight school was sink or swim," recalled Turner. "They threw you into the melee without much instruction."[116] Berke, who lost 4 of his class of 106, could not believe how instructors could demand tight patterns for landing—a practice that enabled them to see students better but also "increased the possibility of a low-altitude stall."[117] Instructors also insisted on very tight formations—a difficult skill to acquire for the novice flyer, as Charles Watry described in his World War II aviation training memoir:

> Beginners in formation flying always over control, fighting to hold the proper formation position with wild bursts of power, followed by sudden

frantic yanking the throttles rearward when it appears that the wing of the lead plane is about to be chewed up by the propeller of the airplanes flying the wing position. Beginners also try to hold lateral position using only rudders. The airplane is likely to wallow through the air like a goose waddling to its pond.[118]

Although not in a jet at the time, Crockett's first accident occurred in just such a manner. He was flying close formation on a final approach in P-39s and getting closer and closer until a classmate named Othel Dixon reported that Crockett's prop was coming into his cockpit.[119] Crockett immediately "dumped the stick forward, broke off his vertical fin underneath" Dixon's airplane, and sliced Dixon's wingtip off. Both pilots survived, with Dixon receiving a mild cut above his right eye.[120] Crockett and Dixon were lucky, but other pilots were not; in fact, midair collisions during formation flights and traffic patterns were the most common form of training accidents.[121] Accidents during takeoffs and landings were also common. One of Berke's worst training memories was trying desperately to get a classmate out of a plane that crashed during a takeoff, being overcome by the heat and fumes, and finally watching his friend burn up.[122] Painful experiences like these tested even the strongest, but they also bonded and unified the men.

A good example of this bonding was the warm relationships the pilots developed with foreign students. The Air Force Training Command trained students from a number of allied countries, including Belgium, the Netherlands, Denmark, France, Italy, and Thailand. Class 52-E, for example, had 188 foreign students out of a total of 745.[123] George Berke's section of 53-E at Williams had 21 foreign students out of a total of 108 students.[124]

Earl Brown formed a lasting friendship with his roommate in Basic, a French Air Force Academy cadet named Pierre Claude. Later in their careers, the two would serve side by side in Europe: Brown as the NATO Air Commander in the Mediterranean, and Pierre Claude as commander of the French Air Forces in southeastern France.[125] Although Paul Turner did not bunk with a foreign student, he "befriended them because they were a lot of fun." Turner even invited a Danish cadet to spend Christmas with his family after the Danish student washed out: "He was in my group," declared Paul, "and I felt responsible for him."[126] Student solidarity, in short, could even transcend differences of nationality.

Language differences, on the other hand, were more difficult to bridge. The instructor pilots tried to speak in short sentences to facilitate communication, but that did not always help. One day during Brown's training, a French student forgot to perform a standard T-6 test known as the GUMP check:

- Gas: to the fullest tank
- Undercarriage: down
- Mixture: full rich
- Prop: full forward

Well, the instructor yelled "GUMP" several times over the radio net to remind him, and the French student bailed out.[127]

Despite language barriers, there is very little evidence suggesting that foreigners were more likely to wash out than cadets. In fact, an analysis of class 52-E by the ATC even suggests that, as a group, foreigners performed better than Aviation Cadets. In all, 32.2 percent of the allied students washed out in Primary and Basic, compared to 41.2 percent of the Aviation Cadets.[128]

At the conclusion of Basic, Aviation Cadets received their commissions as second lieutenants, but the trials of training did not end there. Future pilots still had to endure another twelve grueling weeks of Advanced before they were fully certified as Air Force pilots and could wear the coveted silver wings. Top-ranked students went on to Nellis to learn to fly and fight in the top-of-the-line F-86 Sabre fighter-interceptor; others went to Luke AFB, near Phoenix, Arizona, to become F-84 fighter-bomber pilots, and the rest went to bases like Wichita Municipal Airport to become bomber pilots.

Advanced

> Each Dawn Nellis AFB, Nev., comes to life with a roar—the
> roar of jets taking off for the first day's many scheduled

missions. In nearby Las Vegas, many a red-eyed gambler is still pressing his luck at a gaming table. But at Nellis the men jockeying the F-80s or the F-86s are clear-eyed, aggressive, and alert. They have less need for artificial stimulus to lighten their lives.[129]

—Everett Dodd, "The Tale of 'Tiger,'"
Air Force Magazine, July 1953.

Air Force Magazine and other popular aviation journals glorified the Nellis training program in advanced fighter tactics. Nellis gave pilots an unprecedented opportunity to practice aerial tactics with actual "aggressor" aircraft: a tremendously costly and dangerous method of training, but one which gave U.S. fighter pilots a clear advantage in dogfights over MiG Alley in Korea. "Although the F-86 was a splendid fighter," writes Air Force historian Wayne Thompson, "its overwhelming success against the MiG in Korea resulted in large measure from its superior pilots."[130] Nellis, however, was not the only Advanced training program, nor was it the only one where pilots confronted realistic and dangerous training conditions. At the Luke AFB Advanced Gunnery school, pilots also lost their lives on a regular basis practicing dive bombing and other tactics in the F-84. Overall, jets like the F-86 and the F-84 were complicated planes that required a great deal of practice to fly properly. Unfortunately for the novice trainees, Advanced did not give them much time to get acquainted with new aircraft; instead, it emphasized the advanced aerial techniques a pilot needed to know in order to perform his given role in combat. In short, Advanced, although part of the basic training cycle, was more of a graduate program for the various flying disciplines than a course in fundamentals. The only thing the various Advanced schools had in common was their flight suit orientation, aggressive pace, and hazardous nature.

When George Berke got to Luke, for example, he received no instruction on the Republic F-84: he was simply told to get in the airplane and fly it. The F-84, like the T-33, was a temperamental and underpowered aircraft. The 586-mile-per-hour plane was designed to be a fighter-interceptor, but because of its slow speed relative to the MiG 15, it ended up being used primarily as a fighter-bomber. Pilots had to "carefully calculate the temperature, barometric pressure, and length of the runway before flying," and on hot days, no planes could take off.[131] Nevertheless, many pilots failed to follow the directions and crashed as a result. Students also had trouble dive-bombing with it. In dive-bombing practice, you would line up a certain target on the ground with your gun sight and when they matched, you would "pickle off your bombs." But if you got distracted, the target would never line up, and you could end up flying your plane into the ground, still trying to line up your target—a situation known as target fixation.[132] Despite these risks and dangers, Berke fell in love with the plane after his first takeoff. Unlike the conditionally stable T-33, "the F-84 felt like a stable rock—it was a real fighter."

Like the F-84, the F-86 was also a complicated plane to fly, but certainly not underpowered like the F-84. The fastest models could fly over 712 miles per hour.[133] The F-86 also had many unique features which pilots appreciated, such as a large bubble canopy for enhanced visibility, and a movable horizontal stabilizer for improved control at high speeds (a first for a production-line aircraft).[134]

At Nellis, F-86 pilots spent most of their time practicing the combat formation known as "fluid four" or "finger four." During the Korean War, it was discovered that four was the optimum number for a combat formation of high-speed jet fighters. Formations greater than four tended to get separated too easily in combat, and smaller formations were not as mutually protective. In a flight of four, the flight leader was the "shooter," and all other planes protected him and acted as additional eyes.[135] Although the leader of the second pair was allowed to shoot if for some reason the formation split up, the two wingmen were never supposed to shoot, and the wingmen never left the shooters.[136] This is one reason why only 4.8 percent of the Sabre pilots accounted for over 38 percent of the kills in Korea.[137]

As pilots transitioned to faster and more sophisticated aircraft, not only did their flying skills improve but so did their self-esteem. Without the constant fear of being washed out, pilots in Advanced could begin to assume the swagger of the Air Force pilot. By the time Turner got to Advanced, he believed he was as good a pilot as many of the instructors:

"People just didn't seem to realize that there were different ways of flying this airplane [the F-86]." Tomlinson, likewise, thought he was entering an elite club: "Everybody that wanted to fly a fighter wanted to fly the hottest, fastest, best thing, and that was the F-86 at that time. And we had a number of people that, uh, did get sent to F-84s, and F-80s, but they were trash haulers, you know, I mean we were the elite. We were the crème de la crème. Everybody wanted to be a jet pilot. I mean you go to the bar downtown in Las Vegas, you know . . ." [138] At Advanced, pilots not only had enough liberty time to explore local social venues, but were also generally stationed in cities such as Las Vegas and Phoenix, which were very "accommodating." "Chasing women," declared Berke, "was one of the things you did as a fighter pilot—it was part of the caché and mark of things." [139] According to Tomlinson, "All the girls wanted the jet pilots, absolutely!" [140] But what kind of girls did pilots want? A 1950 article, entitled "Sarge Looks at Today's Cadet," in the *Air Force Times* attempted to answer this question:

> He's 22 years old, and pretty well set on what he expects of a girl. Brunettes with light blue eyes and healthy tans have a slight edge, but physical characteristics are not so important to him as, first, a sense of humor, and second, the ability to "mix" well. . . . One characteristic of the pilot of yesteryear he will retain—he's something special. Something unique—and he wants his date to match him. He wants to have her have, for him, something no one else has or could have, and he wants to be proud—even a little vain—of her. That's not too much to expect for a young man with worlds to conquer, is it? [141]

As the popular Air Force literature suggests, not only did training constantly stress "aggressiveness and confidence," it also made these men feel special by smothering them with arresting, masculine compliments. Adjectives used to describe them in *Air Force Magazine* and the *Air Force Times* included "unique," "special," "different," and "hard living." [142] They were also told that they were "conquerors of new worlds"; the "thin blue line that stands between worldwide tyranny and freedom"; and "the answers to the dark hints that America's youth isn't fulfilling its obligations, that youths are afraid to fly." [143] Not surprisingly, men like Tomlinson who considered themselves shy before becoming pilots emerged from training as the men "all the girls wanted." [144] After all, if they could overcome fear of flying and "conquer" the air, they could certainly conquer the American woman.

This flight suit cockiness which training produced did have a downside as far as the Air Force was concerned: it did not necessarily serve these men well in their role as professional officers in the U.S. Armed Forces. In 1952, the Air Force Training Command, after conducting a series of base inspections, interviews with students, and reviews of reports by elimination boards, concluded that the average student in the training program was "not properly motivated" and "not willing to accept his full responsibility as an officer, leader, and a fighter." [145] The investigation also found that more than 75 percent of Primary graduates wanted to be assigned to propeller-driven aircraft rather than jets. [146]

To counteract this trend, the Air Force implemented a program called Project Tiger. Starting at Nellis in early 1953 and later spreading to thirty-six other training bases, Tiger attempted to instill students with officer skills by "emphasizing crew, weapon, and firepower philosophy" at every stage of recruitment and training. [147] Old recruitment posters luring cadets with promises of golf and swimming in the afternoon were replaced with ones featuring jet fighters and the caption: "Can you take it?" [148] Preflight was extended from four weeks to three months and more emphasis was placed on "leadership and discipline, the development of a competitive spirit, and publicity of outstanding combat and training accomplishments." [149] Throughout all phases of training, students were constantly "steeped in Air Force lore, history, and customs": a bit of a paradox given that the Air Force was only six years old at the time. [150] Other measures included improving instructor quality, indoctrinating Primary instructors in jet aircraft operation, giving all pilots in Primary a "9-hour review in which single-engine jet training was emphasized," and building "esprit de corps and competitive spirit" through the following:

- Flight rooms were converted into "war rooms."
- Student flights were assigned areas in the dining hall as a unit.
- Student quarters were assigned according to flight.

- Academic subjects were attended by flight units.
- Distinctive insignia was developed and publicized.[151]

Finally, Advanced courses were staffed with as many Korean War veteran pilots and aces as possible.[152]

Although Tiger might have appealed to men like SAC commander Curtis LeMay or General Jack D. Ripper, the fictional general in Stanley Kubrick's *Doctor Strangelove,* the program ended up being more hot air than substance. Instructors reacted to the program by placing more pressure on students to perform in-flight maneuvers and making training more of a "sink or swim routine." [153] More aggression and competition in training, in turn, did little to turn students into better officers. If anything, Project Tiger encouraged them to embrace the cocky pilot persona even more. Berke, who graduated from a Tiger program at Luke, sums it up well: training produced an "Air Force full of fighter pilots who were absolute guerrillas when it came to anything else and whose careers ended in disgrace." [154]

When the student pilot finally graduated from Advanced training, he gained more than the title of Air Force "pilot," he gained immeasurable status as well. Only he had the "rated" title; all other officers were "nonrated," in other words, insignificant. Symbolizing his new status were the silver wings he received upon graduation. He would wear these wings on every uniform for the rest of his career, including his shirts and flight suits. Furthermore, as the pilot advanced in the Air Force, these wings, like badges of rank, would change. After seven years, a "senior pilot" star would be affixed to the top of the wings. Eight years later, a "command pilot" wreath would encircle that star. Command, in short, was directly linked to piloting: only pilots could have the prefix, "command," in their official titles because only they could control operational units such as squadrons, wings, and groups.[155] Navigators with fifteen years of experience, by comparison, were called "master navigators." So important were wings that if you walk into the home of any former Air Force pilot (as I have done on numerous occasions) and ask to see his first set of wings, inevitably he will produce them for you. Sometimes they will be framed in the den, sometimes mounted on a desk, but more often than not, they will be hidden away in a top desk drawer where they can be easily accessed but never lost.

With wings, a pilot also acquired a collection of attitudes, ideas, and values that made him different from other types of officers. Unlike Peter Karsten's "naval aristocrat," the Air Force pilot did not enter a "social" elite upon being rated. Military ancestry and institutional traditions were irrelevant to him; instead, elitism in the Air Force was defined by skill, courage, and plane type. If one could overcome the various barriers to becoming a pilot—washouts, accidents, fear, death—one could define oneself as elite, and be a part of the team. Within the Air Force flying elite, the degree of one's elitism then depended on the plane one flew: F-86 pilots were the most elite, followed by F-84s, F-80s, F-51s, B-26s, and so forth.

Unlike Samuel Huntington's or Morris Janowitz's "professional soldier," training also did not create an anti-individualistic, "corporate spirit," or an "organization man" in uniform; instead, it brought out the reverse. Bureaucratic concerns had little meaning for a pilot struggling to master the complexities, dangers, and fears associated with flight. That civilians played an integral role in the training process did not help matters, nor did the egalitarianism of the flight line. Like his flight suit (a jump suit with lots of zippers and pockets but few military markings of any kind), the pilot graduating from training was specialized, informal, and thoroughly functional. Military regimentation and institutional concerns had little meaning. Yes, he had to discipline himself while in the air, but while on the ground, he could let things slide a bit and assume a more casual demeanor. Training had taught him that he would "sink or swim" based on his ability to fly, and that life outside the flight suit was secondary.

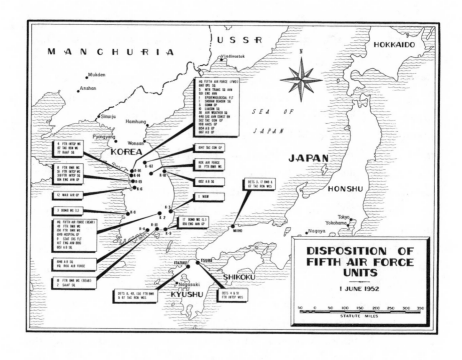

DISPOSITION OF
FIFTH AIR FORCE
UNITS

1 JUNE 1952

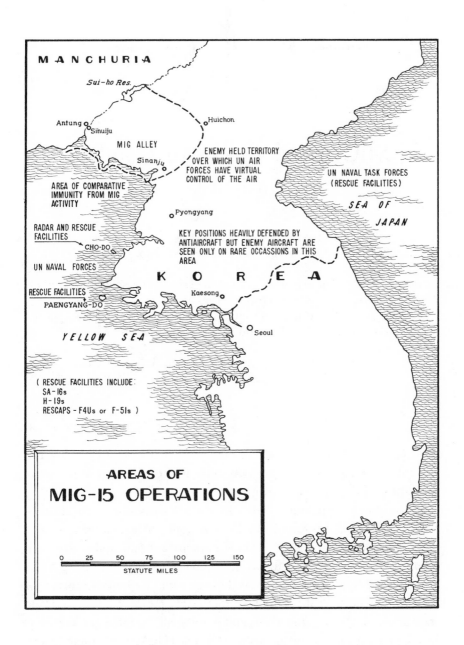

MANCHURIA

Sui-ho Res.

Antung ○
Sinuiju

○ Huichon

MIG ALLEY

Sinanju

ENEMY HELD TERRITORY
OVER WHICH UN AIR
FORCES HAVE VIRTUAL
CONTROL OF THE AIR

UN NAVAL TASK FORCES
(RESCUE FACILITIES)

AREA OF COMPARATIVE
IMMUNITY FROM MIG
ACTIVITY

SEA OF
JAPAN

RADAR AND RESCUE
FACILITIES

○ Pyongyang

CHO-DO

KEY POSITIONS HEAVILY DEFENDED BY
ANTIAIRCRAFT BUT ENEMY AIRCRAFT ARE
SEEN ONLY ON RARE OCCASSIONS IN THIS
AREA

UN NAVAL FORCES

K O R E A

RESCUE FACILITIES

Kaesong ○

PAENGYANG-DO

○ Seoul

YELLOW SEA

(RESCUE FACILITIES INCLUDE :
SA-16s
H-19s
RESCAPS - F4Us or F-51s)

AREAS OF
MIG-15 OPERATIONS

0   25   50   75   100   125   150
STATUTE MILES

4

MiG Alley: Air-to-Air Combat in Korea

Getting ahead in the Fighter Air Force meant shooting down MiGs. —James Hagerstrom, Korean War pilot and ace

In battle, you may draw a small circle around a soldier, including within it only those persons and objects which he sees or which he believes will influence his immediate fortunes. These primarily will determine whether he rallies or fails, advances or falls back.

—S. L. A. Marshall, *Men against Fire*

In 1950, James Hagerstrom was promoted to major; by 1958, he was a full colonel. How does one rise two ranks in the Air Force in the space of eight years? For Hagerstrom, such advancement was achieved by shooting down eight and a half Chinese MiG-15s during the Korean War.[1] As soon as he found out he was going to Korea, Hagerstrom understood implicitly that all of his future assignments and promotions would depend not only on his flying combat missions, but killing MiGs as well. Consequently, he did everything he could to prepare himself for such a task: he started running on the beach, taking courses over and over again on the A-4 gun sight, and reading all the intelligence reports he could get his hands on at Nellis AFB. For Hagerstrom, going to war was not a grim duty to which he submitted reluctantly, but the career opportunity of a lifetime.

During the Korean War, fighter-interceptor pilots like Hagerstrom were motivated to fight for very different reasons than their infantry comrades on the 38th parallel. One cannot, as historian S. L. A. Marshall did with infantrymen,[2] draw a circle around a four-plane element of F-86s and argue that a pilot kills primarily to protect his buddies; aerial killing was almost entirely offensive in nature. Elements of F-86s took to the skies of North Korea and China to hunt and kill MiGs, and the tactics they employed reflected a philosophy of extreme aggression—not one of mutual survival and group protection. Generally, only one plane, the designated shooter, in an element of four actually did the killing: the remaining planes acted as extra sets of eyes and guns for the lead. In fact, the shooter rarely even saw his wingmen in action—often his only assurance that they were behind him was the radio. Pilots, however, generally were under orders to maintain strict radio silence while flying to and from a combat area.[3] Aviation technology and the need to maintain stealth, in short, disconnected the pilot from his comrades. Pilots flew with wingmen, but wingmen were physically separated from the pilot by air and metal: they were not a living and breathing moral presence like a fellow soldier for the infantryman. In the heat of combat, furthermore, it was not unusual for a pilot to become separated from his wingman. According to pilot Bud Mahurin, getting separated during a fight was such a common experience that he instructed his wingman to forget about attempting a rendezvous if he lost visual contact with him during combat. Instead, Bud instructed his wingman to "make any attacks as he saw fit" whenever they got separated.[4]

Group dynamics, in short, played only a small role in fighter-interceptor combat motivation in Korea. The technology of the period militated against the formation of fighting groups. In the end, as Mahurin writes, "A jet-fighter pilot is responsible to himself alone."[5] James Salter, a pilot with the 4th Wing, put it even more eloquently in his autobiographical novel, *The Hunters:*

You lived and died alone, especially in fighters. . . . You slipped into the hollow cockpit and strapped and plugged yourself into the machine. The canopy ground shut and sealed you off. Your oxygen, your breath, you carried with you in a steel bottle. If you wanted to speak, you used the radio. You were as isolated as a deep-sea diver, only you went up, into nothing, instead of down. You were accompanied . . . but they were really no help. At the end, there was no one you could touch.[6]

Because of the highly individualistic nature of air combat, pilots found other reasons to fight besides mutual survival, the chief one being status. For flight suit officers, killing MiGs in Korea, like flying F-86s at Nellis, represented yet another opportunity, in fact the ultimate opportunity, to display their skills and earn kudos within the air organization. As George Berke explains, a pilot's quest for status did not end once his wings were pinned on: "Most people thought that being a fighter pilot was an epitome of sorts, but the reality was that it was just the starting rung of an astonishing meritocracy of skill, brains, and pure guts. Word got around the community about who you were. There were no ballots, but everyone voted."[7] In the fighter-interceptor business, medals, future promotions, and good flying assignments all depended on flying combat missions and shooting down MiGs.

In addition to a desire to climb the Air Force status ladder, some pilots were also motivated to kill for the "thrill of it." Time and time again, whether in interviews or written memoirs, aerial combat was described by pilots as an exhilarating or "peak experience": the language associated with killing was often highly sexual and occasionally orgasmic.[8] Killing, it appears, presented American men with the opportunity to escape briefly from middle-class suburban culture, with its love of domesticity and harmony, and engage in highly stimulating acts of legal violence at the very fringes of Western civilization. For those who managed to indulge the "inner warrior" in themselves, Korea was a transcendent experience. As ace Robinson Risner explained, "Korea was probably the high point of my whole career as far as real gratification is concerned—to be able to participate in air-to-air combat was a thrill."[9]

The War against the MiGs: An Overview

The struggle for U.S. air superiority over Korea was a comparatively minor part of the air war in terms of sorties flown. In all, only 18.6 percent of all U.S. Air Force, Navy, and Marine Corps combat sorties were devoted to the counter-air mission; by comparison, 47.8 percent were dedicated to interdiction, 18.5 percent to close air support, 13.1 percent to reconnaissance, 1.8 percent to antisubmarine patrol, and 0.2 percent to strategic bombing.[10] However, in terms of the popular memory of the war, the fight for air superiority commands center stage. Much of the literature on the war and movies like *Sabre Jet* (1953), *The McConnell Story* (1955), *Jet Attack* (1958), and *The Hunters* (1958) all celebrate the epic struggle between the F-86 and the MiG in the skies of North Korea and China. The Air Force views this chapter of the war to be of the utmost significance in its institutional memory. When one enters the front gate of Nellis AFB, Nevada, the Air Force's premier jet school, one is greeted by a Korean War F-86 mounted on a pedestal; similarly, in the Air Force area of the Pentagon, one can view large paintings of MiGs and Sabres dueling in the sky. Why has so much been said, drawn, written, and produced on this aspect of the war? First, the image of "aerial knights" dueling in the skies is much more romantic than fighter-bombers dropping napalm on villages or B-29s destroying cities and irrigation dams. Second, in Korea pilots battled their foes at relatively close quarters using guns rather than missiles—an alluring image for a nation that relished gun fighting and the frontier. More important, it was also the last American air war that produced aces in large numbers: overall, Korea produced thirty-nine aces whereas Vietnam, by comparison, produced only two. Finally, the only campaign in Korea where America squarely defeated its enemy was in the struggle for air superiority. Unlike the ground war, which ended in a stalemate, or the bombing campaigns, which also yielded rather mixed results, the U.S. war against the MiGs, with its impressive 7:1 kill ratio, was an undisputable victory of American technology and manhood over Communism.[11]

When the USAF first engaged in fighting the Communist forces on the Korean peninsula in June 1950, it did not have to confront the modern MiG-15 jets of the Chinese Air Force. Instead, it merely had to defeat the small, 132-airplane North Korean Air Force (NKAF) crewed by eighty inexperienced pilots. Although the NKAF shot down several American B-26 bombers and even damaged a British Royal Navy destroyer, it was no match for the USAF's Fifth Air Force. In air-to-air combat, Fifth Air Force F-51 Mustangs and F-80 Shooting Stars easily defeated inferior NKAF Yak-9s, a World War II vintage, 415-mph Soviet fighter similar in appearance and capabilities to the U.S. P-39 or the British Spitfire.[12]

However, the early battle for air superiority in Korea was not won by Air Force fighters in the air, but rather by bombers and fighter-bombers which destroyed most of the NKAF on the ground. On 29 June, for example, a flight of eighteen B-26s destroyed twenty-five NKAF planes on the ground and one in the air during a dusk raid against Yonpo Airfield.[13] Similarly, on 5 August, a flight of Mustangs destroyed nine Yaks on the ground at Pyongyang.[14] Efforts like these, along with B-29 airfield cratering attacks, secured almost total air superiority for the USAF's Far East Air Forces (FEAF) by the beginning of August 1950.

On 1 November 1950, however, the entire Korean air situation changed. On this date, six Chinese MiG-15s crossed the Yalu River and attacked a flight of Mustangs and a T-6 Mosquito forward air control aircraft. Fortunately, the FEAF planes managed to evade the MiGs, but the appearance of MiG-15s in the Korean War, as Air Force historian Robert Futrell writes, at once "rendered obsolete every American plane in the Far East."[15]

The small cigar-shaped Soviet-built jet had been developed in the late 1940s by the design team of Artem Mikoyan and Michael Gurevitch, hence the name MiG-15. Its famous swept-wing design was believed to be the result of data captured from the Germans, and its 5,000-pound thrust engine, the result of a close study of the British Rolls Royce Nene engine. Whether it was an original conception or simply a derivative of pirated technology, the 660-mph MiG could fly over 100 mph faster than the F-80C, FEAF's primary jet interceptor in the theater as of November 1950.

To counter the MiG threat, the Air Force transferred top-of-the-line North American F-86 Sabres to Korea. In terms of capability, the MiG-15 was vastly superior to the F-86 in the crucial areas of speed and altitude. One intelligence report written by the 4th Wing stressed that the MiG could "out-accelerate, out-climb and out-zoom the F-86 at any altitude, and enjoyed an estimated minimum 5,000 feet top ceiling advantage."[16] Despite these seemingly overwhelming advantages, the MiG-15 and F-86 were relatively evenly matched as far as technology was concerned. Although clearly slower, the Sabre could out-turn the MiG in level or diving turns below 30,000 feet, and could out-dive it in sustained dives.[17] Because of its hydraulically boosted ailerons and adjustable horizontal stabilizer, the F-86 also had superior lateral and longitudinal control at speeds above .85 Mach.[18] Another special feature found on the Sabre but not on the MiG was the A1CM radar-ranging gun sight: a sight which determined distance from a target with an AP30 radar, and then computed "the proper lead gyroscopically, so that steering an indicator on the windshield aimed the guns for the pilot."[19] Finally, in contrast to the MiG, the Sabre had "heavy armor plate, bulletproof glass, and adequate cockpit pressurization and temperature controls."[20] In short, to achieve a higher ratio of power to weight, the Mikoyan/Gurevitch design bureau sacrificed many features which North American Aviation considered essential for an air superiority fighter. As F-86 pilot Bud Mahurin asserted, "We were driving Cadillacs while they had Fords."[21]

The superb capability of the Sabre combined with well-trained and experienced U.S. pilots—many of whom were aces from World War II—compelled the Communist pilots to fly very conservatively during the initial months of engagement.[22] Most attacks were made from high altitudes and against the rear of the Sabres. In general, the Communist pilots also restricted their operations to MiG Alley—an area "lying between the Chongchon and Yalu Rivers and bounded on the west by the Korean Bay and on the East by a line running roughly between the Sui-Ho reservoir and the city of Huichon."[23] This conservatism was partly due to the short, 100-mile range of the MiGs, which operated out of bases in China; however, it was also due to the desire of the Communist leadership to hide the identities of their pilots. If the MiG pilots operated in areas controlled by the U.N., there was always the danger that shot-down pilots would be recovered by the United Nations, and their Soviet identities discovered. In all, roughly 150 MiGs were flown by Soviet pilots, and all operated out of the Chinese base at Antung, but under Soviet control. Initially, the Soviet Air Force (and the Chinese as well) used the Korean War as "on-the-job training" for new pilots.[24] To maintain plausible deniability, the planes were forbidden to fly within sixty miles of the United Nations lines or over the sea—restrictions that often prevented the MiGs from pursuing damaged planes. Chinese colors were painted on the planes, and pilots were compelled to wear Chinese flight suits and use Chinese call signs while in the air—a difficult order to follow during the heat of battle. Overall, roughly 345 of the 1,000 Communist planes shot down in Korea were Soviet; the rest were Chinese and North Korean. By comparison, the U.S. lost over 3,335 planes, but most of these losses were attributed to ground fire and mechanical problems, not MiGs.[25]

Beginning in late June and early July of 1951, the Communists revised their tactics and started replacing trainee pilots, or "nimwits" as the Sabre pilots called them, with "honchos": instructors and other highly experienced pilots.[26] By autumn, General Liu Ya-lou, the commander of the Chinese Air Force, also began to focus less on engaging Sabres and more on attacking FEAF formations of fighter-bombers and B-29s. To elude the Sabres, Liu Ya-lou sent his MiGs up in "MiG trains" of between sixty and eighty planes. As one of these formations encountered Sabres, flights would break off and battle the F-86s while the main train kept heading south in search of fighter-bombers or bombers.[27]

By September, the trains compelled the Fifth Air Force to halt all fighter-bomber operations north of the Chongchon River, and by late October, after losing five B-29s in three days, the FEAF Bomber Command decided to halt all daylight bombing raids with B-29s, a feat which even the German Luftwaffe had never been able to accomplish during World War II.[28] In its mission reports, the 307th Bomber Wing concluded that "nothing less than 150 F-86's would have been an adequate escort for the bombers"; the Fifth Air Force, though, only had 127 in the entire theater.[29]

For about a year, the MiGs continued to concentrate their efforts against fighter-bombers and used their speed and altitude advantages to avoid Sabre patrols or MIGCAPs (MiG Combat Air Patrols), as the Americans called them. In late December 1952, the MiGs once again altered there tactics and started to challenge Sabres, this time with new "box-in" tactics. When a MIGCAP would call "bingo," the low-fuel state that signaled all Sabres to depart for their bases, one MiG flight would cross the Yalu River and pursue the Sabres while another flight, positioned over the Chongchon, would attempt to meet the retreating Sabres head on, thereby boxing them in.[30] Box-in tactics were eventually thwarted by having MIGCAPs return via the Yellow Sea—an area where MiG pilots refused to fly because of fears that in the event of being shot down, FEAF's highly efficient air-sea rescue would pick them up and discover their Soviet identities.[31] However, the aggressiveness of the MiGs did not subside, and the final months of the conflict were among the most active of the air war.

During May 1953, the combined number of air-to-air sorties flown by both sides peaked at 219 for the month. What is more, between 8 and 31 May, F-86 patrols shot down fifty-six MiGs at a loss of only one F-86, and in June, shot down a record seventy-seven with no losses. Partly responsible for these late successes was new technology. The USAF Research and Development Command and North American Aviation had reduced wind drag on the F-86 by eliminating leading-edge wing slats and introducing a solid leading edge like that found on the MiG.[32] They also improved the thrust of the F-86 by 700 pounds with a new J-47-GE-27 engine, and extended the plane's range by replacing the 120-gallon drop tanks with 200 gallon tanks. These basic improvements increased the F-86's ceiling from 49,600 feet to 52,000 feet, and its speed from .9 to 1.05 Mach.[33] Technological improvements, though, only reduced the major performance gaps between the MiG and the F-86—they did not close them. In the end, what really tipped the scales in the battles over MiG Alley were the superior skills of a select group of American pilots.

The aces, not the average pilots, were the critical ingredient in America's success because simply put, they were the ones who shot down the most MiGs. The top eight pilots shot down 98 of the 757 MiGs destroyed in the conflict. In other words, fewer than one percent of the F-86 pilots shot down 13 percent of the destroyed MiGs. Further, the thirty-nine Air Force aces scored over 287 aerial victories—38 percent of the total. This meant that roughly 5 percent of the pilots were destroying close to 40 percent of the MiGs.[34]

There are several reasons why a small number of pilots did most of the killing: the nature of fighter tactics, rank, situational awareness, and combat motivation. It was determined very early on in the war that the most effective formation for MiG killing was the four-plane "finger four" formation: the high speed of the F-86 made larger formations too difficult to manage effectively. The finger four resembled the four fingers of the human hand, with the index finger being the lead fighter. The intention of the formation was to maximize the defensive and acquisition capabilities of the flight. In theory, only the lead plane would fire on enemy MiGs: the other members of the formation would act as lookouts and guard the lead from MiG attacks. Generally, the second most experienced pilot would fly in the number three position (the ring finger) and act as an alternate shooter. New pilots would be assigned as the wingmen for the one and three men.[35]

The net effect of such conservative tactics was that a small number of shooters and alternate shooters were able to monopolize the kills, while the vast majority of pilots were compelled to perform less glamorous wingman roles.[36] Not surprisingly, shooters were often "old heads," experienced captains or majors, and the wingmen were younger, second lieutenants. In fact, as a junior officer you could very easily serve an entire tour of one hundred missions and never get a MiG.[37] For example, despite seeing six MiGs go down while flying wingman for such famous aces as James Jabara, Pete Fernandez, and Frederick "Boots" Blesse, Earl Brown flew 125 missions with the 4th Fighter-Interceptor Wing between April and October 1952, and only damaged one MiG.[38] Frank Tomlinson, similarly, complained that the "old guys wanted to fly the most missions, and in the patrol sectors where they were most likely to get a MiG." The pressure to get MiGs was, as he put it, "absolutely intense! Uh, it's just like any war, you want to be a killer, and the old heads had all the advantages!"[39]

Besides these tactics, another reason why a small group of men shot down so many MiGs is best described as "situational awareness" (SA). A term coined during the Vietnam War to describe the various physical capabilities of the ace, SA is the ability to perceive quickly and analyze moving objects in a three-dimensional environment. Robin Olds, the commander of the 8th Wing (the "Wolfpack") in Thailand during the Vietnam War, claimed that the key to SA

> is what you can see, retain, anticipate, estimate in a three-dimensional movement of many aircraft. Can you look at an enemy aircraft and know the odds—to get him before someone else if he can get behind you first, and so on? It is a three-dimensional impression you must get in seconds. This is essential in aerial combat. The guy you don't see will kill you. You must act instantly, anticipate the other fellow's motives, know that when you do this, he must do one of several things.[40]

Blesse's first kill in Korea on 25 May 1952 was an example of SA in action. On this day, Blesse spotted two MiG-15s at a higher altitude than he and his wingman. In the next couple of moments, Blesse attempted to close in on the MiGs and compute a "fire solution" before the MiGs spotted him. When they finally did, Blesse was nearly within range to take a shot. The fight, though, was hardly over because at that point the faster MiG could have easily outrun the Sabre by straightening out and continuing to dive. Instead, the MiG turned into Blesse, a move that enabled the slower, heavier F-86 to easily out-turn the MiG and get a clear shot at the plane's rear side.[41] Blesse, in short, had SA, the MiG pilot did not. Not only was Blesse able to see the MiG first, but he was able to compute a workable fire solution faster and more efficiently than his adversary. As Randall Cunningham, one of two aces of the Vietnam conflict, would say, Blesse had a "three-dimensional sense of awareness and feel of time, distance, and relative motion as if they were part of his soul."[42]

Unquestionably, situational awareness played an important role in determining who was to become an ace and who was to become "snake-bit" during the Korean War. However, it took more than SA to make an ace—it also took desire and motivation to kill other people. This desire, as we shall see from descriptions of aerial combat that follow, was fueled primarily by two factors: an intense drive for success and status and an adrenaline-driven desire to "thrill" oneself and achieve a peak experience similar to climbing a mountain, skydiving, or having orgasmic sex.

A Typical Fighter-Interceptor Mission in Korea

A standard mission would begin at first light. After quickly throwing on a uniform, the pilots would wolf down breakfast, typically powdered eggs and black coffee. As unappetizing as this food was—especially for those hung over from too much drinking the night before—most pilots would force themselves to eat. "You always ate breakfast," recalled Tomlinson, "because you might not get another meal for a while, especially if you had to bail out." [43]

After breakfast, the entire mission would be briefed in the Combat Operations Briefing Room. First, the ground situation was described by the ground liaison officer. Then, an intelligence officer briefed everyone on flak, escape and evasion, and rescue procedures. The basic rule of thumb if you were hit was to try to bail out over the Yellow Sea or near the friendly island of Chodo. These areas were patrolled by the U.S. Navy's Seventh Fleet and were therefore much safer for the slow-moving rescue helicopters to operate over than the mainland. For those who had to bail out over the mainland, travel instructions, survival tips, and contact lists were provided, but the chances of avoiding capture in these cases were extremely slim. [44] FEAF Intelligence instructed pilots to head toward the coast, and then paddle out to sea in their survival rafts so that air-sea rescue could pick them up. Not surprisingly, no pilots shot down over the land portions of MiG Alley escaped capture. [45]

After the intelligence briefing, a weather officer would give the weather forecast over the base, the mission areas, and the island of Chodo. He also gave the pilots a list of alternative airfields to be used in the event of emergency landings. Finally, the mission leader would explain the order of the day, or the FRAG order as it was called: "FRAG" literally means a "fragment" of FEAF's daily air order of battle. He would also assign "start-engine times, areas and altitudes to be flown, and special duties to be accomplished." [46] At the end of the meeting, pilots would get flight maps, pasted on cardboard mats for ease of use, and code words to be used in the event of a bailout. Pilots would then break up into smaller groups and conduct informal meetings to discuss their individual roles in the mission. [47]

The briefing, overall, not only informed the pilot of the day's mission, but it also was very much a part of the ritual of aviation combat. Many of these men had seen air combat movies such as *Dawn Patrol* (1936) and implicitly understood the symbolism of the predawn briefing: the danger, the patriotism, and, most important, the fact that some of the men in the room might not return. The emphasis on escape, survival, and evasion reinforced this danger.

If shot down, they would be expected to leave the security of the cockpit and survive alone in a harsh and dangerous environment. According to Bud Mahurin, "There were no known friendly civilians above the bomb line." North Korea was "Indian country" for these men—a harsh and dangerous frontier inhabited by a "savage" foe. To survive in this environment, all men were issued a standard survival kit which contained such items as food, a first-aid kit, and a .45-pistol. However, most men customized their kits to reflect their own personality and fetishes. Mahurin, for example, added "two pairs of heavy white sox, a change of underwear, a .22 caliber Savage folding rifle, and a roll of toilet paper."[48] For Hagerstrom, the survival kit and his personal flight suit became an obsession and a mechanism for managing fear. Before he left the U.S., Hagerstrom purchased a pair of felt-lined Russell moccasin boots and a white bird-cloth flying suit lined with raw silk for maximum insulation. He also carried dried milk, berries, nuts, oatmeal, ten pounds of rice, sterno, a pot, a fold-up camp stove, a monocular, maps, shaving equipment, a sleeping-bag vacuum packed in a picnic-ham can, a shelter-half, and enough sulfa to cure pneumonia three times. In addition, he packed a radio, three batteries, and a special SAC issue .22 caliber Hornet rifle with a muzzle velocity of 4000 feet per second, a range of 100 yards, almost no bullet drop, and no smoke. "The Hornet was the first thing in my backpack," Jim explained, "a pistol won't do it because a patrol with rifles would just stand off at 50 yards and shoot at you." If shot down, Hagerstrom planned to fight off any patrols which came after him until dark, when he could slip away. He had enough food to last thirty days and he planned to hike ten miles a day until he reached the DMZ. Why did he plan so carefully for a bailout? Hagerstrom claims it helped him not to worry: "The difference between panic and fear is pretty tight, and you can spread that line a bit by having one last chance." [49]

After another cup of coffee, many pilots took a trip to the latrines to relieve themselves before the flight. Flight suits had acquired the unenviable nickname of "poop suits," and it was certainly more desirable to dispose of waste before a flight rather than during it. It was also not unusual for anxious or hung-over pilots to throw up before battle. [50] Before one mission, for example, Leonard "Bill" Lilly leaned over the side of his F-86 on the taxiway and threw up; he then went up and shot down two MiGs. [51]

After the latrines, all pilots proceeded to their aircraft to examine the maintenance logs, talk to the ground crew chief, and perform a preflight inspection. [52] From there, the pilot would join his comrades in the locker room to suit up. The atmosphere before a mission was similar to a high school varsity locker room before the big game. "It was almost joyful," claims Earl Brown, "and guys would start to sing while they were suiting up": "Oh we sing, we sing, we sing of Lydia Pinkham, Pinkham, Pinkham, and her love for the human race. Wonderful compound, a dollar a bottle, and every label bears her face, her fucking face." [53] They would also tease one another with such lines as: "Today's the day I'm going to get some MiGs." "How are you going to do it?" another pilot would respond. "You'll never know!" [54]

The joking, though, ended as soon as the pilots hit the flight line and performed their final stationary check, a 360-degree walk around their aircraft. By this time, over three hours had passed since reveille, but there was still more to focus on before takeoff: all gauges, instruments, brakes, and surface controls had to be checked while taxiing out. Take-offs were then conducted in four-plane formations "approximately five to eight seconds apart." [55]

Once airborne, the climb to altitude is made at "near maximum power settings and the element does not move into close formation except to penetrate an overcast." [56] The object here was to achieve a high speed of Mach .88 or above and an altitude of 43,500 feet before hitting MiG Alley. Because the MiG could get above the Sabre at any altitude, speed was tactically more valuable to a flight than altitude, for

Flight suit banter. Second Lieutenant William R. Bowman, First Lieutenant Harold E. Fischer, and Second Lieutenant Edward Sanet of the 51st Wing go over tactics in the barracks. Lieutenant Sanet is "palming" his cigarette in the warrior style. (Courtesy Far East Air Forces)

First Lieutenant Joseph A. Caple of the 51st Wing composes a letter to his wife. Note the rustic conditions of Lieutenant Caple's hootch: dirty underwear in the background, a homemade pine desk, and a tin can ink well. (Courtesy Far East Air Forces)

Pilots of the 49th Fighter-Bomber Group kick back in front of their officers' club, "Auger Inn," April 1951. Note the casual reference to death and danger: in pilot parlance, to auger in means to crash in a tail spin. From left to right: Captain Martin N. Nay, Captain Frederick F. Champlin, First Lieutenant Edward H. Warne, and First Lieutenant Robert M. Allen. (Courtesy Far East Air Forces)

Demon mugs for firewater. First Lieutenant Franklin G. Putney doles out mission whiskey to fellow pilots of the "Screamin' Demon" squadron in the "Auger Inn." This unit just returned from attacking a supply area in North Korea, September 1952. From left to right: First Lieutenant Franklin B. Putney, First Lieutenant William G. Fuller, Captain Theodore Upland, Major Clifford C. Gould, Second Lieutenant Raymond H. Johnson, and First Lieutenant Reed C. Jansen. (Courtesy Far East Air Forces)

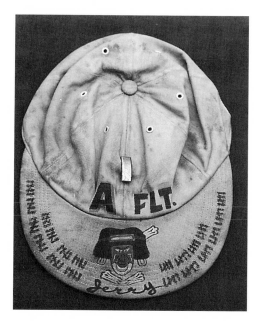

Jerry Minton's squadron baseball cap. After every mission flown, Minton made a hash mark on his visor: pilots were sent home after having flown one hundred missions. (Courtesy Jerry Minton)

Pilot Jerry Minton's house boy, Pak. According to Minton, he swept, did laundry, filled canteens, and polished boots. Each of the pilots in Minton's hootch chipped in a few dollars a week to support him and his sister. "I think he ended up getting paid more than a South Korean general," recalled Minton, "but he was worth more." Minton claims that Pak did not want his picture taken with any pilots because when the North Korean troops captured Suwon early on in the war, they shot the houseboys who could be identified as having worked for American pilots. These troops also broke the backs of several houseboys with their rifle butts. (Courtesy Jerry Minton)

Miss Winnie Wildman, Red Cross canteen supervisor, turns the newly opened Red Cross Club over to Lieutenant Colonel Joseph E. McNally of the 49th Fighter-Bomber Wing, August 1951. The canteen will serve free coffee, ice tea, and doughnuts, but pilots will have to go to the o club for more potent refreshments. (Courtesy Far East Air Forces)

Staff Sergeant Richard Crowell takes time out of his busy schedule as an F-80 crew chief with the 51st Fighter-Interceptor Wing to grab a cup of hot coffee from Red Cross girl Elizabeth Truner. November 1951. (Courtesy Far East Air Forces)

In this picture, members of Fifth Air Force units in Korea attend Easter services. In the foreground, an F-86 pilot gets ready to taxi down the runway and continue destructive attacks against North Korea. (Courtesy Far East Air Forces)

it emphasized the Sabre's rate of closure when attacking and reduced the MiG's rate of closure when the tables were turned.[57]

A basic MIGCAP or "fighter sweep" contained either nine or twelve elements spread across MiG Alley. At least two elements would fly directly opposite the large Chinese air base at Antung, nicknamed "Antung Air University"; other elements might be placed between Antung and the Sui Ho Reservoir; and still others, east of the reservoir or farther south as a backup.[58] These sweeps were often vectored to MiG flights by two radar stations—one just above Kimpo Air Force Base known as Dentist, and another on Cho Do, known as Dentist Charlie.[59]

There were several tactical problems the Sabres confronted while in MiG Alley. First, their patrol time was extremely limited due to the 200-mile distance between the F-86 bases near Seoul and MiG Alley. F-86s, consequently, only carried enough fuel to loiter over the Yalu River for twenty minutes; however, aggressive pilots like Hagerstrom would try to "whittle down" their "bingo" state. When a pilot transmitted the bingo code word to his flight, it meant that he had only enough fuel to get back to the base, and would have to break off from a combat patrol. A high bingo was 1,500 pounds of fuel and a low bingo was 1,100 pounds, but Hagerstrom quickly discovered that these guidelines were conservative. "It was ridiculous to come up and only spend twenty minutes over the Yalu," he explained, "so I made a few calculations of my own and determined that I could make it back to base with 600 pounds: just to be safe, though, I used an alarm clock to tell me when to head on home." Nevertheless, Hagerstrom often "pushed the envelope" well beyond his own self-imposed 600-pound limit: on a mission where he shot down a MiG, he pushed it to 300 pounds, and on another, he actually ran out of gas taxiing away from the main runway.[60]

Another problem which the Sabres faced was limited maneuverability at high altitudes. In the thin air of the stratosphere, oxygen-breathing jet engines begin to lose power, and a quick turn or a burst of gunfire from the 50-caliber guns could cause an F-86 to lose speed and altitude in a hurry. Consequently, MIGCAPs flew racetrack patterns and made broad, 90-degree turns.[61]

The final and perhaps the most vexing problem for the Sabre pilots was target acquisition. In general, the MiGs were very reluctant to "mix it up" with Sabres. The Sabres, therefore, often had to sneak up on the MiGs from behind to get a shot in, but this was no simple task. Clear air and lots of sunshine made spotting a MiG extremely difficult. Without visual references, the human eye tends to focus on a point eighteen inches in front of the nose. Often, sunlight reflecting off an aluminum fuselage was the only visual cue that a MiG was nearby, and your eyes constantly played tricks on you: a speck of dirt on the Plexiglass canopy, for example, could easily be mistaken for a distant MiG. Some pilots carried binoculars to improve their chances of spotting MiGs. Hagerstrom, before he left the States, had a special pair of half-mirrored, distance glasses made which enabled him to see at twenty feet what an ordinary person would see at ten. The optometrist told him they might permanently ruin his eyes, and he replied: "I don't give a shit." [62]

As soon as a MiG was spotted, it became a race against time to maneuver to within 2,000 yards of the MiG, position the gun sight, and get a kill in before the bingo point was reached. F-86s only had enough fuel to patrol MiG alley for twenty minutes, and any dogfighting limited that time even further.

Upon return to base, a pilot would immediately be debriefed on the day's activities. If the nose of his plane was black from gun smoke (an indication that an aerial battle had been fought), he would often be met on the tarmac by the squadron leader or even the wing commander and be asked to go over the kill as he emerged from the airplane. Later, more formal debriefings would occur in the operations hut, and on occasion "mission whiskey" or other spirits would be offered to the pilot by the flight surgeon to settle his nerves. The flight surgeon gave the pilot several ounces of whiskey for every mission flown, and generally this whiskey would be awarded to the pilot in large volumes at the end of every month; but occasionally, the spirits were actually doled out after a mission. "Thank God the doctors were also aware of the limits of human endurance and gave us a ration of whiskey to be used at the completion of every mission," recalled Mahurin. "If it had not been for the whiskey ration and the rest leaves in Japan," he claimed, "we would have had frequent crack-ups." [63]

F-86 pilots flew roughly three missions a week and one hundred missions per tour. When a pilot completed his hundred-mission tour, he was immediately sent home.[64] After every thirty missions flown, a pilot was given an Air Medal, and after one hundred missions, a Distinguished Flying Cross. If a pilot managed to do something spectacular like shoot down five MiGs, a Silver Star was awarded.[65] Status in the Air Force, in short, was directly related to performance in combat and missions flown.

The Characteristics of the Ace

As mentioned previously, seniority and rank did indeed improve a pilot's chances of getting a kill: the higher your rank, the better your chances of being assigned to the number one "shooter" slot in the flight. Another characteristic which facilitated MiG killing was the ability to discriminate objects at far distances and think in a three-dimensional manner. However, SA, rank, and seniority alone did not make an ace. Most Korean War pilots had excellent vision, but only a select few found and killed MiGs. Conversely, not every ace was an "old head." James Low was just six months out of flying school when he became America's seventeenth jet ace.[66] Killing, in short, took more than luck, rank, or even pilot skill; it took desire and intense aggression.

The intense desire to get kills is best demonstrated by the pilots' willingness to push the capabilities of the aircraft to the limit, a limit wingmen would often not cross. On 3 October 1952, for example, the two wingmen in Major Blesse's flight withdrew from a chase, ostensibly due to lack of fuel. Blesse and his alternate shooter, however, pressed on until a dangerously low fuel state forced them to withdraw from the attack. While returning, Blesse encountered two additional MiGs, pursued them, and got a kill; his alternate, though, headed home. In the end, Blesse had to bail out over Paengnyong Do when he ran out of fuel.[67] Blesse, in short, was willing to expend all of his fuel, sacrifice an airplane, and endure the dangers inherent in a bail out just to "get a MiG."

Similarly, Captain William Guss, a Marine attached to the 4th Wing, was also willing to "push the envelope" to get kills. On 4 November

1951, Guss observed two MiGs at his 9 o'clock position. He then maneuvered behind the aircraft and fired a short burst at the number two MiG. Next, Guss pursued that plane for "fifteen minutes through a violent and continuous lufbery [a tight, vertical spiral], firing throughout the encounter" until the MiG finally "snapped into a flat spin and the pilot ejected." [68]

Another example of how much determination it took to get a kill is the ace Robinson Risner. After two months of service in Korea, Risner departed for Tokyo for a three-day leave. That night he learned from another pilot that the MiGs were flying again in Korea: the MiGs flew in cycles and would often stand down for a week before flying again. Rather than enjoy his rest and relaxation, Risner took the next plane back to Korea and arrived at Kimpo Air Force Base at two in the morning. He slept for one hour and then headed out to the alert shack to get on the next flight. Because Risner's flight was a quick reaction, "hot-shot" flight, every pilot in the flight was already at his aircraft, ready to roll when the klaxon finally sounded.

When the flight reached Pyongyang, four MiGs crossed under their noses, but the American attack was soon interrupted by another flight of MiGs which attacked them from the rear. Rather than breaking off the fight, Risner allowed the attackers to bear down on him and used a scissor maneuver to force them to overshoot him. [69] Once a MiG was in his gun sight, Risner "ate him up" with his 50-caliber guns, causing the MiG to stall. In order to simply stay behind the MiG, Risner had to chop his engine to idle and throw his speed brakes—a move which in turn caused Risner to stall and start spinning. As Risner recalled, "I managed to control the rudders just enough to recover and plant another machine-gun burst in the tail pipe of the MiG—a burst which tore the tail off the MiG and forced the pilot to bail out at 31,000 feet." Risner remembered thinking to himself, "This is my first kill; I really nailed him, and it was almost by accident." But it was *not* by accident; Risner *made* this kill happen. He cut his leave short, missed a good night's sleep, and once in battle, refused to break off the fight no matter how dangerous it became. [70] Risner, in short, had that key ingredient necessary to become an ace: desire! As fellow ace Frederick Blesse put it in his famous pamphlet on Korean War fighter tactics, "No Guts, No Glory," Risner had the will to "get in there and mix it up."[71] He had the guts to achieve the glory.

The notion that MiG killing had more to do with desire and courage than luck or seniority is a central theme of James Salter's novel, *The Hunters*. At one point in the story, an established ace in the outfit, Ausman, explains to the novel's protagonist, Cleve Saville, that a pilot "can play it safe and never get into a tight spot," and probably "go home after a hundred missions with the usual medals and, who knows, maybe a couple of victories, just by waiting for the sure things." On the other hand, he continues, "You can take chances, and you'll probably be a hero when you get back. And you'll probably go back. It just depends on what you want most. You'll see for yourself. After ten missions everybody is an expert."[72]

As Ausman alludes, there were quite a few men who chose not to mix it up. In fact, pilot Bud Mahurin complained that out of the one hundred pilots who attended any given pre-mission briefing, only eighteen "could actually be depended upon to mix it up with the enemy and perhaps do some shooting." The other eighty-two "would fly into the combat zone but for some strange reason never see the enemy or fire a gun."[73]

Hagerstrom once flew with a vice commander of the 4th Wing, a South African colonel, who called an attack off as soon as Hagerstrom spotted MiGs.[74] According to Hagerstrom, this man just wanted to get his one hundred missions in and did not want to get "his pink body" anywhere near actual shooting.[75] "It sounds great to be a fighter pilot," Hagerstrom complained, "but when you see those 30-millimeter cannon balls coming at you (and it only takes one to blow the tail of an airplane off), then people say wait a minute, this is a little too sporty for me, and then they back off."[76] For Paul Turner, similarly, a lack of "sportiness" in one of his wingmen caused Turner to get shot down. Turner was maneuvering to shoot down a MiG and thought his wingman, who had withdrawn, was covering his "tail": "He never called me or did a goddamn thing and so here I was pulling behind number two and expecting to be told when there was any danger or anything and this dog food manufacturer decided he was going to turn around and go home, and didn't even say bullshit or anything else."[77] In the end, Turner was shocked that a wingman would abandon his shooter, but incidents like this one were not as unusual as Turner imagined. Hagerstrom experienced this type of behavior twice, and Salter, also a pilot with the 4th, wrote extensively about it in his novel *The Hunters*. According to Salter's protagonist, Cleve Saville, pilots "were accompanied [by wingmen] . . . but they were really of no help."[78]

Not only was it dangerous when a wingman abandoned you, but it also greatly complicated the kill confirmation process. Ordinarily, a wingman would confirm a kill if it did not show up on the shooter's gun camera film, a common occurrence. However, if a wingman was not around to witness a kill, as was often the case with aggressive flyers like Hagerstrom and Turner, kills would not be entered onto the squadron claims board. After Turner's wingman retreated, he managed to pull a quick scissor maneuver and "nail" the horizontal stabilizer of the MiG that shot him.[79] Unfortunately for Turner, his ship eventually caught fire, forcing him to bail out, and he never got the claim confirmed. Furthermore, this was not the only occasion where confirmation was a problem for Turner: "As far as the Air Force is concerned I never got a MiG, but as far as I'm concerned, I got three."[80] Hagerstrom, after one mission where he got separated from his wingman, was told by Royal Baker, the Wing commander, that he "was not going to get a confirmation unless he had good film." About that time, the crew chief, who was putting the chocks under the airplane, said, "Colonel, let me show you this," and there was a chunk of MiG-15 wedged in the leading edge of the airplane. Baker looked up and replied: "I'll confirm it."[81]

As Hagerstrom's and Turner's experiences demonstrate, aerial combat often required one to risk becoming separated from a wingman to get a kill. Aces were not only willing to "go-it-alone," but were even willing to break standard rules of engagement for the sake of a kill. Although pilots were directed not to cross the Yalu River into China unless they were in "hot pursuit," some of the more aggressive pilots regularly patrolled north of the Yalu. In 1952 and early 1953, U.S. planes would often attack MiGs as they were taking off or landing from Antung.[82] Blesse described the "unofficial" rules of engagement for aces as follows:

"We were forbidden to cross the Yalu River but we did it anyway; we had to if we were going to protect the fighter-bombers. One rule specifically ordered us not to strafe MiGs on their airfields, all of which were across the river—an absolute no-no. If he was flying, OK, shoot him down, but if he was even rolling down the runway, no dice, because that's really ground attack." [83] Hagerstrom once flew fifteen feet over the alert pad at Antung at nine-tenths the speed of sound just "trying to get the MiGs off the ground." [84]

In addition to breaking rules, aces were always willing to extend their tours and fly on holidays for an extra opportunity to kill a MiG. Even though Blesse complained that the huts, roaches, poor food, uncomfortable bunks, and lack of women made Korea a "lousy" place to be, he "put in for another twenty-five missions" of overtime in an attempt to become an ace.[85] For aces, aggressiveness also extended to sacred holidays. On Christmas, for example, Hagerstrom volunteered to be on defense alert because he had a hunch that the MiGs might fly on that day. Sure enough, his element got a radar plot, and Hagerstrom got a MiG on Christmas Day. He had his "pipper lined up on the tail pipe" of a MiG at 50,000 feet, but he knew that if he shot, he would stall. Suddenly, the MiG pilot looked over his shoulder, saw Hagerstrom's F-86, and kicked his plane into a spin. Before Hagerstrom could fire, "the guy bailed out at 45,000 feet on a 20-degree below zero day, and froze to death on the way down." [86] The wind-chill factor, according to Hagerstrom, would have made it feel like 100 degrees below zero. Wind chill or not, there would be no "peace on earth and goodwill towards men" for Hagerstrom on that Christmas Day; instead, there was merely the image of a MiG pilot slowly freezing to death during a thirty-minute parachute ride to earth.

In March 1953, Hagerstrom knew he would be transferred out of theater or to fighter-bombers in a couple of days. He refused to go quietly. With only 4.5 MiG kills to his credit, there was still hunting to be done. He needed a kill and the ace status it would confer. He delivered the following speech to his men: "Gentleman, I've been living on coffee; I haven't been sleeping; I've got to do this thing; I'm gonna do it; and if you don't want to go with me, that's fine, I'll understand. We are going to go up there and give it one good college try south of the Yalu, and if we don't scare anything up, I'm going after them today."[87] As it turned out, he shot down two that day just outside of the Antung air complex in China. However, he did not stop there. On his last day in Korea, Hagerstrom was in the operations hut in his dress-blue uniform waiting for his C-47 flight to Tachikawa to arrive. A friend in "ops" suddenly came over to him and told him that four aircraft were needed over a sensitive area. "I'll do it," said Hagerstrom, "and I turned to the ops officers and told them we have an instant mission: you're two, you're three, you're four, and Sam Kratz will be the leader—that's me." The radar operator then vectored them into a flight of twenty-five MiGs, and Hagerstrom got one.[88]

The Dynamics of the Kill

We see from the experiences of fighter pilots like Hagerstrom, Turner, Mahurin, and Blesse that none of them were fully cognizant of the fact that what they were doing over MiG Alley was killing *people,* not planes. Fast-moving aerial warfare in jets tended to remove the individual from the process of killing. Risner, who believed that Korea was the "high point of his entire career," describes it as a "clean, impersonal" form of combat: "It's not dirty, like down in the trenches, and there is no hand-to-hand combat. When people die, you don't see it. I saw a few buddies go down, and I saw MiG pilots go down, but you're not aware of the blood and pain."[89] Blesse is even more blunt: "Later, after three or four victories, I was surprised how cold and calculating I had become. At times, I almost felt ashamed. I never thought I'd get that way but to be honest, I never wanted it any different. I could come back with every detail, altitudes, maneuvers, sun position, clouds, everything! Better still, it wasn't instinct flying. I was thinking my way through each flight."[90] For Blesse, the mechanics of combat flying were so complex that he could psychologically distance himself from the act of killing by immersing himself in technical details. Hagerstrom also rationalized the killing process by disconnecting the enemy pilot from his machine: "I never shot directly at the pilot, nor did I shoot anyone dangling from a parachute."[91] For Hagerstrom, there was a distinct difference between blowing a plane to pieces with your guns and firing at a pilot. Aviation technology depersonalized killing and allowed Hagerstrom to absolve himself of any and all responsibility for his actions. So pervasive was Hagerstrom's obsession with the technical aspects of killing that even when one of the men in his own wing got shot down, he focused on the technical mistakes which caused that pilot's death rather than grieving for the loss of a friend and comrade: "Screw it, it happens, get on with it. Learn something from everything that happens. That's the most important thing to do."[92]

Another pilot who chose to see killing in technical rather than moral terms was Bud Mahurin. After his first aerial victories in World War II, he claimed: "I was so excited that the thought of having killed two human beings didn't enter my mind. In the first place, I had been spurred to action out of anger; in the second place, the planes I had just shot down were objects, not people."[93] Mahurin, like Hagerstrom, was too elated over the thought of joining "the charmed circle of aces" to worry about death and killing.[94]

Given this detachment from the darker side of war, it is not surprising that Hagerstrom and other pilots actually enjoyed combat and the adrenaline rush it gave them. Blesse describes this peak experience as follows: "The one thing that never left me was the intense, gripping anxiety and excitement that occurred when I saw some kind of movement which indicated the enemy pilot had seen me and one of us wasn't going home. That remained and has to this day been the greatest thrill of my life."[95] A significant clue that many pilots derived intense pleasure and excitement from aerial kills is the sexual language they use to describe it. Scholars in the field of cultural studies argue that connections between "seemingly unrelated categories of experience" can be found in the symbolic codes of cultural phenomena, language, and discourse.[96] For example, Elaine Tyler May and Allan Brandt show a link between sexual power and military power during World War II by analyzing nose art. Scantily clad or naked women on fighter planes, these authors claim, suggest "a power to destroy the enemy." In the context of the air war in Korea, a similar interrelationship between war and sexuality can be found not only in nose art, but in the language that fighter pilots use to describe combat. Not only are plane parts and planes compared to genitalia, but rape, sodomy, and violation imagery directly link killing with male dominance, homoeroticism, and power. Orgasmic language, similarly, connects killing to the adrenaline rush or thrill many felt after getting a kill. Feelings of sexual frustration and impotence, by contrast, relate to the failure to get a kill.

Hagerstrom and others, for example, constantly talked about "violating" Chinese air space in "hot pursuit" of MiGs—as if shooting down a MiG in China was somehow the equivalent of a violent rape. Some kill imagery even had homoerotic and sadomasochistic overtones: "Three or four scissors later," exclaimed Hagerstrom, "I was on his ass and hit him." [97] Because violation could also occur in reverse, a pilot's own wingman was expected to cover his "rear" at all times.

Once a MiG was sighted, the process of maneuvering in for the kill was described in terms of "lining" the pipper up with the other guy's "tail pipe." That "pipper" is also a slang word for penis can hardly be ignored, nor for that matter, can the connection between the tail pipe and the anus.

Like plane parts, occasionally entire planes took on an anthropomorphic sexual identity. The lower performance F-84, for example, was described by George Berke in a novel about fighter pilots in the 1950s as a second-rate prostitute:

> Oh don't—
> Give me an F-84;
> That bitch is a ground lovin' whore;
> She'll tumble and roll;
> And dig a deep hole;
> Don't give me an F-84. [98]

In another section of the novel, roles are reversed, and an actual sexual act with a prostitute becomes aeronautical: "He lay down on the bed spread-eagled. Marcey knelt between his. . . . They were down in the quick check area, getting the last look over. He watched them move the control surfaces. The crew chief gave the thumbs up." [99] Just as a takeoff is roughly equivalent to sexual climax, so too are kills. In *The Hunters*, the physical sensations Cleve Saville feels when he gets a kill—namely, a "wild pipper," senseless cries, and a ballooning heart—bear an uncanny resemblance to sexual climax:

> Cleve was behind him, on the inside, turning as hard as he could. The bright pipper of his sight was creeping up on the MiG, jerkily, but moving slowly up to the tail, the fuselage, the wing root. He squeezed the trigger. The tracers arced [sic] out, falling mostly behind. There were a few strikes near the tail. He could hardly hold the wild pipper where it was but somehow he moved it forward, it seemed only inches more.... He fired again. His heart ballooned in his throat. He shouted into the mask, not words, but a senseless cry. Solid strikes along the fuselage. There was a burst of white flame and a sudden flood of smoke. The MiG pulled up sharply, climbing. It was slipping away from him, but as it did, he laced it with hits. Finally, trailing a curtain of fire, it rolled over on one wing and started down.[100]

In another instance, Imil, the wing commander, draws a direct connection between aggressive sex and getting a fifth kill:

> "I remember when I came down that day. What a feeling! The whole world wasn't big enough for me. You know what I mean."
> "Right," Pell agreed impulsively.
> "I had this girl. Know what she said?"
> "No."
> "Be a bloody ace tonight, that's all." He held his fist and forearm up [a locker room symbol for sex] and laughed.[101]

Sex and death were inextricably linked in this highly charged, male environment of fighter "jocks." It was as if the act of creation and killing had become one and the same.

Like chasing women, a failure of a pilot to catch a MiG was tantamount to sexual failure. When Charles "Chick" Cleveland was "snakebit" during one particularly intense day over MiG Alley, he lamented to Blesse: "If they sawed a woman in two, I'd get the half that eats."[102] Failure to get a kill, in short, was equated to being denied the genitals of a woman.

In *The Hunters*, Cleve Saville, the book's hero, also was tormented over not getting MiGs. For Saville, his courage and skill were the most important things in his life. Everything else that he valued—"the good women, the crewmen eager to serve, the respect"—depended on his ability to demonstrate these fighter qualities by shooting down MiGs.[103] When he could not accomplish that end, "he could sense the ebbing respect," especially from women.[104] However, when he finally did make a kill, he "never felt so fine." In one brief moment, his entire reason for existence was confirmed: "He knew then that he would never lose."[105]

In the clear-cut world of the fighter-interceptor squadron, success, simply put, was defined by killing. As Salter writes: "There were no other values. It was like money. . . . MiGs were everything. If you had MiGs you were a standard of excellence. The sun shone upon you. The crew chiefs were happy to have you fly their ships. The touring actresses wanted to meet you. You were the center of everything—the praise, the excitement, the enviers."[106] On the other hand, if you did not kill MiGs, "you were nothing."[107] Clearly, such a world appears vapid to the outsider, but at the same time there was a liberating Nietzschian appeal to it. In contrast to the white-collar world of the 1950s described by C. Wright Mills and other cultural critics, one did not rise in the "fighter business" by one's ability to patronize one's boss and sell oneself in the "great salesroom"; rather, the Korean War fighter Air Force was almost a pure meritocracy. If you could kill MiGs, it did not matter whether you were a James Low fresh out of flight school, or a more experienced pilot like Frederick Blesse or James Hagerstrom—you still rose within the organization. Few pilots who shot down five MiGs or more left Korea below the rank of colonel.[108] Rank, in the end though, was not all that these flight suit officers were after. Kudos, status, and peak experiences were far more important. Pilot James Brooks explained it in this manner: "It feels extremely good to saddle up to that officers' club and know you have applied yourself a little beyond normal; you stand a bit taller than most of your peers."[109] Blesse, after he got his fifth kill, claimed that it was the "realization of a dream I had since I was a kid, and over the years came to mean more to me than becoming a general officer in the Air Force."[110]

─ · · 5 · · ─

Headhunters and Fighting Cocks:
The Fighter-Bomber in Korea

In James Salter's novel *The Hunters* (1956), Cleve Saville, an F-86 fighter-interceptor pilot, is obsessed with one thing: killing MiGs. Although Saville had already distinguished himself as a fighter pilot during World War II, he realized when he got to Korea that he would have to shoot down MiGs to maintain his status as a superior pilot. He was not arriving in Korea as a second lieutenant straight out of flight school, but as a veteran captain and flight commander. Consequently, it was imperative for him to shoot down at least as many MiGs as any other pilot in his flight. "If he did not get MiGs he would have failed, not only in his own eyes but in everyone's. Talking to Corona, to Daughters, to anybody, it was only too plain. They said it meant nothing, but their denials were a confession. They expected a great deal from him. He was the old hand." [1] To ensure success in this quest, Saville chose his missions very carefully and only flew when he thought he might see combat, "deciding often at the last minute, trusting what was now a hardened, vicious instinct." [2]

When he managed to get a MiG, he was literally on top of the world, but when he failed and other pilots got kills, he could "sense the ebbing respect": "Cleve had come to see, so had everyone else, how rigid was that casting. There were no other values. It was like money: it did not matter how it had been acquired, but only that it had. That was the final judgment. It was magisterial. MiGs were everything. If you had MiGs you were a standard of excellence."[3] Even the prospect of sex with a beautiful woman in Tokyo was no substitute for getting kills. Just as Cleve is about to embark upon a romantic interlude with a young Japanese woman in Tokyo, he discovers that there had been a big air fight while he was on leave; immediately, Saville leaves the woman to return to his unit. After missing such a big fight, "he felt like a man washed overboard a thousand miles from shore."[4]

Despite his obsession with MiGs, Saville in the end fails to shoot down a total of five MiGs and become an ace. Unlike Pell, a younger pilot in his flight, Saville lacks the ruthlessness to become a successful jet ace. Saville, in several instances, is unwilling to abandon a wingman in trouble to get a MiG. For Saville, looking out for the welfare of his fellow pilots is more important than personal gain.

Good intentions in the end, however, get Saville nowhere. After shooting down his fifth MiG, Saville is denied the victory because his wingman, Hunter, the only person who can confirm the kill, crash-lands and dies. In a bitter twist of irony, Saville then confirms the victory for Hunter, and Hunter is awarded a posthumous Silver Star. On his next mission, Cleve Saville is killed when Pell, his wingman for this mission, abandons him to shoot down a MiG. The book concludes with the new ace Pell disingenuously telling a reporter that Saville was a "great guy," and a "brother" to him.[5]

Like Saville, Tindle, the protagonist in Walt Sheldon's *Troubling of a Star* (1953), is equally troubled by his personal predicament in Korea.[6] However, Tindle is an F-80 fighter-bomber pilot, and thus his troubles are quite different than Saville's. Whereas Saville is status anxious, Tindle is distraught over his job as a killer of men, women, and children on the ground. Sheldon's novel begins with Tindle returning from forward air control (FAC) duty on the main battle line.[7] As a ground-based FAC, Tindle had the opportunity to witness napalm attacks at close hand and was very disturbed by what he saw: men similar to himself being slaughtered in an inhumane fashion. Hence, when he returns to his outfit, he does not look upon his remaining missions as opportunities to get kills; rather, he sees them as trying ordeals which he must endure at all costs. Throughout the rest of the novel, Tindle tries to reconcile his desire to be a good fighter-bomber pilot with his angst over the holocaust he feels he is inflicting upon his fellow man.

Immediately upon his return from FAC duty, Tindle worries if he will even be able to kill, but then assures himself that he would: "There would be no other choice. Like the woman had said when rape was inevitable—that was lieutenant Rossi's remark that day he couldn't pull out and knew he was about to cream into a mountain—'It's inevitable,' Rossi had said, 'I might as well relax and enjoy it.' "[8] Like Saville, though, Tindle learns that simple rationalizations do not always work in war. On his first mission after returning, Tindle discovers that inflicting death is indeed a personal choice: one can easily allow one's rockets or napalm to miss a target. However, "live and let live" strategies like this carry penalties of their own. When Tindle fails to hit his targets on that mission, he is immediately confronted by an angry wing commander, who accuses him of being jittery and afraid to fly: it takes steady nerves to lay down a bomb load on target. Thus, Tindle is trapped. He can either continue to fly and engage in "immoral" killing, or he can submit to an FOF charge and never fly again. If he chooses an FOF discharge, though, he would end up denying himself of the only thing he was good at—flying an airplane. "The fact was, he wasn't fit for much anything except flying a combat airplane. He'd spent more time learning that, after all. And he had the feeling that he had never really properly learned another goddamn thing in his twenty-nine years of existence. So what kind of life was that, where a man learned only one thing, and spent his whole life doing just that, doing nothing but getting better at one thing."[9] Allowing himself to be labeled as an FOF coward would also place him in the same category as Major Ronsdale, a man who had lost all respect for himself and who literally and figuratively was impotent. For Tindle to maintain his individuality and manhood, he must live with his turmoil and continue to drop bombs on innocent people. Only death or an honorable transfer to a noncombat assignment can fully resolve his inner turmoil.

In the end, Sheldon's novel falls victim to a Hollywood-style ending, and Tindle is spared from his predicament by circumstance. After Tindle's aggressive wing commander barely escapes death, he decides to leave the Air Force and take an administrative position with a church. However, before leaving, he offers Tindle a desk job as a final act of Christian charity and goodwill, and Tindle accepts it without gratitude.

As this brief literary comparison reveals, the lot of the fighter-bomber was much different than that of the fighter-interceptor. Both types were casual, individualistic, flight suit officers. However, fighter-bombers like Tindle were much more concerned with surviving their combat tour honorably than competing with fellow pilots for status symbols. Unlike fighter-interceptor pilots, fighter-bombers pilots were not ranked individually by number of kills achieved. Rather, their self-worth was very much connected to the accomplishments of their units: number of bridges destroyed, troops killed, railroad tracks cut, and so on. One could not paint a red star on one's aircraft or call oneself an ace for napalming a concentration of railroad laborers. All a fighter-bomber could hope for was to survive his tour and return to the U.S. with a Distinguished Flying Cross—the standard reward for flying one hundred missions.

A close study of the fighter-bomber raises a number of interesting questions. Why was the mission of the fighter-bomber more difficult and dangerous than that of the fighter-interceptor? How did the fighter-bomber pilots motivate themselves to fight and kill in the absence of tangible rewards and status symbols? How did this situation affect morale, and how did commanders attempt to offset potential and actual moral problems by building unit pride? These questions will be examined in this chapter. Readers unfamiliar with the operational history of the fighter-bomber campaigns in Korea, however, may wish to read Appendix 1 before reading on.

The Hazards of the Job

The life of a fighter-bomber pilot was hazardous and often short. Typically, fighter-bomber pilots flew lower-performance planes and exposed themselves daily to more hostile ground fire than the typical fighter-interceptor. Overall, only 147 Air Force planes were lost in air-to-air combat; by comparison, over 816 planes were shot down by ground fire.[10] As Raymond Sturgeon, a pilot with the 35th squadron of the 8th Group, put it, "I had friends in 86s who never saw a MiG their entire tour, but we got fired on every mission with high-powered guns that shot golf balls at you." [11] Sturgeon's squadron lost "a pilot or two" every week, and losses like these were not unusual. Perrin Gower, another pilot in Sturgeon's squadron, claimed that five of the ten pilots he shared his hut with were killed, and Howard Heiner, a pilot in the 12th Squadron of the 18th Wing, remembered one week when seven pilots in his squadron were shot down.[12]

Far and away the greatest danger to the fighter-bomber were anti-aircraft (AA) weapons.[13] The Communist AA effort was concentrated to cover the areas south of the Chongchon River that the MiGs did not patrol. Bridges were especially well defended, but even along standard stretches of track, the Communist forces deployed anti-aircraft emplacements every four miles. Communist anti-aircraft artillery included So-viet-built, radar ranging, 85-millimeter guns capable of hitting targets as high as 25,000 feet. According to FEAF intelligence reports, as many as four Soviet AA divisions were operating these guns throughout North Korea.[14] However, the weapons that pilots feared most were not these big guns, but small caliber 37-millimeter automatic weapons operated by regular Chinese and North Korean troops. As Perrin Gower explained: "In Korea, most people were killed by flak and automatic weapons fire. No member of [my] outfit was ever shot down by a MiG. On one mission against Sinanju, we would send seventy-two airplanes against a target. The big black puffs at 30,000 feet didn't bother us. What bothered us was the 37-millimeter stuff. You would drop your bombs and fly out at the deck level to avoid automatic weapons fire."[15]

M. J. Bailey, a pilot with the 7th Squadron, 49th Wing, similarly claimed that it was not the MiGs that bothered him, but the AA fire. In his 22 June 1952 diary entry, he wrote: "A flight of 16 of us went to Sinuiju airfield on a bombing job. I took my flight in second and things were really getting hot. The F-86s were keeping the MiGs busy for us. At 11,000 feet we had one layer of black flak and a layer of white at

6,000. I tried to keep the flight out of as much as possible. Everyone got out without a hole. This mission really had me scared—it's been so long since I've been up north." [16]

MiGs, in spite of the trains, were kept away from the fighter-bombers by large patrols of F-86 fighter-interceptors: the interceptors would fly at high altitudes above the fighter-bombers and attack any MiGs which attempted to attack. "We basically held the MiG pilots in contempt because they never came down to fight," recalled Howard Heiner. "They didn't want to fight because it was always fifteen to one." [17]

Small caliber anti-aircraft weapons presented such a dangerous threat for the fighter-bomber because they were indiscriminate and easily hidden in so-called flak traps. Regional militia and repair troops would guard important interdiction routes by creating large barriers of small-arms fire. These troops also strung wire cables between hills to thwart low-level attacks, and created elaborate ambushes using tanks as bait to lure U.N. aircraft into carefully configured "kill zones of automatic weapons." [18] In June 1953, for example, Heiner's flight fell victim to just such a flak trap on a standard armed reconnaissance mission. His flight leader, Don Forbes, spotted a truck and started a 45-degree bomb run with his number two man (Heiner was three in this flight). Automatic weapons suddenly popped out from behind camouflaged foxholes and commenced firing upon Forbes and his wingman. The number two man went straight in, and Forbes got hit in several places, but managed to crash-land his plane safely behind friendly lines. [19]

After the mission, a staff officer tried to blame Forbes for the death of his wingman, but Heiner immediately jumped in and told this particular major that "he was very much out of order," a remark which under ordinary circumstances could have earned Heiner an Article 15 or even a court martial. However, rather than punishing Heiner and Forbes, their wing commander ordered them to Tokyo to "cool off." [20] In a combat environment, the rules are different: flight suit attitude was tolerable. Heiner believed he was the "best pilot in Korea," and viewed operations officers as "administrators" who had no business telling either him or Forbes how to fly. [21]

Unlike Heiner's wing commander, this operations major did not fully understand that death in a fighter-bomber outfit often came in an indiscriminate fashion, and that pilot error was rarely if ever involved. Superior flying could not warn you of hidden flak, nor could it necessarily save you in a typical bomb run. All a pilot could do was minimize his exposure to fire by employing a steep angle of attack in a bomb run; however, exposure was still unavoidable. Such daily, involuntary risk taking made fighter-bombers much more fatalistic than their fighter-interceptor brethren. Whereas pilots like Hagerstrom could maintain a level of optimism if they considered their own pilot skills to be better than their adversary's, fighter-bombers like Bailey lived a life of uncertainty, praying every day that their luck would hold out. On leave in Tokyo, he wrote: "Returned to the BOQ and thought of you very much darling. Wonder if and when I'll see you again. Yes, 'if' enters into it more than you realize."[22] Two days later, Bailey returned to base "just to find out that the squadron lost two men in three days." One pilot, who was hit by flak and went right in, had been expecting his first child very soon.[23] Raymond Sturgeon (35th Squadron, 8th Group) similarly believed with "absolute certainty" that he would die in Korea when he found out he would be flying fighter-bombers. Hence, when Sturgeon left, he broke off his engagement with his fiancée: "No way was I going into combat with a wife. When I said good-bye to my mother and dad, I didn't think I would ever be back—no doubt in my mind that I would ever be back."[24]

In addition to ground fire, slower planes and dangerous payloads made the life of the fighter-bomber pilot more hazardous than that of the fighter-interceptor. The first generation of combat jet aircraft had more than a few bugs in them, and fighter-bomber detachments received the oldest and least mechanically sound aircraft in the inventory. The F-80, for example, required an elaborate water injection system just to take off from many of the rather short runways in Japan and Korea. Water injection worked like a primitive after-burner: water was injected into the combustible mixture of the engine, giving it three or four hundred more pounds of thrust. The F-80's wing tanks also had a propensity not to feed well. Bailey, on one mission, had to shoot drain holes in them with his Colt 45 so that he could land without the danger of blowing up.[25]

Like the F-80, the F-84, the other workhorse for fighter-bomber outfits, had more than a few mechanical problems. E. R. James (182nd Squadron, 136th Group) remembered one week when his squadron lost two aircraft due to wing collapses—one plane carried the wing commander and the other carried his deputy. Because of this accident, James's wing was grounded for four weeks until their early model F-84 Ds could be replaced with F-84 Gs, an improved model with a stronger wing.[26]

Not only were many fighter-bomber aircraft more dangerous to fly than the state-of-the-art F-86, they were also less forgiving due to the dangerous payloads they carried. Bailey, for instance, described how a tire blowout upon takeoff created a spark which in turn ignited the napalm bombs of his friend's F-80. This pilot, Lieutenant Reacer, ended up with burns on 70 percent of his body and died a week later.[27]

The Unrewarding Mission of the Fighter-Bomber

In addition to being more dangerous, the mission of the fighter-bomber tended to be less rewarding than that of the fighter-interceptor. A village bombed was not the same as a MiG destroyed—no visible status symbols were awarded and rarely was the press interested in hearing bomber stories. Aces such as James Jabara and Joseph McConnell had their pictures plastered in such national magazines as *Life, Look,* and *Time,* and McConnell's story was even turned into a major motion picture. Fighter-bombers, on the other hand, only received attention in service-oriented journals, such as the *Air Force Times* and *Air Force Magazine:* napalming a village or a suspected troop concentration was hardly as romantic as shooting down a sleek MiG. No titles, parties, or awards were given for bombing five villages. In fact, a fighter-bomber only received a party after his death or his hundredth mission—whichever came first. The hundredth-mission party varied from squadron to squadron, but it generally consisted of a "victory pass" over the base by the hundredth-mission pilot, followed by a photo session and a champaign reception on the tarmac. The more common party, though, was a "shoot-down party." According to Perrin Gower: "Every time someone got shot down, they threw a party and got completely stoned. Ostensibly it was a wake, but really it was a celebration to celebrate the fact that it wasn't you." [28] Survival, in short, was the major reward for the fighter-bomber and the only status symbol he could look forward to during his tour.

The differences between the two types of missions are perhaps best illustrated by the pilots' descriptions of combat. Douglas Evans, a pilot with the 4th Fighter-Interceptor Group, wrote a glowing moment-by-moment account of his first brush with a MiG in his memoir, *Sabre Jets over Korea:*

> I closed in and positively identified the T-tails and mid-wings, then picked on the number three man, who was straggling, and spanned him with my manual Mark 18 sight. A short burst and hits! The jerk never moved, so I held the trigger steady, and did that buzzard light up. There were flashes all over him with rips appearing in the metal skin along with puffs of smoke and hunks of metal flying off.
>
> I can't really describe the sensations I felt, but I suppose they were the same as those experienced in all air wars at their first kill. I was tremendously excited—tight as a knot in the guts, mingled with an odd feeling of awe that all this was happening. As if I was sawing wood I just sat behind him (I was trying to do everything at once and didn't span properly), held the trigger, and clobbered him as my nose moved around. [29]

Bailey, by comparison, described his first successful bombing mission in rather lackluster terms: "Napalmed and strafed two villages north west of Pohang. This is guerrilla activity area and may have been their headquarters. We destroyed 40 houses, 100 troops, and a small ammo dump." [30] Clearly, Bailey viewed his first combat mission in far less heroic terms than Evans; in fact, his attitude toward the fighter-bomber mission was ambivalent at best. Bailey, however, was not alone in his ambivalence. Heiner described his DFC (Distinguished Flying Cross) mission as a "massacre": "I saw troops running and people who I was about to eliminate and we just went up and down this row of trenches killing everyone in our path." [31]

As Bailey and Heiner's remarks reveal, it took effort on the part of the individual pilot to perceive the "people" they were killing as "targets." Bailey rationalized the destruction of a civilian village by defining it as a guerrilla headquarters. He also rarely used the word "kill" in his descriptions. Bailey described another attack on civilians as follows: "Let down just NE of route and hit 5 ox carts, 5 cows, 1 truck, and about 10 laborers repairing a road." [32] Ironically, despite the lack of remorse which Bailey showed toward "enemy" civilians, his feelings toward civilians on the other side of the battle line were quite compassionate: "It's been hot as hell and just as dusty. Hope for rain as the rice crop is failing fast. I wonder how these people are going to make out if the crop fails?" [33]

Bailey, though, was not alone in perceiving civilians north of the bombline as "the enemy." Other pilots justified their attacks by labeling civilians as "disguised troops" or as "supporters" of enemy activity. One pilot interviewed by the Operations Analysis Office of the Fifth Air Force stated that civilians were being used as human shields. "If I saw any signs of civilian activity in the village, I assumed that there were enemy troops there as well. I've seen instances where there might be as many as 100 civilians dressed in white usually. The majority of these would be men, and I do believe that the enemy did use the civilian population as cover and mingled with them in villages." [34]

Another pilot used a series of crude syllogisms to justify his slaughtering of innocents: "If we saw civilians in the village—just because they look like civilians—from an airplane you can't tell whether he's a civilian or a soldier. Anything in North Korea I consider an enemy. They're definitely not on our side, therefore I have no mercy. If I saw people in a village, why, I consider them troops or supporting troops. Anything supporting enemy troops is an enemy of ours; therefore, I consider it worthwhile to strike it." [35] Clearly, the distinctions between combatants and civilians were blurred on purpose by pilots in an attempt to rationalize their often gruesome job.

In *Troubling of a Star,* Sheldon captures the dilemma of the fighter-bomber well and reveals how language was an important means for pilots to justify their actions. For example, a "mass of huddled, terrified human beings" became a "target," and a "bewildered poor slob of a man who never wanted anything but a few meals and a woman to sleep with" became a "troop concentration." [36] Similarly, Jerry Minton, a pilot with the 80th Squadron (the "Headhunters"), insisted several times that a little town along the Chinnampo estuary he napalmed was a "troop concentration point" even though he had "no idea where the intelligence came from." [37] "I know that sounds horrible to someone who hadn't had that experience, and you probably get visions of My Lai and everything," recalled Minton, "but believe me there was heavy flak there and it was a concentration point." [38]

As Minton's reference to My Lai alludes, the job of the fighter-bomber was often messy and brutal. Napalm, for instance, will stick to anything it touches and burn flesh straight down to the bone. Upon impact, it sounds like "tearing silk amplified a thousand times," and there is almost no escape from it: it will flow behind parapets and into foxholes, burning everything in its path. [39] As low-level attackers, fighter-bombers generally witnessed much of their attacks close-hand. According to one pilot interviewed by the Fifth Air Force Operations Analysis Office: "I have been around villages that didn't appear to have any life whatsoever and dropped two napalms in there, and saw a lot of activity immediately in the buildings. People would leave the cover of the buildings and surrounding hills." [40]

Raymond Sturgeon also confirmed that "up-close-and-personal" views of "mass killings" were routine: "I can't say I enjoyed it. You're there and that's what you do, but some guys absolutely loved it. I've seen guys come back and brag about shooting a woman with a package on her head and watching her blow up. We were instructed to hit civilians because they did a lot of the work, but I just couldn't do it. Other guys did and it just turned them on. It was nothing to get 150 KIAs [killed in action] in a strafing run." [41] For Sturgeon, dropping napalm and strafing people was a difficult job; yet he was highly motivated to fly missions and finish his tour. "We wanted to get out there and do the best job we could do," exclaimed Sturgeon. "You never heard of a guy just going up and dropping his bombs and getting the hell out and counting another mission." [42]

Combat Motivation

Sturgeon and most fighter-bomber pilots were highly motivated to fight and fly for career reasons. For the most part, these men were reserve pilots whose only hope of securing a permanent commission in the Air Force was to successfully complete a combat tour.

Like Tindle in *Troubling of a Star*, Sturgeon believed he was not fit for much else except flying; therefore, he volunteered for combat to secure a place for himself in the postwar Air Force: "I was career all the way, and a combat tour in Korea was a necessary ticket punch." [43] William Elder, the commander of the 8th Fighter-Bomber Wing in Korea, also understood that combat flying in Korea would be pivotal to his career: "I am convinced that my checkout in jet aircraft in Korea was the turning point in my career, at almost the midpoint of that career (15.5 years). For without it I would not have been considered nor assigned the 8th Fighter-Bomber Wing or the air divisions which followed. During the last half of my 32-plus years of active service, I was assigned to command positions at air division level or higher, the only exception being a two-year tour as Inspector General, Air Defense Command." [44] Although service in fighter-interceptors was preferable, "it was known that if you came out of fighter-bombers alive, you had served your purpose." [45]

Besides careers, another motive for fighter-bombers to perform their job was peer pressure. In the tight-knit flight suit culture of the fighter-bomber wing, one could not easily shirk one's duty. Fighter-bombers attacked targets one after another in formations of four. Once you were lined up to attack, it was very difficult to avoid combat without making a complete spectacle of yourself to your close friends. On the mission in which Don Forbes was shot down, for example, Heiner knew he would probably get hit as soon as he saw Forbes's wingman plow into a mountain; nevertheless, he followed Forbes in because Forbes ordered him to, and to disobey such an order would have disgraced Heiner in the eyes of his flight. Like Tindle in *Troubling of a Star*, Heiner saw no way out of his predicament; only the flight leader had the power to call off an attack.

Because of the flight leader's pivotal role, he was chosen not on the basis of rank, but on the basis of experience. "The combat veteran was respected in Korea," remembered George Berke, an F-84 pilot, "and he not only led the flight regardless of rank, but also helped plan the operation." Flight suit values, in short, often took precedence over institutional rules and regulations. As Berke put it, "The spirit of Korea was 'Let's do it the best way, and forget the bureaucratic stuff.' "[46]

In addition to succumbing to peer pressure, many of the pilots interviewed took pride in directly aiding U.S. troops on the ground by flying close-air support missions. Robert Pomeroy, a T-6 forward air controller who was hit thirteen times in sixty-four missions, compared his lot with that of the ground soldier and concluded that he had no excuse to complain:

> I knew how to dig foxholes and I had seen lots of movies of guys being burned to death by flame throwers and their guts torn apart by artillery shells. And in a lot of ways what we were doing was cleaner and neater, less messy and less dangerous than what the front-line soldiers had to do 24 hours a day. I also had a cowboy streak in me to support the Army in the best and most first-class way it could be done, and that involved exposure and that was just part of it.[47]

Bailey, similarly, claimed that it was a "very wonderful sight" to napalm Communist soldiers near an advancing column of American troops. Ironically, given the Air Force's near obsession with interdiction, Bailey found these missions to be fruitless: "I flew the most useless mission of the war today. Went to the Yalu just by China to bomb a portion of a bridge. The photo was taken just twenty days before but there was a beautiful pile-type bridge a quarter of a mile up the river which was brand new. We hit the target but didn't ever give them 'one way traffic.' Four men and four planes to knock out a bridge that can be repaired in two hours."[48] Minton, similarly, complained about rail-cutting missions, another a staple of the Air Force's interdiction effort: "The whole squadron could go in and try to cut a railroad track and might not get one good cut."[49]

Despite their belief in the futility of interdiction, Bailey and Minton completed their hundred-mission tours because in the final analysis they believed in the U.N. cause. They also understood implicitly that their Air Force careers depended on completing their hundred-mission tours and having a Distinguished Flying Cross above their pockets to prove it.

Fear of Flying

Not everyone, though, made it to his hundredth mission. In addition to being shot down, many soldiers had to be transferred back to the States because of FOF and other mental illnesses.

Due in part to their more dangerous and less rewarding mission, FOF and other mental illnesses were far more prevalent in fighter-bomber pilots than fighter-interceptor pilots. According to flight surgeon Lucio Gatto, FOF was a vehicle for these men to receive attention in what was otherwise a thankless job.[50] It was also an outward manifestation of the stress and hazards of the job. As Pomeroy put it, these men "were not afraid of flying, they were afraid of dying."

In general, FOF cases tended to be older reservists with wives and families at home. In a study of 186 Korean War FOF cases, H. A. Schultz noted that all but three were reservists recalled to active duty, and 90 percent had been trained in World War II.[51] In terms of rank, most cases were first lieutenants and captains with a few majors and lieutenant colonels. The average number of combat missions flown before FOF struck was eighteen. Additionally, most pilots had served two to three months in Korea before being referred for psychiatric treatment.[52]

In short, pilots afflicted with FOF were not "green" troops but experienced combat aviators who "cracked" under the pressures of sustained combat in fighter-bombers.

In one case, a pilot with thirteen missions completed ran into the flight surgeon's tent in the middle of the night and began acting agitated and delusional. The flight surgeon "instituted immediate supportive treatment which included heavy sedation, complete reassurance, and, as the patient recovered, ego strengthening discussions."[53] This patient recovered after two days of intensive therapy.

Another case involved a twenty-five-year-old pilot who had flown twenty-six combat missions on a temporary-duty status. He then went on inactive status for six weeks. When he returned, he expressed "a great deal of verbal anxiety about returning immediately to regular flying." He also asked for a couple of check rides with a veteran pilot, and flew erratically during combat flights. This man was then referred to psychiatric review and diagnosed with anxiety.[54]

A third interesting case involved a twenty-nine-year-old married fighter-bomber pilot who had flown thirty-five combat missions and then requested to be grounded (an action which eventually helped relieve his symptoms). This man had lost two of his best friends — one in a mission on which he had flown. The pilot subsequently became depressed, lost weight, and could not sleep. Finally, he requested leave to ponder his situation. While on leave, he became more anxious and depressed. He also contracted gonorrhea from a prostitute and "cried bitterly when he came to the flight surgeon for treatment."[55]

In all three of these examples, FOF resulted after a substantial number of combat missions had been flown. Periods of idleness also appear to be a contributing cause of FOF. In the latter two examples, time spent away from flying exacerbated FOF symptoms. As flight surgeon Robert Lifton put it: "In Korea, our experience has been that enforced idleness is an external factor much more damaging to morale than enemy activity. . . . Most pilots are anxious to complete their missions and get home quickly. When grounded by poor weather for any length of time, they feel a sharp loss of their 'sharp edge' and fear getting 'stale.' "[56]

To combat FOF and other forms of mental illness, some squadrons assigned a flight surgeon to live with each flight. According to E. R. James, this allowed pilots to have "access to him on off-hours, and conversations with him were quite soothing."[57] Conversation alone, however, was often insufficient. Flight surgeons also supplied pilots with liberal supplies of "mission whiskey" to keep their nerves at rest while they were not flying. According to pilot Dean Price of the 80th Fighter-Bomber squadron: "At the beginning of the war, the flight docs were handing out one-ounce bourbons at the end of each mission. It was claimed it was needed to steady the pilots' nerves. But they were also flying 5–6 + missions a day, and by midafternoon they couldn't find anyone sober enough to fly! That policy didn't last too long before they started to give you a whole bottle for each 25 missions." [58] As this example illustrates, alcohol was the psychiatric drug of choice during the Korean War: it was used by flight surgeons, who often had no training in psychiatry, to cure everything from anxiety to depression.

Another strategy for bolstering morale and motivating fighter-bomber pilots was to instill in them a sense of unit pride: commanding officers accomplished this end through the skillful manipulation of unit logos, folklore, and history.

Morale Building

For fighter-interceptor unit commanders, unit pride was not an issue—pilots knew that they were "hot stuff" and received confirmation of this status both through the press and by the reverential treatment offered by the Air Force community. Fighter-interceptor pilot Douglas Evans, for example, had the following reception when he landed at Komaki air base in Japan:

> When we got out of our 86s at Komaki and walked into base ops to file for Kimpo, everybody just gaped in awe at us. After all, we were the only 86 Sabre outfit in the war, the big MiG hunters, and considered very hot stuff wherever we went—especially heading back for combat. I had on my new boots with my flying suit tucked in them and felt like I was really hot stuff—in the best outfit and best assignment in the world. Boy, it was a great feeling, and I made the most of it. [59]

Fighter-bomber pilots, by comparison, were referred to derogatorily as "straight wings" at the officer clubs in Japan and Seoul. This nickname came from the straight wings of their F-84s and F-80s: by contrast, the higher speed F-86s had the more aerodynamic swept-wing configuration. [60]

Because fighter-bomber pilots did not have the high status that came with flying the most advanced fighter of the war and shooting down MiGs, unit pride took on a much more significant meaning for these men. To bolster unit pride, some squadrons developed colorful and sexy logos for their aircraft and flight suits. Squadrons also had special baseball caps and beer steins made. Finally, unit history and lore were carefully recorded and used by unit commanders.

While fighter-interceptor pilots also sported baseball caps in Korea, the phenomenon was even more popular in the fighter-bomber units. Each squadron custom-designed and ordered its own cap from Japanese manufacturers. Jerry Minton, a pilot with the 80th Squadron, still displays his cap in his den: the cap features his "Headhunter" squadron patch, his flight designation, and one hundred black hash marks to denote missions flown.[61]

Like caps, colorful and erotic unit logos were a vital part of morale building. Some squadrons, for example, chose animals of prey: the symbol for Sturgeon's squadron was a black panther; for the South African squadron, a "Flying Cheetah." Other squadrons adopted a sexual theme such as "the Foxy Few," the logo of the 12th Squadron of the 18th Fighter-Bomber Wing. Heiner's squadron, the "Fighting Cocks," went so far as to have Walt Disney design its logo—a rooster with boxing gloves. This logo was emblazoned on aircraft, flight suit patches, and even squadron beer mugs—mugs which were proudly hung in "The Cockpit" (the Osan officers' club).[62]

Walt Sheldon, in *Troubling of a Star*, pokes fun at these "sacred cows" in the character of Colonel Straker, the wing commander. In a Patton-like speech to the outfit, Straker announces his plans to develop a logo that would improve morale and remind the wing of its major mission—killing. After much thought and contemplation, Straker chooses "the Manhunters" as the logo and orders it to be displayed on all base signs, aircraft, and uniforms.[63] "The Manhunters," argues Straker, would motivate his men to kill more people than any other wing in the war.

The Manhunters logo is a thinly veiled allusion to the 80th Squadron's Headhunter logo. During World War II, Captain Edward "Porky" Cragg, the squadron commander in New Guinea, commissioned crew chief Yale Saffro, who had worked before the war as an artist for Walt Disney, to design a symbol for the unit. Saffro promptly designed a patch which supposedly resembled a New Guinea headhunter. In Korea, this symbol was ubiquitous: it was emblazoned on caps, signs, beer mugs, jackets, and flight suits. So popular and sacred was the patch that when the Air Force attempted to add the motto "Audentes Fortuna Juvat" (Fortune Favors the Bold) to it in 1971, Headhunters rebelled by tearing all but the Juvat word of the motto off their patches. For these flight suit officers, a change in their squadron patch was acceptable only if it was done on their terms. In fact, the harder the higher echelons attempted to keep the full motto on the patches, the "more entrenched the single-word Juvat title became (to the point of covering the Wing Commander's flight suit with Juvat patches each time he hung one on the line to dry)."[64]

In addition to patches, fighter-bomber commanders also attempted to build morale by decorating their aircrafts with unique and unorthodox paint schemes. Raymond Sturgeon's commander, Levi Chase—a gruff World War II veteran who gave all new pilots a speech about how he had "five hundred missions in World War II" and knew what he was doing—had his personal plane painted in garish colors: one color for each squadron in his wing.[65] Chase then flew this colorful plane on three "max effort" missions against Pyongyang; he won the Silver Star for his efforts; the other members of his flight merely received air medals.[66]

Chase was not alone in his attempts to instill pride by sharing risks with his pilots. Fifth Air Force commander Glenn O. Barcus boosted morale considerably by flying a mission against Pyongyang Radio. On 1 May 1953, Barcus broadcast the following message from his F-86, appropriately labeled "Barcus Carcass":

> Attention all Communists in the Pyongyang area. This is General Barcus speaking. I have a message for you from the Fifth Air Force. These little attacks today against military targets in the Pyongyang area are our response to your insulting lies over Pyongyang radio. In the future, every time you make derogatory remarks about the Fifth Air Force you can expect our answer with bombs against military targets in your area. The attacks will be with ever-increasing severity. This is all now, but we will be back every time you broadcast filthy lies about the Fifth Air Force. Goodbye now. This is General Glenn O. Barcus.[67]

In addition to developing colorful logos and flying missions, fighter-bomber wing, group, and squadron commanders relied heavily on unit folklore as a vehicle for instilling their outfits with pride. The 67th Fighter-Bomber Squadron, for example, took pride in the fact that their unit was organized explicitly for duty in the Korean War. According to their squadron newsletter, the Fighting Cocks were "conceived in haste, born in obscurity, and have risen from the unknown to write a fateful page in history." [68] Interestingly enough, this fateful page concentrates more on the squadron's close air support missions than its interdiction attacks. For the fighter-bomber, supporting front-line troops was seen as much more honorable than napalming Korean villages or cutting railroad tracks. The newsletter emphasizes throughout that the contribution of the squadron "cannot be expressed in words of praise, but only in the hearts of the men in the front lines, who daily watched the squadron's relentless attacks against the enemy weaken and drive him to cover." [69]

The Fighting Cocks were proud of their first commander, Major Lou Sebille of Pontiac, Michigan. On his fifth mission, Sebille's plane was heavily damaged in an attack on an armored unit near the Pusan perimeter. Rather than bailing out, he dove his plane onto an enemy halftrack, destroying himself, the halftrack, and numerous troops in the process. [70] To honor Sebille, who posthumously received a Medal of Honor for his efforts, the squadron created a trophy in his memory to be awarded to the "unit credited with making the most accurate bombing runs." [71]

Like the 67th Squadron, the Foxy Few of the 12th Squadron relied heavily on unit history to uphold the morale of the group. They boasted that theirs was the first official USAF combat squadron to see action in Korea. [72] The Foxy Few also traced their lineage back to the World War II Flying Tigers. Consequently, they painted tigers' teeth on their aircraft—a tradition that was also carried over to the Vietnam and Gulf wars.

Legends like Sebille and the Flying Tigers were an integral part of the institutional memory of squadrons like the 67th because they provided members of these groups with a sense of history and mission. However, when history failed, direct competition with F-86 pilots often provided the necessary tonic to keep a fighter-bomber outfit in high spirits. Sturgeon recalled how one F-80 pilot trailed the ace Francis Gabreski during a victory pass over the Suwon air base—a tradition that Francis Gabreski indulged in after many of his kills. Although he flew a vastly inferior plane than Gabreski's F-86, the F-80 managed to stay right on his tail during the entire performance—and made Gabreski the laughingstock of the 8th Wing.[73]

On another occasion, the 8th Wing competed with the 51st to see who could get a flight of fighters to K-14 faster in the event of an alert. Pilots of the 8th sat in their F-80s all day until the alert finally came and they launched. The 51st Wing, by comparison, was so confident that its faster F-86s would win that they waited for the alert in their hammocks. In the end, the F-80s carried the day—an event that did wonders for unit pride. As Heiner put it, it "was all these crazy things that helped you survive."[74] These things ranged from beating fighter-interceptor pilots in competitions to wearing red scarves and blowing sampans over with jet exhaust for "sport" after missions. However, far and away the greatest pressure relief valve was the drinking in the officers' club—one of the many base-life issues that will be explored in the next chapter.

When George Berke, Raymond Sturgeon, Howard Heiner, M. J. Bailey, and a great many other pilots joined the Air Force in the late forties and early fifties, they truly believed that they would eventually fly top-of-the-line fighter-interceptors against the best planes in the Communist inventory. For the lucky few in the 4th and 51st Wings, their dream came true, but for most jet pilots, dropping bombs and napalming villages became the order of the day. The day Berke discovered he would be flying fighter-bombers in Korea, he stormed into his commander's office at Williams and said: "I didn't join the Air Force to burn gooks." His commander replied: "Get used to the idea!" Although taken aback at the time, as Berke made his way up through the ranks he came to realize the "tremendous wisdom in that statement": "The fighter-bomber was the real Air Force—it was what we really did the job with."[75] The most common jet fighter experience in Korea was an interdiction attack against a heavily defended railroad bridge, not a duel to the death with an angry MiG-15. In fact, many of these fighter pilots never had the privilege of getting a kill, let alone becoming an ace. Some never even saw a MiG. Instead, fighter-bomber pilots were shot at on every mission and lost many of their comrades. However, they could boast of killing more enemy troops per mission than most aces killed during their entire tours. In return for their efforts, fighter-bomber pilots received a Distinguished Flying Cross and a party. Through it all, most fighter-bomber pilots remained proud and let their flight suit attitudes sustain them. In the end, they knew that if they made it, there would be a role for them to play in the Air Force and its future wars.

6

Thunderboxes and Sabre Dancers: Base Life and Recreation in the Korean War

Every morning in Korea, George Berke and the twelve other pilots in his barracks would wake up and yell in unison, "1-2-3: We hate this fucking place!" What these men hated was living in unfurnished, poorly heated huts, defecating in slit trenches, and showering outdoors in the middle of the winter. They also despised the dusty, dirty, bombed-out Korean countryside.

However, despite their primitive conditions, Berke and other flight suit officers did not suffer from extreme deprivation in Korea. Cheap Asian labor alleviated many of the major hardships of base living. For example, "house boys" cleaned barracks and latrines, laundered everyone's uniforms, and stayed up all night to ensure that oil-burning heaters kept burning. Korean waitresses served pilots in the mess, did their dishes, and tended bar at their clubs.

In addition to cheap labor, pilots received extra pay and other benefits that enabled them to compensate for base hardships with lavish vacations in Japan. These benefits included free meals, free medical attention, and base exchanges loaded with inexpensive jewelry, liquor, and electronic goods from Japan. While on leave, pilots stayed at Air Force-subsidized hotels and ate inexpensively at officers' clubs. In fact, the only popular "commodity" which was not subsidized was prostitution, but

116

even that was cheap due to the weak economies of Japan and Korea in the 1950s.

Finally and most importantly, Korea represented an escape from the ceremonious and increasingly rigid environment of continental U.S. Air Force bases. Although the Air Force was still the most informal service, air bases in the continental United States were becoming increasingly more formal during the 1950s. For example, the old military tradition of "calling" was being revived: when an officer arrived at a new station, the other officers on base were expected to call formally upon the new arrival at his house and present an engraved calling card. Many U.S. bases also had dress codes that prohibited officers from wearing T-shirts and other informal attire when they were off-duty. Coat and ties were mandatory in officers' clubs.[1] Korea, by contrast, demanded no such formalities. When an officer arrived on station, he was assigned a bunk and expected to scrounge for a blanket or sleeping bag. Furthermore, the best description of the Korean War dress code was eclectic. A pilot could wear anything from fatigues to flannel shirts—whatever suited his needs. He could show up at the officers' club after a mission, smelling like a goat in an old flight suit and be welcomed. If he wished, he could drink himself drunk, and no one would think any less of him the next day. Similarly, while on leave, he could sleep with prostitutes even if he was married. In short, his only responsibility was to fly and fight: bases were merely a place to park one's aircraft, rest, recuperate, and prepare oneself for the next mission.

Korea: Its Climate and Topography

The Korean peninsula combines rugged mountainous territory with an extreme climate. Shaped like Florida and containing about the same amount of territory as Minnesota (85,000 square miles), the Korean peninsula is 540 miles long at its longest point and an average of 150 miles wide south of Seoul. Japan lies 340 miles away across the Sea of Japan. China and Russia border it on the north.[2]

The land itself consists primarily of mountains. In the north, peaks can be found as high as 9,000 feet, and in the south, as high as 6,000 feet. In between the mountains are narrow valleys, coastal mud flats, and rice paddies. Korea also has a host of rivers: the Yalu forms its northern border with China, the Han flows through Seoul, and the Naktong flows "west and south around the town of Taegu and then east to empty into the Korean Strait near Pusan."[3] The latitudes of Korea are the same as the eastern seaboard of the United States between New York and North Carolina. The seasonal temperatures in South Korea are similar to those in Connecticut or New Jersey: hot and humid in the summer and cold in the winter. The major difference between the two regions is the Korean monsoon period—a very rainy spell that occurs during the summer.[4]

Upon arriving in Korea, the pilot, fresh from jet training in Arizona or Nevada, was not only shocked by this climate but also by the poverty of the country and its wartime devastation. Raymond Sturgeon's first impression was typical: "The country was horrible. If you had a shovel, you were rich. Seoul looked like something out of World War II. When I got over there, I knew why I was there—to stop them [the Communists]!"[5]

George Berke, similarly, was struck by the bareness of the landscape: "The country was completely deforested and ugly and they used shit for everything."[6] Major Dean Hess, an F-51 pilot who founded the first Air Force-sponsored orphanage in Korea, complained of the many orphans near his base at Yongdungpo:

> The orphans would cluster like flies around our garbage cans, into which the men scraped their trays three times a day. It was both heartbreaking and nauseating to see these ragged children lean over and dip their swill with tin cans, trying to scoop up choice morsels from our garbage. Most of them had scabs and skin infections on their faces, and inflamed and running eyes. . . . They were all over the field during the day, but at night they disappeared, probably back to the ruins of Seoul.[7]

Paul Turner, who used to drive one of the mess hall girls to her home every night, was appalled by her "bombed-out nothing of a house" near his base at K-13 in Suwon.[8] Most Korean towns, in short, had very little to offer in the way of amenities for the typical pilot. As Berke put it, "You could go into Taegu but the poverty was such that you wouldn't go—if they served you meat, it was probably dog."[9] So underdeveloped was the countryside that the Air Force actually warned its airmen not to eat the local food. The human excrement used to fertilize vegetables was known to cause intestinal cysts. The unsanitary slaughtering techniques of the Koreans made meat equally hazardous.[10]

Like the local food, the Korean countryside was also dangerous. During 1950, guerrilla activities tied down 30 percent of U.N. military forces.[11] Dewey Sturgeon, who left his base at Suwon only twice during his entire tour, remembers driving to a nearby base at Yongdungpo and worrying about snipers during the entire drive. Dean Hess, a pilot and base commander who arrived at Taegu early in the war, ordered the air police at his base to set up four .50-caliber machine gun emplacements around the perimeter of the base to guard against guerrillas. After he noticed guerrillas signaling to each other with mirrors in the nearby hills, Hess personally led a company of air police on a patrol of the territory around the base. After this failed to flush out the guerrillas, he asked a 40-millimeter anti-aircraft gun unit to help him out: "I pointed out this mountain, and they laid a dozen shells right on its top—no more lights ever flashed from it."[12]

Because of the danger of guerrillas and snipers as well as the impoverished conditions of the countryside, most pilots rarely ventured forth from their bases. When they had leave, they went to Tokyo; when they were on duty, they tended to remain on their "blue island." In fact, for many flight suit officers, the base and Korea were synonymous: "When you were in Korea," exclaimed Sturgeon, "there was nothing except the base."[13] Almost everything one needed to live could be found there: shelter, food, sports, movies, variety shows, shopping, education, hobbies, bars, and even a few Western women or "camp followers," as they were often called.

The Bases

When the Korean War began, there were only two airfields in Korea suitable for jet aircraft—Suwon and Kimpo (both were near Seoul). These fields, along with the eight smaller fields in the country, had been built by the Japanese during World War II. Kimpo and Suwon had modern concrete runways; another airfield, Pusan, had a 4,900-foot runway of concrete wash on four inches of rubble, and Taegu had a 3,800-foot clay and gravel strip. The remainder of the fields, however, were sod—a surface suitable only for light propeller-driven aircraft.[14]

Although jet aircraft could operate from bases in Japan, the extra fuel spent traveling over the Sea of Japan meant that these planes had only ten minutes to find and destroy targets on the Korean peninsula. Hence, the development of Korean airfields was one of the Air Force's highest priorities in 1950, but the obstacles to such development were often tremendous. Because many fields were built on rice paddies and soft clay, drainage and soil stability were a major problem. When Taegu was improved in the summer of 1950, the 822nd Engineer Aviation Construction Battalion and five hundred Korean laborers had to excavate five to ten feet of clay along the entire length of the 4,300-foot-long runway. Then they had to fill this excavation with crushed gravel before concrete could finally be laid down.[15] Other hindrances included shortages of construction materials, engineering troops, and equipment.

Despite these obstacles, the Fifth Air Force, in May 1951, launched major construction programs at five air bases. This initiative included the construction of 9,000-foot runways at Taegu, Kunsan, and Suwon. Logistically, it was cheaper to hire Korean laborers and build modern runways than to rely on expensive jet-assisted takeoff bottles—a device that enabled jets to take off from shorter runways by increasing their thrust.[16] However, newer and longer runways alone did not solve the operational problems involved with jet aircraft. A jet wing consumed as much as 125,000 gallons of fuel each day. Hence, tank farms and fuel pipelines were also required. To maintain these aircraft, hangars had to be built. To guard the hangars against sabotage, bases had to be encircled with barbed-wire fences, guard towers, and mine fields. Finally, control towers, operations huts, parking stands, revetments, anti-aircraft positions, radar sites, and a host of other miscellaneous buildings had to be constructed before a base could become fully operational. Consequently, Korea-based wings conducted most of their aircraft maintenance at rear-echelon bases in Japan. For example, the 4th Wing housed a maintenance squadron at Johnson Air Force Base near Tokyo, the 27th and 51st Wings used Tsuiki (an old Japanese naval field on Kyushu); and the 49th Wing stationed its maintenance group at Itazuke.[17] When a plane required serious maintenance, a pilot would be assigned to fly it to one of these bases for an overhaul. This system not only eased the logistical demands in Korea, but enabled pilots to travel to Japan more frequently.

Life in the Hootches

Given the intensive runway construction demands of the new fighter bases in Korea, the lowest priority project for Air Force and Korean construction crews was living quarters and latrines. Early in the war, conditions were very primitive. Ranald Adams, who flew F-82 Twin Mustangs from the beginning of the war until early 1951, lived in an unheated tent and slept in all of his clothes to stay warm.[18] Dean Hess, likewise, slept on the ground in a small tent, and stuffed clothing into his sleeping bag to enhance its insulating properties.[19]

As the front stabilized, the Air Force gradually constructed more permanent living quarters, or "hootches" as they were commonly called. At Taegu, the Air Force contracted Korean laborers to build stucco buildings, but these structures quickly deteriorated under the extreme climate of Korea. Hence, the Air Force switched to steel World War II-style Quonset huts and "tropical shell" prefabricated wooden huts built in Japan.[20] Tomlinson defined his tropical shell as a "chicken coop" because it had a bare wood interior and lots of screens along its sides.[21] Turner's hut, by comparison, was a Quonset hut with sandbags along its sides to protect the occupants from air attack.[22]

Unless they were majors or higher in rank, pilots shared hootches with anywhere from six to twelve other pilots. To create a modicum of privacy in these single-room, open structures, each pilot would construct a cubicle for himself with packing crates and other debris. For a bed, pilots slept on air mattresses over GI-issue cots and used Army blankets or sleeping bags to stay warm at night. Heat was provided by an oil-burning stove that stood in the center of the hootch. Decorations consisted of pictures of wives, sweethearts, and pin-up girls or, as Tomlinson put it, "the usual graffiti that warriors take to war."[23] James Salter, in *The Hunters,* offers a particularly graphic description of the hootch of his protagonist, Cleve Saville:

> It was a large room, but crowded, with a wall of sooty white. There was a debris of furniture that had been made from the wood of packing crates: wardrobes, cabinets, a ponderous table, and several awkward chairs. A mosaic of women in clippings of every size was on one wall from the ceiling down almost to the floor, and four or five feet wide. Cleve was overwhelmed by the litter. The windows had occasional squares of cardboard for missing panes, and not much light came through them. . . . It made entering the room like coming into a den.[24]

Whether they lived in tents or huts, pilots constantly complained of the poor heat, bad ventilation, and poor furnishings. Furthermore, even newer accommodations lacked such amenities as electricity and running water: showers and latrines were strictly outdoor affairs.

Howard Heiner described his latrine as a trough with no partitions and a "big tin which was dumped every once in a while."[25] Douglas Evans's latrine had shoulder-level boards to ensure some privacy, but it was still "torture" to use. The cold air encouraged "you to hold it and bake it as long as possible."[26] At K-10, a stream flowed underneath the latrine and carried its contents to the nearby rice paddies.[27] This latrine, incidentally, was a "40-seater thunderbox" where pilots sat "shoulder to shoulder, cheek to jowl," on a long wooden bench with holes in it.[28]

Because of the imposed intimacy of the latrines, jokes and humor flourished in them. Mickey Rorke, a South African pilot attached to the 18th Wing, constructed a wooden boat filled with paraffin-soaked newspapers, lit it on fire, and launched it on the stream which passed under the latrine.[29] Another South African pilot, Brian Martin, claimed that the 18th Wing's Korean cleaning woman insisted on cleaning their latrine during the morning "rush hour": "She would arrive at that critical period with her mop and bucket to clean the block. Without fail she would stop in front of each occupant who was seated on the latrine and bow in a polite and dignified manner. The men each returned the compliment by rising off the roughly constructed bogholes with their trousers round their ankles and bowing to her with great aplomb and solemnity!" [30]

Some found that the rustic conditions of the bases brought the units closer together. Douglas Evans actually preferred his Korean base to ones he had served at in the United States: "I liked the feeling of living in a tent community," Evans explained, "the simple, friendly closeness— like camping out—that just doesn't exist on a fancy 'established' base." [31] He also enjoyed wearing fatigues—"the only sensible way to go in this alternating dust and mud." [32] Tomlinson, likewise, enjoyed the casual nature of life: "Everybody was on a first-name basis, and everybody partied together in everybody else's houses." [33]

Dayrooms and O Clubs

Two institutions (besides the latrines) that helped foster this casual, flight suit collegiality were the squadron dayrooms and the officers' clubs.

The dayroom was the building where individual squadrons posted flying assignments and unit statistics. Statistics consisted of categories such as number of kills, targets destroyed, and ordnance expended. It was also a place where pilots received briefings and waited for a mission when on "ready alert." Radios in the room allowed pilots to listen in on air battles in progress and also warned them of MiG infiltrations. Some dayrooms even had equipment rooms where pilots could change into their flight suits. Not surprisingly, this hut was a nexus for on- and off-duty pilots during the day. It was also one of the few places on base reserved for squadron activities alone: the officers' clubs were shared by all the officers of a wing. As a consequence, each squadron attempted to fix up its dayrooms and transform them from drab operational buildings to comfortable flight lounges.

The 16th Squadron of the 51st Fighter-Interceptor Wing, for example, organized an ad hoc construction crew consisting of pilots, off-duty members of the supply squadron, and several Japanese carpenters to build their new hut at Tsuiki in December 1951. This ad hoc crew used two tent frames as the foundation and constructed the rest of the building from salvaged rock, wood, cloth, and paint. They also constructed a front porch on the outside and equipped the inside with "a small bar, writing tables, card tables, and plenty of chairs."[34] Dewey Sturgeon's squadron, the 35th of the 18th Group, improved its dayroom with an enlarged picture of Marilyn Monroe and a Ping-Pong table: "It was right out of M*A*S*H."[35] Kenneth Koon actually hauled in stone and built a working fireplace and a corner bar for the 67th Squadron's dayroom. He then flew to Tokyo and purchased a refrigerator and vinyl upholstered chairs to "make it even more desirable." "We couldn't serve alcoholic beverages in there because that is where we got ready for missions," recalled Koon, "but we had soda, juices, etc."[36]

In addition to using it as a lounge, dayrooms were used for parties, promotion ceremonies, Ping-Pong tournaments, or simply as a comfortable place to read or write letters home. Heiner's lounge on the flight line of Osan hosted many after-hours parties: "The officers' club was for all the squadrons but our lounge was for the 12th Squadron only."[37] The 4th Wing held all promotion ceremonies in the lounges. After the ceremony it was customary for the newly promoted officers to brace officers of lesser rank and "bark crisp clear orders to their less fortunate colleagues." Rank, in short, was not something to take too seriously in a flight suit environment.[38] Everyone relaxed together, drank together, and played Ping-Pong together. According to Tomlinson, only colonels and high-ranking operations officers were bestowed with the traditional military title of "sir."[39]

Epitomizing the casual environment of the dayroom was the customary Ping-Pong table. The 4th Wing dayroom was equipped not only with a table, but also with benches for spectators.[40] Pilots, suited up and waiting for missions, enjoyed Ping-Pong because the game relieved stress and demanded good hand-eye coordination—qualities that were critical in flying a fighter aircraft. Not surprisingly, the best Ping-Pong players tended to be the best pilots. "Boots Blesse and Chick Cleveland," according to Earl Brown, "were the best Ping-Pong players and the best pilots" in the 4th Wing.[41] According to Cleveland: "I could beat anyone in the squadron except Boots, and he took great pleasure in whipping me in front of other pilots. If I was reading or drinking coffee when he marched in, I knew what was coming. He would pick up a paddle and ask me with a smirk, "How's your Ping-Pong today, Lieutenant?" It was good but not good enough, and I thought I knew how those enemy pilots felt when Boots got behind them. It was kill or be killed."[42]

Although Ping-Pong, conversation, and relaxation were the most common activities in the dayroom, many pilots also read. Each flight in the 4th Wing collected its own assortment of magazines and paperback books and would trade reading material with other flights.[43] Most wings also had small libraries that were run by Air Force special services personnel. As of October 1952, the base library at Kimpo had over four thousand books, and a monthly withdrawal of nearly fifteen hundred books by 542 borrowers.[44] The 51st Wing's library instituted a paper-back book exchange in December 1951. Under this policy, if you brought a paperback book to the library, you could exchange it for another one.[45] According to Douglas Evans of the 4th Wing, pilots in his flight were so involved in their books that "all conversation would cease while each one was buried in some story."[46]

While the dayroom was a primary place for pilots to relax and socialize during the day, the officers' club, or "o club," was where most pilots spent their evening hours. Unlike the dayroom, the o club served no operational purpose—it was used solely for drinking, eating, and socializing. In fact, it was the central party place on most bases—a place to indulge in the primary off-hours ritual of flight suit culture: drinking.

On Kenneth Koon's first day at Osan, Colonel Martin, his wing commander, told him that "Korea was the easiest place in the world to become an alcoholic: it was extremely cheap and available every-where."[47] Lack of other activities as well as a shortage of women on bases made "booze the primary recreational activity."[48] Whereas beer was bought locally, liquor was imported to bases from the rear-echelon maintenance bases in Japan. The 4th Wing would hire C-47 pilots to fly plane loads of liquor from its rear-echelon base at Tsuiki to Kimpo. Pilots ferrying planes back to Tsuiki for maintenance would also bring back as many fifths of liquor as their flight suits would carry. The 80th Squadron went so far as to cut doors in a spare set of wingtip fuel tanks to carry booze from its rear base at Itazuke to its forward base at Suwon. According to Pilot Dean Price, "Our F-80s didn't have enough fuel to make it from K-13 (Suwon) to Itazuke without tip fuel, so we'd land at Pusan to refuel. On the trip back we'd load the tips with rice beer, usually Asahi, and land again at Pusan for fuel for the trip home. You could get about four cases of beer in each trip. After about three trips we'd have enough for a squadron party."[49] They would also stick them in baggage wing tanks.[50] The o clubs would pay for liquor and other supplies by collecting dues from users and also by charging small fees for drinks. At most bases, all drinks were twenty-five cents.[51]

In addition to serving drinks, some clubs doubled as officers' messes. Woodrow Crockett often would have a steak dinner with all the fixings at his o club at Suwon.[52] By comparison, Kenneth Koon would spend most of the time at his squadron's club, "The Cockpit," drinking. According to Koon, "That's all there was—the mess hall was for eating."[53] In Koon's wing, the 18th, each squadron had its own beer mugs with the squadron insignia emblazoned on them.[54]

Ace James Hagerstrom did not partake in the drinking: "I wasn't going to go up and play with the MiGs unless I was 100 percent!"[55] For Hagerstrom, the pilots who drank a lot were "insecure." Hagerstrom's teetotaling was the exception rather than the rule. Most flight suit officers drank regularly. Kenneth Koon, a light drinker, typically would have a couple of martinis at his club when he was not flying. Perrin Gower, by comparison, would often drink until three in the morning and fly at six-thirty. According to Earl Brown, Leonard "Bill" Lilly, after one heavy night of drinking, leaned over the side of his F-86 and threw up.[56] He then went up and shot down two MiGs.[57] Hungover pilots would combat their queasiness by adjusting the oxygen setting on their breathing apparatus to 100 percent. "Oxygen was pure medicine," remembers Sturgeon. "It could cure queasiness and hangovers instantly."[58]

No group of flyers had a more notorious reputation for drinking than the South African Cheetah Squadron attached to the 18th Fighter-Bomber Wing. "The South Afs definitely consumed the most booze," recalled Kenneth Koon, "but they seemed to have a better innate consumptive capacity."[59] The Cheetahs not only turned most of their squadron debriefings into two or three mission-whiskey bottle parties, but also

built their own club known as "Rorke's Inn." Mickey Rorke founded
the club because he thought the 18th Wing's club "lacked atmosphere"
and charged too much for drinks. Hence, he built a bar out of ammunition cases next to his bed and initially stocked it with ten dollars worth
of liquor purchased at the British exchange in Pusan. Later, the Cheetah
squadron built a small wood and corrugated-steel building for the establishment. Charles Scott Shaw, a chaplain with the squadron, described it
as follows:

> We had our own pilots' pub, a cozy little room started by one of our
> gallant pilots, Mickey Rorke. There was a storm water drain adjoining the
> pub, and to gain access one had to cross Rorke's Drift, as it was called, on
> a narrow plank. During winter nights Rorke's Inn, with its dartboard and
> good companionship, rang with music and laughter, but it was a sobering
> thought to remember that one had to walk back across the plank in the
> chilly night air after a few drinks! If you fell into the drift, you landed in
> the ooze and slime. One or two fellows did fall in and were not given a
> chance to forget it. They were ostracized for a week afterwards! A doctor,
> so the story goes, was thrown into Rorke's Drift. The pilots were feeling a
> little touchy and tender after returning from a particularly grim mission.
> The doctor, with a complete lack of tact, had entered the pub and trium-
> phantly announced that he'd acquired a canvas bag for the bits and pieces
> of the body of the next pilot to crash. The doctor and his canvas bag were
> thrown into the slime of Rorke's Drift.[60]

Sadly, Rorke's Inn outlasted its owner. On 15 May 1951, Rorke
crashed into a B-26 parked at the end of the runway of Pusan on his
third mission of the day. Rorke's napalm bombs then ignited, killing him
and enveloping both aircraft in a large fireball.[61]

Given the young age of many of the pilots and their lack of responsibilities other than flying, drinking and partying often got out of hand,
as the Rorke's Inn episode demonstrates. Perrin Gower describes these
episodes as follows: "We had parties and broke every glass and beat up
the club officer. We would get on the wing commander's house and
yell, 'We hate this fucking place.' I just couldn't imagine that kind of
environment being re-created. Fighter pilots had very little responsibility—they were only responsible for themselves and their wingmen. This
is very different from the infantry."[62]

In an environment where pilots were shot down daily, drinking provided an important escape from the danger and boredom of the war. Douglas Evans and members of the 4th Wing would occasionally play kick the can with empty beer cans in their club, known as "Swig Alley." [63] In one famous game, "The stove got hit and the chimney fell down—oh, wonderful. Someone threw up out the window (an activity referred to as 'laughing at the ground') and another barely made the door before 'laughing,' which made a rather slippery entrance. One of the boys spun in, so we parked his carcass on a mattress in the corner." [64]

On another occasion, members of the 4th engaged in a full-fledged barroom brawl, complete with bodies flying through the air and broken furniture. Evans, who called the behavior GCA (gone completely ape), "got gashes on the side and back that looked like [he had] fallen in barbed wire." [65] Brown, who sat on the board of the 4th Wing's club, claimed the rowdiness got so out of hand that the board stopped ordering glasses and made everyone drink out of tin cans.[66] The o club in Korea, unlike the dayroom, was not a place accorded much respect. Rather, it was more akin to a gymnasium or a locker room—a stark contrast to officers' clubs on stateside Air Force bases.

In the 1951 edition of *The Air Force Wife,* an etiquette manual for young military brides, Nancy Shea describes the typical Air Force officers' club as a place for dances, bingo games, family night buffets, private parties, and other forms of entertainment.[67] According to Shea, the club was a place where a pilot could take his wife for fine dining and genteel company. "Club parties and dinner dances," she writes, "are not USO parties; they are dignified forms of entertainment where all social amenities, including proper dress, are observed." [68] Clubs which hold "informal dances with juke-box music border on the honky-tonk variety of road house entertainment and are certainly not up to the standards of officers and their wives." [69]

The Korea club, by comparison, was strictly a flight suit affair: a casual, male-only drinking lair unadulterated by Air Force wives and military rigmarole. As Salter described Kimpo's Swig Alley in *The Hunters:* "No two men were dressed alike. There were overcoats, leather jackets, woolen sweaters, and even a few plaid shirts. The room was a small one filled with smoke and shouting. Beer cans and glasses were strewn on the tables." [70] Not surprisingly, many pilots preferred the culture of the Far East Air Force to its stateside equivalent. Howard Heiner enjoyed his "independent and belligerent" lifestyle in Korea, but decided to quit the Air Force as soon as he returned to the United States. "When I got back to the States," he recalled, "I ran across a social element which I as an individual couldn't stand and totally rejected: everyone had to give a command call to the officers' club and socialize." [71]

"Round Eyes"

The casual and occasionally excessive lifestyle of the Korean War fighter pilot was the product of many factors, including the stress of war, ample free time, and the primitive conditions of most bases. However, as both Shea and Heiner suggest, the absence of American women in general and Air Force wives in particular enabled pilots to engage in many excessive activities with near impunity. Except for the Korean women domestics, Korean War air bases were populated almost exclusively by men. The only American women on base were the occasional Red Cross doughnut girl, the Air Force or Army nurse, and the United Service Organizations (USO) showgirl. These women were called "round eyes," [72] a racial slur which contrasted their round eyes with the narrower Korean variety.

The most typical "round eye" was the Red Cross woman. During World War II, the Red Cross recruited three thousand women to assist in improving the morale of overseas troops. These women served coffee and doughnuts, performed skits, organized parties, and played board games with GIs. Some were stationed at Red Cross clubs on military bases, but many served in the over 319 clubmobiles that traveled to isolated units. A clubmobile was a mobile canteen equipped with coffee urns, doughnut ovens, and an audio system for music. Some even had movie projectors. During the D-Day invasion, these mobile clubs served 200,000 doughnuts and over 5,000 gallons of coffee to participating soldiers.[73]

When the Korean War broke out, the Red Cross continued this

tradition by opening a club at Pusan in November 1950. In the spring of 1951, additional clubs were established at Pusan East, Suwon, Kimpo, Taegu, and Kunsan air bases.[74] Each of these clubs had an average of three clubmobiles and a staff of ten—two women for each clubmobile and four to staff the club. During the first twenty months of the war, sixty women were recruited as Red Cross club workers; several months later, the staff peaked at eighty.[75]

After breakfast in the mess hall, Red Cross women left the base for the forward positions. They would drive the clubmobile from one front-line position to the next, handing out doughnuts, performing skits, playing games, and talking to the GIs. The clubmobile would return to base by five; the women would then eat dinner, complete their daily paperwork, and go to bed. If a Red Cross woman worked in a club, she would perform tasks similar to the clubmobile worker. The only difference was that her work was continuous. Each stationary club served as many as two thousand people a day. At K-9, the 100 by 20-foot club had blue leather chairs, five writing tables, six lamps, a piano, and a Ping-Pong table. Its plaster walls were painted "a soft, cool green," and decorations consisted of "red and white construction paper above the windows and on the lamp shades."[76] At the club, Red Cross workers served coffee, led sing-alongs, hosted Ping-Pong tournaments, and put on theme shows such as "Monte Carlo Night," "Carnival Night," and the "Air Race" (an adaptation of horse racing).[77]

The hectic schedule of the Red Cross women made socializing with officers very difficult. At most bases, the "round eye" quarters were strictly off-limits to flight suit personnel. Some base commanders went so far as to erect barbed wire fences around the quarters and assign air police to guard them.[78] Moreover, all of these women had an obligation to the Red Cross to refrain from any activity which might be considered morally improper. According to a recruitment flyer, the Red Cross recruited the "highest type of American girl for Clubmobile units in Korea," and each was expected to be a "responsible representative after working hours as well as on duty time."[79] When their behavior fell short of exemplary, controversy could erupt. For example, a rumor about a Red Cross woman who allegedly infected an officer with a venereal disease was investigated by the Red Cross and the Department of Defense for one year. Concerned about the Red Cross's reputation, Robert Lewis, the vice president of the American Red Cross, tracked the rumor to an artillery officer named Francis Stevens, and sent representatives to interview Stevens personally. The story was determined to be a rumor, and a written statement was taken from Stevens to exonerate the Red Cross.[80] In another instance, a U.S. Army soldier accused Red Cross club women of drinking excessively at a Christmas party for Korean orphans at a Red Cross club in Korea:

> I really felt ashamed that I was an American. Several reasons, I guess. The thing that irked me was the drunken shrieks, curses, and ravings of those Red Cross bitches. They were soused to the gills and made fools out of themselves. It seemed to me that one day out of the year they could act decent and sober, especially in the presence of a nun who had devoted her ideals and was sacrificing so much for others. I wonder what the Korean sisters thought of those species of American women.[81]

This letter sparked an investigation by the president of the American Red Cross. Although this investigation also failed to uncover any inappropriate behavior by Red Cross staff members, every staff person who attended the party was interviewed before the case was finally closed.[82]

As these two examples illustrate, Red Cross women were held to very stringent moral standards: any moral breach could result in a broad-based investigation. Consequently, Red Cross workers tended to be cautious in their social relations with men. On nights that she did not work, Red Cross worker Jessica Hunter "would go to a movie, a choir practice, have a living-room date, or just wash and write home."[83] Drinking at the o club was definitely not on Hunter's list of after-hour recreational activities, despite the fact that the club was the social center of any base.

A final factor that discouraged dating was the age of most Red Cross women. For the most part, Red Cross women were older than many of the younger flight suit officers. Thirty of the sixty women sent by the Red Cross to Korea between November 1950 and June 1952 had World War II experience, all were over twenty-five years old, and most were over thirty.[84] Hence, most were interested only in the older, commanding officers. Paul Turner claimed that the Red Cross women at Suwon "usually hung out in Colonel Gabreski's room. They sold us doughnuts and coffee, talked to us, and it was nice to see a round eye around there; they were camp followers." [85]

The other type of Western woman to which pilots were exposed was the USO showgirl. The 4th Wing, for example, would typically host one or two shows a month. In February 1952, Betty Hutton performed in her bathing suit in the middle of the frigid Korean winter.[86] In October, Danny Kaye highlighted a show, and in February 1953, two shows entitled "Breezing Along" and "Room Service" were performed for a crowd of five hundred onlookers.[87] Pilot Curlee Satterlee enjoyed the USO shows so much that he would shoot pictures of the entertainers and then give the photographs to them the next day. Unfortunately, not all of the stars were always grateful for his efforts. During one show headlined by Mickey Rooney, Satterlee stayed up all night developing pictures for Rooney. The next day, he presented the five-by-seven pictures to Rooney only to hear him say, "They're too damn small," and throw them on the floor. "That was the most distasteful moment in my career," recalled Satterlee.[88]

Although stars like Rooney often headlined USO shows, the standard USO entertainment workers put on memorable shows, too. William Van den Bos, a South African pilot, recalled one show where USO women sang "popular songs in the style of the singers who made them famous": "Julie acted as MC . . . Peggy combined singing and dancing; Rosanne was an acrobatic dancer, while Terry accompanied them all on the piano accordion. The applause that they received was well deserved." [89] That evening, Van den Bos and several other pilots managed to persuade these four women to accompany them to a party at a nearby base: "We and the four girls piled into a jeep and headed for the thrash. Whiskey flowed freely and there was much singing by the girls, the American officers, and ourselves." [90] Van den Bos's experience, in the end, was rare. Most USO women were on base for only a day or so, and social time was limited and circumscribed. As was the case with Red Cross women, there were never enough USO girls to go around. As Turner put it,

"They were nice to see and talk to, but that was the extent of it: there were just too few of them."[91]

Prostitution

Because of the shortage of women, pilots who desired sexual relations often turned to prostitutes. While many pilots refrained from openly discussing the issue, evidence of prostitution can be found in the medical reports of the various wings. During the first five months of 1951, the venereal disease rate of the 51st Wing ranged as high as 7.14 percent in January to a low of 2.35 percent in May.[92] In January 1952, the rate soared to 8.12 percent. Ninety-five of the 117 cases were known to have been contracted in Japan—a fact which lead the base flight surgeon to conclude "the rest and relaxation leave system is contributory, in that it allows frequent exposure of Suwon Air Base personnel in Japan."[93] Despite the prevalence of VD in Japan, flight suit officers and even enlisted men actually considered Japan to be a better place to solicit the services of a prostitute. "It was looked down upon even for an enlisted man to go with a Korean prostitute," recalled George Berke.[94] Furthermore, many wings placed surrounding Korean villages "off-limits." The 51st Wing placed Suwon off-limits and ordered Paul Turner to patrol the city in a jeep and hunt for violators—a job called "pussy patrol."[95] The 18th Wing did not place its nearby village of Osan "on-limits" until May 1953; it did so only after all base personnel and "probable contacts" were administered antibiotics as a prophylaxis.[96] Clearly, the Air Force believed Korean prostitutes to be disease ridden even toward the end of the war. Consequently, Japan remained the favored spot for illicit sexual activity. Rest and recuperation (R&R) leave became known as I&I—intoxication and intercourse.[97]

Flight crews generally received six days of leave in Japan every six weeks. For pilots, leaves were staggered on an individual basis. Some pilots like Hagerstrom rarely took leave, while others, like Satterlee, went to Japan almost weekly.[98] The most frequented houses of prostitution were in Tokyo and at rear-echelon maintenance bases. Tsuiki, for instance, had a famous whorehouse appropriately called the "Sabre Dancer." Every pilot interviewed in this study had at least heard of the Sabre Dancer and many admitted to frequenting the place. Paul Turner remembers the Sabre Dancer as a "gorgeous" place only two stops from Tsuiki by train: "There were lots of nice people there, the girls were a lot of fun, and there was always dancing, singing, etc."[99] Turner claims that one of the girls even lent him money when he ran out. "It was thoroughly enjoyable. It was just like a bunch of people hanging out in a singles bar. At Tsuiki, the officers recommended it as the place to go. It was just for officers and transient pilots."[100]

As this statement implies, the line between girlfriend and prostitute often blurred in Japan. John Verdi went so far as to write, "These girls were not prostitutes."[101] George Berke, who wrote a fictitious manuscript about flight suit officers during the 1950s, described Air Force whorehouses as "clubs." "You could keep a bottle there," writes Berke, and "the madame poured your drinks and dispensed chat."[102] If you were a squadron commander, the madame might even sleep with you, as was the case with Sam, Berke's protagonist. Sam, however, not only slept with the madam but treated her like a "wife": "He was a good husband and treated her like a good wife. When he was done [ejaculating] and she was nice and slippery he brought her off with his hand. . . . The next time they went she gave him a french anyway and they made love like real people."[103]

To heighten the realism of these "marriages of convenience," officers would rent a single prostitute for their entire leave and take them to country resort hotels. Perrin Gower, who visited Myoshi's Bordello in Tokyo as soon as he arrived from the States, would go on R&R every three months. First, he would stop in Tokyo and find a beautiful "girl" (a prostitute); then he would go "to some suburban, small hotel with maybe six rooms, and just relax there in the beautiful setting."[104] For a nominal fee, Gower could flee from the war and re-create domestic life.

Interestingly enough, this domestic interlude is a theme found in both *The Hunters* and *The Troubling of a Star*. In *The Troubling of a Star*, Tindle spent his R&R sitting with his "girlfriend" by a sliding Japanese window, smoking quietly and looking at the rain. In *The Hunters*, Cleve

Saville similarly spent his vacation with a nineteen-year-old girl in an artist's house in the hills outside of Tokyo.[105]

To facilitate these idyllic experiences, the Air Force leased hotels in the countryside. The 4th Wing leased a total of 136 spaces in rest hotels for enlisted men and 84 spaces for officers.[106] The 18th Wing leased a hotel called the Fujiya for officers only. The Fujiya had 221 rooms and was located in the heart of Hokone National Park, a park famous for its natural hot springs.[107] The 18th Wing also reserved a C-124 Globemaster, appropriately labeled "the cocktail courier," to transport the two hundred service personnel who took leave every week. The Globemaster's weekly runs continued until the plane crashed on 18 June 1953, killing 129 airmen in the world's worst air disaster to date.[108]

Although many pilots wanted to do nothing but find an attractive prostitute and relax in a countryside resort hotel, some refrained from prostitution altogether and chose to relax at a rear-echelon base or Tokyo. Berke, a newly married pilot with a pregnant wife in the States, claimed to talk to girls, but that was it: "I was with a bunch of guys who were going to be faithful to their wives."[109] M. J. Bailey, similarly, not only refused to engage in prostitution, but was morally outraged. At Tachikawa, he was appalled to see "girls hanging around trying to pick any one up, white or black, for 1,000 Yen (about $2.75)," and guys "grabbing them and being so public about the whole thing—it sure looks dark and dirty."[110] Men like Berke and Bailey, in short, had to find alternative forms of entertainment while on leave. Bailey spent his leave shopping and sightseeing in Tokyo.[111] Howard Heiner stayed at an Air Force hotel in the countryside and read novels.[112] Other pilots visited the Turkish baths at Onsan or enjoyed "the Nicki Gieke, or Round Theater similar to the Lido in Paris." The Nicki ran twenty-three hours a day and was never empty.[113]

Because food at many bases in Korea left a lot to be desired, a priority for many pilots on R&R was to escape the powdered eggs and gristly stews of Korea and find a good American meal.[114] In this regard, the o clubs in Japan were very accommodating. The club in Tokyo served steak and lobster.[115] Brown boasted of the good food served at the Tsuiki club.[116]

In addition to o clubs, pilots, anxious to avoid any type of Asian food, also frequented other American clubs in Tokyo. The University Club featured a roof-garden terrace and live, big-band-style music. Douglas Evans recalled, "The view of the city and expanse of lights at night from the roof-garden terrace made a much more agreeable impression than the daytime's street-level madhouse." Evans also thought that the "swell" Japanese band sounded just like the Glenn Miller Orchestra.[117]

Another popular pastime in Tokyo was shopping. Cameras, radio equipment, and pearls were all popular items. For as little as two hundred dollars, a pilot could buy a double string of "perfectly matched cultured pearls" from traveling Mikimoto pearl salesman.[118] Most pilots, however, purchased jewelry and other gifts at their local base exchanges, where discounts were even greater. Kimpo's BX often sold over seven hundred dollars worth of jewelry a month during the war.[119] Whenever a new line of stock came into the BXs, men would line up several hours before store opening to purchase choice items.[120] Like similar establishments in the continental United States, some base exchanges also had snack bars attached to them. The snack bar at Kimpo served "hamburgers, sandwiches, hot breakfasts of ham and eggs, and ice cream with its companion products of milk shakes and sundaes."[121] The Kimpo BX also sold beer by the case, and lots of it. As of February 1952, it was selling an average of 750 cases a month to a base population of one thousand.[122]

Because of perquisites, such as base exchange discounts and subsidized hotels, money was rarely a problem for pilots on leave. In addition to their standard officer salaries, pilots also received two hundred extra dollars a month in flight pay. Tomlinson and James, both of whom sent most of their money home to support dependents, still had enough money left over to purchase new automobiles when they returned to the States.[123] "Money was never a problem," remembers Roy Lottinger. "I never spent a penny of my flight pay—it all went to investments."[124]

Indigenous Workers

The gracious, albeit rustic, lifestyle of the flight suit officer was not only the result of high incomes and low expenses, but also the product of the colonial relationship these men established with the local populations in Japan and Korea. In addition to performing prostitution services, low-paid, indigenous workers built air fields, worked in messes, cleaned barracks, and did laundry for officers. These workers, in essence, liberated flight suit officers from the everyday drudgeries of military life and enabled them to live a life reminiscent of the nineteenth-century colonial experiences of British officers in India and Africa.

In May 1951, the 51st Wing employed 1,748 indigenous workers at its Tsuiki base. Most of these employees (1,381) worked on the operational areas of the base—namely, the runway; 104 in the mess; and 263 in the officers' barracks.[125] The 4th Wing employed over five thousand Koreans in October 1951—mostly to improve runways. These workers were housed in a labor camp adjacent to Kimpo field which bore an uncanny resemblance to a forced labor camp: a barbed-wire fence surrounded the camp, and passes were required to enter and leave it.[126] If a worker was fired, the pass would be given a special stamp to prevent him or her from ever being employed again by the U.N. or by the South Korean government.[127]

Ostensibly, actions such as these were designed to prevent theft and sabotage. Turner, for instance, had a lot of film stolen, and Berke suspected that many of the Koreans were "up to no good": "We didn't mind calling most Koreans 'Gooks' because they didn't like us, and we didn't like them. They had a colonial mentality: anything you could steal from Americans was okay."[128]

In particular, Berke was upset with the Koreans for stealing the wallet and rings of a pilot who crashed just outside his base.[129] Dick Clifton, a South African pilot, remembered one occasion when a Korean worker removed the safety clip on the arming wire of one of his bombs—a move which armed the bomb and nearly blew up him and his plane. The air police caught the saboteur soon after this episode and "dealt with him appropriately."[130] Presumably, they shot him. Similarly, a "neat-looking woman" who ran Berke's o club was suspected of spying by the Korean Army. "One day," recalled Berke, "the Korean Army came in and took this woman behind the club and shot her." [131]

Despite occasional spying and thievery, most pilots greatly appreciated the work Koreans performed and they treated them well, albeit paternalistically. For his Quonset hut of twelve, Turner had two teenage houseboys to keep the place clean. The pilots adopted boys as "part of the family." They were invited to all parties, and food and clothing would be given to them on a regular basis. [132] Tomlinson bought his boy a bicycle. [133] According to Crockett, his houseboys were paid thirty dollars a month, six dollars more than a Korean colonel received. Crockett also kept his messboy in his hut because the boy claimed the labor camp at Kimpo was unsafe. [134] The extent to which many pilots liked the children, many of whom were orphans, was demonstrated not only by the pay and gifts they gave them, but also the compliments they lavished upon them. Douglas Evans's comments are typical:

> Kim has shown us all a lot by his diligent efforts with his schoolbooks in his spare time. That kid wants to get someplace when he grows up after this war is over. Sometimes when I'd watch him studying, I'd think about some American kids, how they take their comforts for granted and barely try in school. Here is this Korean kid with no home, his country torn up by war, taking care of himself, studying his books and full of ambition and hope. I feel that his attitude is probably the best reward we'll get for being over there. [135]

Clearly, Evans held his houseboy Kim in the highest esteem. Paternalism, though, was not always benevolent. Despite giving gifts to their boys, Turner's hut insisted on calling them "Leaky Dick" and "Pom Pom Wa." Turner thought nothing of it: "Everyone had American nicknames because everyone was named Kim." [136] Berke's hut paid their houseboy extra not to eat kimchi because it smelled; however, none of them realized that kimchi (a mixture of pickled cabbage, hot pepper, and fish paste) was the national dish of Korea. [137] Cultural sensitivity, in short, was sorely lacking, and many pilots easily adopted a colonial attitude toward the indigenous population. Dean Hess, who hired seven girls, aged fourteen to sixteen, to work in the officer's mess at K-24 (Pyongyang East), was proud that his "men could sit at tables and be waited upon like time-honored warriors of old."[138] He also felt no remorse about working these children "like beavers" or about the fact that they gave up their Korean names for American ones.[139] Exploitation, for Hess, only existed in the sexual sphere. As long as Hess ordered his men not to make any sexual advances toward the girls, he felt perfectly comforted with the fact that he employed young children for menial tasks even though laws that forbade such practices existed in the United States. Hess saw it as a mutually beneficial relationship: "We developed an affectionate and protective attitude toward these gay, giggling young-sters that somehow mellowed our harsh, cold male world."[140]

Base Jobs

In the United States, pilots were often assigned demanding nonflying jobs to fill their time when they were not flying. Before the war, for example, Ranald Adams was a supply officer and was personally liable for all the supplies at his base. "The job was so difficult," complained Adams, "that the officer before me had a nervous breakdown and had to be carted off in a straight jacket."[141] In Korea, by contrast, these jobs were neither demanding nor time consuming. Free time, therefore, also contributed to the pilots' excessive partying and recreation.

Tomlinson spent a few hours a day as a unit historian. Howard Heiner did occasional paperwork for the maintenance squadron. Earl Brown helped manage the officers' club and worked in intelligence. Perrin Gower was in charge of on-the-job-training for enlisted men.[142] However, Chick Cleveland held the most creative job title: "squadron athletic officer." Cleveland was in charge of duties such as building and painting a Ping-Pong table in the squadron ready room.[143] Except for squadron leaders and operations officers who planned missions, the extra duties assigned to "junior birdmen," as Tomlinson explained, "were designed to keep you busy, and keep you out of trouble."[144] Gower's attitude toward his job was typical: "I didn't understand it and didn't spend much time on it."[145] Overall, most pilots performed their nonflying jobs only on days they were not flying, and even then would never spend more than five hours at it.[146] For flight suit officers, flying was their job, and the ground was a place to play and relax.

Bedcheck Charlie

No examination of base life in Korea would be complete without a discussion of the "Bedcheck Charlie" raids—raids later made famous by their appearance in several episodes of *M*A*S*H*. The term "Bedcheck Charlie" was coined in World War II and originally referred to the light German aircraft that bombed Allied airfields in England under the cover of darkness. In Korea, Bedcheck Charlies were propeller-driven biplanes that attacked U.N. airfields at night. They were a source of both amusement and anger on bases. Nightly Charlie raids denied pilots of much-needed rest and also occasionally damaged equipment with the worked-over mortar shells and hand grenades they dropped. However, most officers found humor in the raids and looked upon them as their own personal "fireworks show."

The Bedcheck Charlie raids began in June 1951 and continued throughout the war. The basic plane used was a PO-2, a Russian-manufactured aircraft that was first developed in 1927 as a two-seat trainer and later used as "a reconnaissance bomber, an ambulance, freighter, crop duster, and glider tug."[147] These vintage planes had a top speed of 96 miles per hour and were made of fabric, paint, and wood. Because of these antique qualities, the planes were very hard to track and shoot down. Jet interceptors were too fast to shoot them down, and the PO-2, flying at tree-top level, could navigate down narrow valleys to avoid radar. Radar also had great difficulty picking them up because their fuselages consisted mainly of wood and painted canvas, which are undetectable by radar.

To combat Charlies, the Air Force added more anti-aircraft weapons around airfields and experimented with several different "Charlie Killers" during the course of the war. At Kimpo, the base commander attempted to intercept the PO-2s with Marine AD Skyraider aircraft, a "hard nose" B-26 with fourteen forward firing machine guns, and an armed T-6 trainer.[148] Jet F-94 night fighters were also used until one crashed in an April 1953 intercept mission. However, the best Charlie-killing aircraft were the Navy and Marine F4U Corsairs. In July 1953, Navy Lieutenant Guy Bordelon shot down five Charlies in a ground-based Corsair and became the first "Charlie ace" as well as the only Navy ace of the war.[149]

In addition to sending special interceptors after Bedcheck Charlies, the Air Force also launched several intensive bombing campaigns against small airfields in and around Pyongyang. During June 1951, B-29s, B-26s, and F-80s attacked all fifteen of the airfields around Pyongyang. In July 1953, Sabres of the 8th Wing destroyed two Charlies on the ground at an airfield near Pyongyang. So intensive was the U.N. airfield-suppression effort that the North Koreans had to maintain sixty-nine airfields just to operate thirty aircraft. This effort, according to a Chinese inspection group, was "far beyond the financial power of Red China to support."[150]

Although costly for the North Koreans and Chinese, these raids were occasionally quite effective. On 16 June 1952, Bailey witnessed a raid against Suwon that destroyed one F-86, damaged nine other Sabres, killed one officer, and wounded five airmen.[151] In October 1952, a PO-2 raid on the friendly island of Chodo killed five Koreans and wounded one American. On 15 June 1953, a Charlie even bombed South Korean president Syngman Rhee's mansion.[152] A typical raid, however, caused very little damage. For example, on New Year's Eve 1952, three PO-2s bombed Kimpo, created lots of noise and confusion, but caused no serious destruction. The 4th Wing's after-action report reads as follows: "The entire raid was quite a spectacle especially when the ack-ack opened up. The black sky looked like Coney Island on the Fourth of July but none of the raiders were hit. For all the good he did, 'Bedcheck' should have stayed on the ground and enjoyed his vodka. Except for lost sleep, damage to the base and equipment was negligible."[153]

As Tomlinson recalled, "He would come over and you'd hear the grenades go off, but he never did any damage to anything, just kept you awake and that sort of stuff."[154] Perrin Gower even looked forward to Charlie attacks. "We loved Charlie," he exclaimed. "He was great sport."[155] When the alarm sounded, Gower and his companions would go out with their drinks and watch the AAA and tracers. To Gower and other flight suit officers who were accustomed to risking their lives,

"Bedcheck Charlie was largely a joke—a harassment thing." [156] The Air Force, though, never was able to solve the problem completely. For future wars, the Far East Air Force would have to devise a much more sophisticated air defense system to deal with heckler raids than the one that existed in Korea. Since jet interceptors were largely useless against these planes, the Air Force concluded that it would have to rely more on radar-guided anti-aircraft artillery in the future. It also learned that it would have to develop a better aircraft identification system so that the guns could fire as soon as possible. [157]

Whether a pilot flew fighter-interceptors or fighter-bombers, time spent on base and on R&R was an obvious break from the war. Unlike ground troops, who fought around the clock, aviators returned to relatively safe and comfortable bases at the end of each mission. It was because of these intermissions from the war that pilots could indulge in so many recreational activities. Military perquisites and cheap indigenous labor not only facilitated this indulgent lifestyle, but in many respects were its linchpins. Without indigenous workers to perform personal services, flight suit officers would not have had nearly as much time to drink or play Ping-Pong. Cheap prostitution even enabled pilots to purchase women for long periods of time—periods so long that many of the pilots mistook these business deals for real relationships. Finally, cheap liquor purchased at base exchanges in Japan and Korea, coupled with lots of boredom, fueled the excessive drinking in which many pilots indulged at their o clubs.

Additional components to the flight suit lifestyle of the Korean War pilot besides time, labor, and benefits were the lack of supervision and the casual nature of camp life. There were no Air Force wives to curb the roadhouse atmosphere of the o club. Military conventions and discipline were out of place in a base where everyone walked around in fatigues or flight suits, shared a forty-seat thunderbox, and played Ping-Pong in the ready room. But then again, military rigmarole in the Korean War Air Force was secondary. As long as pilots performed their missions well, they could partake in rowdy off-hours partying—and many did.

7

Life after Korea

In 1969, a gray-haired Frank Tomlinson climbed into the cockpit of a Special Forces AD-1 Skyraider at Nakhon Phanom air base in Northern Thailand and took off for what would be the last mission of his Southeast Asia tour. The mission was a pre-dawn strike against Communist forces in the Plain du Jars area of Laos. Although Tomlinson was now a full colonel and could have retired from the Air Force years ago, he was flying a propeller-driven, Korean War-era fighter in one of the most hazardous areas of operation in Southeast Asia. He was having the time of his life. As he puts it: "I was at the tail-end of my tour and I was invincible!"[1] Tomlinson was having "so much fun" that he decided to go for several passes over a supply target as the sun was coming up over the horizon. On his third pass, he was "zapped": "I got two rounds right in the front of the engine, and the oil started coming out. So, I cleaned the wings and headed for Udorn. I had to shut the engine off right over the field. And there was a cloud layer below me, so I set up a big turn, went down to the clouds and rolled out right where I was supposed to be."[2] Although Tomlinson knew it was against regulations for him to attack Laotian targets during daylight in a slow-flying AD-1, his flight suit bravado got the best of him, and he made a "dumb" error.

Tomlinson, however, was not alone in allowing flight suit attitude to influence his behavior as well as his career after Korea. As we shall see, the flight suit culture resonated in the post-Korean War careers of the 12 flight suit officers whose social backgrounds were explored in chapter 2. Although Air Force careerism is not the focus of this book, I will explore this theme even though the primary purpose of the chapter is to let the reader know what some of these officers did after Korea.

Robinson Risner

Robinson Risner[3] left Korea with eight MiGs to his credit, and a strong determination to remain in the Air Force. On his first postwar assignment with the 50th Wing in Hahn, Germany, he received a coveted regular commission. From then on out, Risner would no longer have to worry about reductions in force because as an ace with a regular commission, his future in the Air Force was secure.

In 1956, Risner transferred to George AFB, Victorville, California, to fly the follow-on fighter to the F-86—the F-100 Super Sabre. Risner's unit, the 34th Fighter-Day Squadron, was chosen to evaluate the Super Sabre's high-altitude capabilities. On one such mission, the valves on Risner's pressure suit malfunctioned, and the suit accidentally inflated at about 60,000 feet. Risner could barely move his arms, and had to use every bit of his strength to control the plane and make an emergency landing. At the hospital, doctors discovered that this mishap had ruptured one of his heart valves. They explained to him that he would probably never fly again. However, the injury healed in time, and this flight suit officer once again requested to be put on flight status.

In 1957, Risner was selected to fly the Charles A. Lindberg Commemoration flight from New York to Paris. Flying the F-100 Super Sabre, Risner made it to Paris in 6 hours and 38 minutes. This flight could have been the crowning moment of Risner's career, but there would be many more interesting episodes for this officer.

After attending the Air War College and serving as a staff officer with the Commander in Chief, Pacific (CINPAC), the now thirty-nine-year-old Risner managed once again to get back into the fighter business. The year was 1964, and Risner was assigned to the fly F-105 Thunderchief as a squadron commander with the 18th Fighter-Bomber Wing at Kadena Air Base, Okinawa. This was Risner's first experience with fighter-bombers, but he did not shy away from the challenge. Instead, he set out to be the most aggressive pilot in his unit.

In 1965, Risner transferred to Korat, Thailand, to participated in President Lyndon Johnson's air campaign against North Vietnam dubbed Operation Rolling Thunder.

On Risner's last day in Okinawa on 19 August 1965, he had a strange premonition for the first time in his twenty-two-year flying career, which convinced him to settle his affairs and make a tape for his wife and children. On it, he told his wife and four sons "never to give up hope" if he got shot down because he "would do everything within his power to get back." Indeed, Risner would return to the States, but it would not be for another seven and a half years.

At Korat, Risner's flight suit attitude quickly made him unpopular with his crew chief. During one week, his aircraft was hit on four missions out of five. On a mission against a radar station in North Vietnam, Risner's plane took a bad hit behind the cockpit, forcing him to bailout over the South China Sea. Fortunately, a rescue seaplane was nearby and picked him up within minutes of the bailout.

The next day, General Joseph Moore, the commander of the Second Air Division, ordered him to Saigon. At Saigon, Moore met Risner on the tarmac and immediately ordered him into the back seat of a T-39. Moore knew that desperate measures were required to keep this flight suit officer from pushing himself too hard. Moore ended up flying Risner personally to Clark Air Force Base in the Philippines, for three days of golf, steaks, and air-conditioned quarters. However, this ticket to paradise did not have the desired mellowing effect.

When Risner returned to Korat, he went right back to the same grueling routine until finally his luck ran out. On a routine mission against a surface-air-missile sight near Than Hoa, Risner flew low over the target and took a bellyful of 23-millimeter cannon rounds. He ended up in a low-altitude ejection over North Vietnam. Risner would spend the next seven and a half years of his life at the Hoa Lo Prison in Hanoi, more commonly known as the Hanoi Hilton. While in Hoa Lo, Risner served as the senior officer, and was severely persecuted for petitioning the Vietnamese authorities for better living conditions for his men. Not only did the Vietnamese beat and torture Risner, but they also subjected him to four years of solitary confinement. Through it all, according to Risner, he never lost hope that he would one day see his family. He would often tap Psalm 23 in code to cheer on the flyers in adjacent cells. In the last months of imprisonment, he helped organize church services for the men.

Risner was repatriated in February 1973, and happily found himself flying F-4 Phantoms by August. Risner ended his Air Force career as a brigadier general in 1976 at the Fighter Weapons School at Nellis Air Force Base, where he served as vice commander.

Risner retired in Texas, and began working closely with Ross Perot, first as a motivational speaker in the Texas War Against Drugs program and later as the campaign manager for veterans in Ross Perot's presidential campaign. Risner's last flight in a fighter plane occurred in 1990; he was sixty-five years old. A friend sent an F-16 to fly him to a formal dinner at Nellis AFB. Not one to be a mere passenger, Risner convinced the pilot to let him fly the aircraft both ways. After the journey, Risner fondly reflected, "The F-16 was a tremendous aircraft, but my personal favorite to this day is the F-86."

Earl Brown

Of all the officers interviewed in this study, Brown had the most successful military career. He became a lieutenant general and attributes his meteoric rise in the Air Force establishment to two factors: fighter service in Korea and Vietnam, and pure luck.

After Korea, Brown flew F-86s and later F-102 Delta Daggers at McGuire AFB, in Wrightstown, New Jersey. In 1960, he went to Zaragoza AFB, Spain, where he flew F-102s with the 431st Squadron. The 431st, known as the Red Devils, transitioned to F-4 Phantoms in 1964 at George AFB, and then transferred to Ubon, Thailand, in 1965. In Thailand, Brown flew fifty interdiction missions against targets in North Vietnam and Laos.

After fifty missions in the Vietnam War, Brown attended the Armed Forces Staff College in Norfolk, Virginia. He then took command of the 53rd Tactical Fighter Squadron at Bitburg, Germany. According to

Brown, "Commanding a fighter squadron was the best job in my entire career."[4]

In 1969, however, Brown's luck ran out and he was transferred back to Thailand, this time to Udorn to serve in the 432nd Tactical Reconnaissance Wing. With this wing, Brown flew another fifty missions in F-4Ds and RF-4Cs, a reconnaissance version of the F-4. On this tour, he saw much more flak than during his earlier missions. During his one-hundredth mission, Brown was escorting a reconnaissance flight near the Mughia Pass, when his plane took a round that knocked out one engine and lit up his instrument panel with warning lights. Brown's strategy was to fly the disabled aircraft toward the Thai border and then bail out. He describes the episode as follows:

> We flew past a small village, dropping less than 500 feet. Len [his back seater] went out first and I followed. The system is almost idiot-proof. The seat ejects from the airplane, the pilot is ejected from the seat, and the parachute opens, all automatically. Hanging in the chute, I saw the ball of flame where the F-4 impacted the ground. Below me, Len appeared to be drifting toward the fire. I was watching him when I realized how close to the ground I was. I landed on both feet, started to fall backwards, then sat down on the survival pack, which I had forgotten to release, and came to rest with my back against a tree. A helicopter had come from Nakhon Phanom to pick us up. We were about three miles from the base. As Len and I walked down the road toward the chopper, he turned to me and said: "You know somethin', Brownie? We're too old for this stuff!"[5]

That was his last mission. A month later, he left Udorn for Tokyo and then flew a refurbished F-4 to George AFB: "I pulled into a parking spot on the ramp, finally home safe from the war, and stop cocked the engine. Best of all, there was Gloria with Nancy, Lou, and Bill [his wife and children] waiting to see me home."[6]

In 1970, Brown was assigned to be the assistant to the Assistant Secretary of Defense for Manpower Reserve Affairs at the Pentagon and promoted to the rank of full colonel. While there, he met many influential people, including Chappie James, the first black four-star general in the Air Force. He also set up a program for bases to share underutilized facilities with local communities.

In 1973, Brown was transferred to the Air Training Command at Reese AFB, in Lubbock, Texas, as an operations director, for two years. He then became base commander of Williams AFB, where he was promoted to brigadier general in 1975. During his time at Williams, he also took the Industrial College of the Armed Service's course by correspondence and attended the Advanced Management program at the Harvard Business School.

As a brigadier general, Brown's first assignment was as base commander at Andrews AFB from 1975 to 1978. During the bicentennial year, he hosted over one hundred heads of state at Andrews. In 1977 he became head of the Air Force Security Police for eighteen months. He then took over the Aerospace Weapons Center at Tyndall AFB, Florida. In this job, Brown oversaw the testing of the Air Force's newest weapons and lived in base housing right on the beach. As he put it, "I knew then that I had died and gone to heaven." [7]

Brown's next job as head of the Seventeenth Air Force elevated him to "an even higher level of heaven—commanding all the fighters in Europe." His final job with the Air Force was as head of NATO Air Forces in the Mediterranean, where he worked closely with Admiral Crowe, the future chairman of the Joint Chiefs. Brown retired from the Air Force in 1985 as a lieutenant general after thirty-four years of service, and now works as a docent with the National Air and Space Museum. [8]

Woodrow Crockett

Like many black officers in the 1950s, Woodrow Crockett chose to remain in the military after the Korean War. As an officer and a pilot, he believed he would have a much more rewarding career in the Air Force than in the civilian sector. The Air Force, however, was not devoid of racial stereotyping, and Crockett discovered that the higher he rose, the more his skin color became a factor in his assignments—especially those in the area of equal opportunity.

After Korea, Crockett attended the Air Force Command and Staff College at Maxwell AFB, Alabama. When he graduated, Major Crockett was assigned to McGuire AFB, New Jersey, as a wing installations officer. This job placed him in charge of three radar sites and eighteen units of base housing—hardly a choice assignment for a veteran fighter pilot of two wars. Nevertheless, Crockett put great effort into his job and soon attracted the attention of the commander of the 26th Air Division, Brigadier General Thayer Olds. Olds saw potential in Crockett and chose him to be the deputy commander of the 2nd All-Weather Fighter Squadron, an F-86D unit. When Crockett left the unit in 1955, he was squadron commander.

In 1957, Olds assigned Crockett to the 26th Air Division Headquarters as an operations officer. A year later, Crockett landed a coveted slot as an F-106 test pilot at Edwards AFB, California. The F-106 Delta Dart, part of the Air Force's "Century Series" of fighters, was designed to fly at speeds in excess of Mach 2, and was dubbed by many at the time as the "ultimate interceptor."[9] As a test pilot, Crockett flew one of the fastest fighters of the time, had his own T-33 for personal transportation needs, and was slated to be the first F-106 squadron commander. Unfortunately, his luck ran out and in one of those strange twists of fate not uncommon in military careers, Crockett ended up at McGuire again, this time as an air defense operations officer.

When John F. Kennedy was elected president in 1960, Crockett was assigned to the National Guard Bureau in the Pentagon to assist in integrating blacks into the Air National Guard. The position called for a World War II veteran, a West Point graduate, and a pilot experienced in Century Series aircraft. Because Crockett met two out of the three qualifications, he was chosen to be the first minority officer on the Guard Bureau Staff. This job required him to travel to Guard bases across the country to ensure that adequate efforts were being made to recruit blacks into the Air Guard.

In 1965, Crockett went to Oslo to work in the headquarters of the NATO Northern European Air Forces. Three years later, the Air Force asked him to go to Vietnam to fly the AC-47 gunship known as "Puff the Magic Dragon." As a veteran fighter pilot of two wars, Crockett was not interested in driving a multi-engine, World War II vintage aircraft. Instead, he opted to return to the Guard Bureau until his retirement as a lieutenant colonel in September 1970.

After his retirement, he continued to work for the National Guard Bureau as a civilian Equal Opportunity Officer until 1977. Since then, Crockett has been active in the Washington, D.C., area public schools as a guest lecturer on the Tuskegee airmen. He also is an avid tennis player who twice won the senior doubles championship in Virginia. In 1994, as part of the D-Day anniversary celebrations, President Bill Clinton invited Crockett to escort him and British prime minister John Major to the aviators' wall at Maddingly Cemetery in Cambridge, England. At the celebration, CNN zoomed in on his red Tuskegee Airmen Association jacket and beamed his image around the globe while the *New York Times* placed his picture on the front page of its June 5, 1994, issue. Because of this publicity, the association awarded him with the Noel Parrish Award for the Tuskegee airman who had done the most for the organization during the year. Crockett lives with his wife in northern Virginia.[10]

Frank Tomlinson

After the Korean War, Frank Tomlinson was in "hog heaven." He had saved over seven hundred dollars of combat pay and immediately purchased a 1949 Pontiac for three hundred. With a car, money in his pocket, and wings on his uniform, he also became attractive to the local women who lived near Grandview AFB, in Grandview, Missouri, his first duty assignment. "It was kind of neat to date a lieutenant who had money, a car, and wings, and could take women to the Officer's Club and other marvelous things."[11] In addition to enjoying his new status as a veteran fighter pilot, Tomlinson worked in Group Operations at Grandview and eventually flew with the 326th Fighter-Interceptor Squadron, an F-86 squadron and later an F-102 Delta Dagger squadron.

In 1959, Tomlinson attended the Squadron Officers' School at the Air University at Maxwell AFB. He then flew F-102s with the 317th Squadron in Galena, Alaska. Most of his missions there involved intercepting Soviet bombers which strayed into U.S. air space.

In 1965, he went to work for the Air Force Inspector General at

Norton AFB, in San Bernardino, California. At Norton, he was assigned to inspect the "planes no one else wanted to inspect—O-1 Bird Dogs, A-1 Skyraiders, C-47s, and Defoliant Ranch Hand planes."[12] During this tour, Tomlinson went TDY (temporary duty) to Vietnam in 1966 and 1967, and flew three combat missions in A-1s. By 1968 Tomlinson was "fed up" with the Inspector General's office. As a flight suit officer, he wanted to fly combat missions in fighters. Hence, he volunteered to fly A-1s with the 56th Special Operations Wing at Nakhon Phanom Royal Thai Air Force Base in Thailand, affectionately referred to as "Naked Fanny" by the flight suit officers who served there.

At "Naked Fanny," Tomlinson "chased trucks and bombed elephants" in Laos. He also flew "Sandy/Firefly" missions with the 602nd Squadron. Sandy missions involved flying cover for downed pilots, and Firefly missions were night interdiction missions in northern Laos. Tomlinson was doing a Firefly when he was nearly shot down over the Plain du Jars in 1969.

As in Korea, base life in Thailand was very comfortable for Tomlinson. Although Nakhon Phanom was a dusty, riverside air strip with very few sheds when the war began, by 1968 the base had been completely refurbished with an 8000-foot concrete runway, new buildings, party hootches for the squadrons, and even a swimming pool. Tomlinson shared his quarters with one other pilot, and hired a Thai woman to do all his cleaning.

After flying 145 missions, Tomlinson finally accepted a transfer to Oslo, Norway, in 1969 to develop a tactical air control system for the Royal Norwegian Air Force. He stayed in Norway until 1973, when he was promoted to full colonel and transferred to Andrews AFB. At Andrews, he performed a variety of administrative jobs with the combat support group. Finally in 1978, he was assigned to the FAA as Chief of the Emergency Operations Staff. While there, he developed a command, control, and communications system (c^3). Tomlinson's experience with the FAA helped him secure his first and only civilian job in 1983: a position with Rockwell International Civil Government Accounts. This job involves developing similar c^3 systems for the U.S. Customs Service,

Border Patrol, Coast Guard, and FBI. With Rockwell International, he has traveled to Latin America and even visited Laos to help set up drug interdiction communications systems.

In addition to working, Tomlinson is an active member of the F-86 Sabre Pilots Association, the A-1 Association, and the Air Commando Association (an association for retired Special Forces pilots).[13]

Robert Pomeroy

After he left the Far East, Robert Pomeroy was transferred to an F-80 unit at Shaw AFB, South Carolina. A year later, his unit transferred to Sembach Air Base, Germany, where he served as a flight commander. In 1954, Pomeroy was in line to move up to the position of operations officer, but instead was assigned to Allied Air Forces Southern Europe in Italy to be the aide to the commander, General Lawrence Craigie. At Naples, Pomeroy attended all briefings and gave opinions when asked.

In 1957, Pomeroy returned to Shaw AFB as an assistant operations officer for the 432nd Tactical Reconnaissance Wing, an RF-101 Voodoo Unit. Pomeroy was then selected in 1958 to join the military studies department at the Air Force Academy as an instructor. From there, he attended the Royal Air Force Staff College at Andover, England, in 1961 and then taught for two years at the Royal Air Force College at Cranwell. This latter assignment proved detrimental to his career because the Royal Air Force had a tougher officer rating system than the USAF. Nevertheless, he took the assignment, coached basketball, led the band, gave lectures in military history, and was even made "All Cromwellian" when he left. In short, it was one of the "best" assignments of his career.

From 1964 until 1966, Pomeroy worked at the Pentagon in Reconnaissance Operational Requirements. In 1966, he was selected to serve as the deputy executive officer for the Office of the Undersecretary of the Air Force. While there, he worked for Norman Paul, Townsend Hoopes, and John McLucas. Of the three undersecretaries, Hoopes proved to be the most difficult to work for. Hoopes was one of the few high-ranking Pentagon officials who opposed the Vietnam War. For Pomeroy, this position was untenable: "If we were going to be doves, we should have been doves and gotten the hell out of there, but if we were going to be hawks, I wanted to damn well do it. I hated the piecemeal approach. I wanted to get in there and fix it and not complain.[14] Although Pomeroy disagreed with Hoopes, they did have a cordial working relationship or, as Pomeroy put it, "We agreed to disagree."

In 1969, Pomeroy attended the Industrial College of the Armed Services and also went to night school at George Washington University's business school. A year later, he finished his M.B.A. degree and also trained in the RF-4 in preparation for a tour in Vietnam. "By this time," recalls Pomeroy, "I had lost many of my friends in the war and was against it, but I felt I owed it to the service to go." [15] Pomeroy served in the Seventh Air Force Headquarters at Tan Son Nhut Air Base, Saigon, as the chief of reconnaissance in electronic warfare. In this position, Pomeroy helped formulate "FRAG" orders and choose targets for the Seventh Air Force.

Besides working in headquarters, Pomeroy also flew fourteen missions in the RF-4 before a bout with hepatitis caused him to be transferred back to the United States. Rather than returning him to Vietnam, the Air Force posted Pomeroy to the strategic studies department of the U.S. Army War College in Carlisle, Pennsylvania, as a professor. From Carlisle, he went to the Supreme Headquarters Allied Powers Europe (SHAPE) in 1975 as a plans and policy executive officer. Three years later, he was made U.S. National Military Representative (NMR) to SHAPE. As the NMR, he was the unofficial mayor of the U.S. community at SHAPE and the link between that group and the international community. Pomeroy also ran the dependent school system at SHAPE as chairman of the dependent school council, and organized all large celebrations, including the annual Fourth of July picnic.

Pomeroy retired from the military in 1979 as a full colonel. He accepted a position as deputy director for the Air Force Aid Society, where he worked for seven years. The Air Force Aid Society is supported by contributions from Air Force personnel, and provides emergency, no-interest hardship loans to Air Force personnel.

Paul Turner

After approximately a year in a Chinese-operated POW camp in North Korea, Paul Turner was released during the "Little Switch" in June 1953.[16] During his long ride back to the U.S. on a troop ship, Turner decided that he wanted to continue his flying career. Hence, when he arrived home, he immediately volunteered for an assignment as an Air Force test pilot for North American Aviation in Inglewood, California. While there, he flew the T-28B, but did not fly fighters because North American "thought he was too young."[17]

In 1955, Turner finally got back into fighters as a test pilot at McClellan AFB, where his tests included the F-86F, the F-84F, and the F-100. Turner also flew multiengine aircraft, such as the C-47, the C-119, and the KC-97.

From McClellan, Turner went to Guam in 1959 as a test pilot and chief maintenance officer, but returned a year later to work for the Winter Olympics in Squaw Valley, California. The Air Force allowed him to take leave for this event because it believed his involvement would be good publicity. His primary responsibility was to manage the athletes' section of the arena.

Following the Olympics, Turner worked for a year as a maintenance officer at Minot AFB, South Dakota, and then attended the University of Colorado as an Air Force Institute of Technology (AFIT) student; he received an electrical engineering degree in 1963, and a master's in 1964.

After he graduated from AFIT, the Air Force asked Turner if he would go on detached duty with the Federal Aviation Administration (FAA) as a major. Although Turner's first choice was to fly fighters, he took the assignment anyway and "thoroughly enjoyed it."[18] The FAA allowed Turner to fly civilian jets, investigate accidents, and write regulations. "I was their jack-of-all-trades," he recalls, "and I wrote papers on air traffic control, altimetry, and maintenance which are still used today."[19] It also gave him civil aviation training, which he eventually would parlay into a civilian career with the National Transportation Safety Board (NTSB).

Turner went to work for the NTSB in 1970 after a final three-year tour as an operations officer with the Alaska Air Command. At NTSB, he examined the performance of aircraft during accident sequences. In addition to analyzing plane crashes, he also flew aircraft and inspected pipeline explosions, shipwrecks, and train wrecks.

In 1987, he retired from the NTSB and set up a consulting business for voice cockpit data recorders. His company, called PiCiT, also does forensic work in audio for the FBI and the Department of Justice—rape cases, bribery, and extortion. Despite a history of broken ribs and bones, Turner still skis two weeks a year. He also fishes during the summer from his 28-foot motor boat.[20]

Jim Bailey

M. J. Bailey left the Korean War with three battle stars, three air medals, a Distinguished Flying Cross, and a strong desire to stay in the fighter business.

His first postwar assignment was with the 93rd Squadron at Albuquerque flying alert against UFOs. A year and a half later, he flew with the 15th Squadron out of Davis-Monthan AFB, in Tucson, Arizona. In 1954, he was transferred to NORAD (North American Air Defense Command) at Cheyenne Mountain, Colorado, where he worked in operations tracking Soviet aircraft that violated North American airspace.

In 1958, Bailey traveled to Ottawa to serve as a radar site inspector for the Air Force. His last assignment in the Air Force was from 1961 to 1963 with the Air Defense Command as an operations officer. Like Crockett, Bailey had an opportunity to fight in Vietnam but opted instead for retirement. As he recalled, "I felt after Korea and World War II that I had pushed my luck—I had kids and my reaction times were getting slower."[21]

After military retirement, Bailey worked as an airport manager at Long Beach Airport and then as a real estate agent at Whidbey Island in Washington state until 1988, when he retired from civilian work. He lives with his wife in Diamond Bar, California, and enjoys hunting and fishing.[22]

George Berke

After Korea, George Berke opted to remain in the Air Force and pursue a career in fighter-bombers.

His first postwar assignment was as flight commander with the 401st Fighter-Bomber Group at England AFB, Louisiana. After ferrying a plane over to Belgium, however, he immediately put in for a transfer to Europe. To him, Europe was where he thought most of the action would be, and he was impressed by the caliber of the tactical fighter units there, especially those in England.

When Berke arrived at his first NATO assignment at the Royal Air Force Base (RAF) in Manston, England, in 1956, the 92nd Squadron (81st Wing) was on full alert for the Suez crisis—each F-84F was fully loaded with nuclear ordnance and guarded by an air policeman and a German shepherd. The squadron commander told Berke to call his wife and tell her he would be sleeping in the hangar until the crisis ended. This was Berke's orientation to life as a NATO nuclear strike pilot in the 1950s.

Berke stayed with this unit until April 1958, when his squadron was transferred to RAF Bentwaters. At Bentwaters, Berke also began flying the F-101A Voodoo: a supersonic, nuclear strike aircraft noteworthy for the fact that it was incapable of delivering conventional munitions. According to Berke, "We only planned for a one-way, max penetration mission: we saw ourselves as the Top Guys." [23] This belief was confirmed by the fact that Robin Olds, a famous World War II ace, and Chappie James became leaders of the wing.

In 1960, Berke's career changed dramatically. Under the Air Force Institute of Technology Program (AFIT), a program designed to improve the educational quality of the Air Force officer corps, Berke was assigned to the University of Wisconsin at Madison to earn a master's degree in English. He was thirty-three years old when he entered the program, and, as he recalled, "It was a real shock—I was no longer on call twenty-four hours a day." [24] From there, he was assigned to the Air Force Academy as an English professor.

Although Berke found his master's degree program stimulating and enjoyed teaching cadets at the Air Force Academy, his professorial career was an anomaly for a fighter pilot. Around the academy, he was referred to by his fellow professors as a "fighter jock." Paradoxically, when he returned to Bentwaters in 1965, his fellow flight suit officers nicknamed him the "poet" or the "professor." Back at Bentwaters, Berke served as an operations officer for the 92nd Squadron and assisted the squadron in their transition to the F-4C Phantom: the "hottest" plane of the Vietnam War era. In 1966, he became chief of operations for the 81st Wing until 1968, when he was transferred to Vietnam.

"A lot of people went to Vietnam because it was good for their career, but I wasn't interested in it for that reason," recalled Berke. He had been a fighter pilot all his life and believed that it was his duty to accept a combat tour. As Berke put it, "They say that if you take the king's shilling, you gotta go to war."[25] Berke did not lobby for any particular job because he was too superstitious and did not want any personal responsibility for his war assignment; instead, he allowed the computer to assign him.

The computer picked the 633rd Special Operations Wing at Pleiku in South Vietnam. When he arrived, he expected to find a fighting outfit similar to the 58th Fighter-Bomber Wing in Korea; instead, he discovered a miniature version of the Pentagon: "Every officer at the Pleiku tactical operations center was a lieutenant colonel, fully qualified to direct the entire air campaign."[26]

While at Pleiku, Berke flew the C-47 "Goony Bird": it "was the lowest of the low" for a fighter pilot. Nevertheless, Berke welcomed the job of driving a World War II-era flying cab. In contrast to the overly automated F-4, the C-47 was pure "brute strength and manual controls."

In October 1968, Berke finally received the assignment for which had trained his entire career—a combat assignment in F-4 Phantoms at Danang. At Danang, Berke flew interdiction and close-air support missions with the 389th Tactical Fighter Squadron.

Berke left Danang in February 1969 and went to work as a senior duty officer at Tan Son Nhut AFB, the nerve center for the air war in Vietnam. It was this final headquarters assignment which most disillusioned Berke about the war. As a flight suit officer, he was frustrated that Air Force doctrines of "surprise, concentration of force, and mobility were being thrown out the window."²⁷ He was also appalled by how officers lived. In contrast to Korea, where everyone lived in drafty shacks, many Air Force officers in Vietnam lived in air-conditioned trailers and swam during their off-hours in Olympic-sized pools. There were also more forty-year-old lieutenant colonels in this war than second lieutenants. Despite his disgust, Berke did not regret his tours in Vietnam: "They allowed me to become part of a defining event for my generation."²⁸

Berke left Vietnam in August 1969 to serve as an operations officer at Andrews AFB, Maryland, and retired from the Air Force in 1970. Since then, he has worked in a variety of consulting jobs—most in defense-related areas. At present, he is the president of Execuserve International, Inc., a firm which assists high-technology companies in conducting business in eastern Europe. He also is active with the 58th Fighter-Bomber Association and the Confederate Air Force. On weekends, Berke dons a flight suit and flies missions for the Civil Air Patrol in northern Virginia, where he resides.²⁹

Howard Heiner

Howard Heiner is unique among the pilots interviewed for this study because he is the only one who chose to leave the Air Force immediately after his Korean War enlistment. Unlike many of the pilots, though, Heiner had a four-year degree when he entered the service and a strong desire to return to his chosen profession: forestry. However, he did not completely divorce himself from the Air Force upon discharge. He continued to fly fighters in the Air National Guard until 1963, when he retired as a major.

Heiner started work as a forester for a private lumber company in 1955. He left the company in 1969 as an assistant manager responsible for finances and production. In 1969, he decided that he wanted to serve overseas as a forestry consultant with the United Methodist Church. Between 1969 and 1992, Heiner consulted and taught forestry at the college level in Bolivia, Mexico, Libya, Chile, Somalia, and Nicaragua. During these overseas tours, he claims he "lost his innocence about U.S. foreign policy."[30] He witnessed three civil wars in Bolivia between 1969 and 1971. He was in Chile during the Pinochet coup, and was placed under house arrest for a year for aiding political prisoners trying to escape Pinochet. These experiences, claims Heiner, compel him "to define himself as antimilitary at present."[31]

Currently, he is the Washington, D.C., representative on environmental issues for the United Methodist Church. He also recently attended the Earth Summit in Rio De Janeiro as a delegate for the United States Department of State. His specialization is forestry and deforestation.[32]

Raymond "Dewey" Sturgeon

Raymond Sturgeon never volunteered to fly bombers after Korea. However, as luck would have it, his first assignment after the war was in the B-47 program at Pinecastle AFB, Florida. Sturgeon "fought like mad" to get out of this assignment and even went so far as to fly up to Albany, Georgia, to talk to the commander of the 31st Wing, a man named Dave Schillings. After Sturgeon stormed into his office and exclaimed that he was a "a fighter pilot and wanted to fly fighters," Schillings, a World War II veteran, took an immediate liking to Sturgeon and secured a transfer for him to Albany, Georgia, to fly F-84s and later F-100 Super Sabres.

In 1958, Sturgeon was transferred to Itazuke, Japan, to fly alert missions for the Formosa crisis with the 8th Wing. Sturgeon stayed with the 8th Wing until 1962, when he was transferred to Seymour Johnson AFB, North Carolina, to fly the F-105 Thunderjet, or "Thud" as it was often called. Originally designed as a nuclear strike fighter, the F-105 eventually became a workhorse fighter-bomber in Vietnam. The F-105, though, proved to be extremely vulnerable to groundfire and surface-to-air missiles—over seven hundred were lost during the course of the war. "If I had stayed in the F-105 program,"[33] explained Sturgeon during his interview, "I probably would not be talking to you right now."[34] The Thud was also renowned for its maintenance problems. During his three years at Seymour Johnson, Sturgeon got the plane on the runway only twice, and both times he had to abort.

In July 1965, Sturgeon transferred to F-4s, and was slated to go to Vietnam. However, because his two sons were blind, the Air Force offered to send him to Hanscom AFB, Massachusetts, on "humanitarian grounds." Sturgeon took this assignment under the conviction that he had already served his country during the Korean War.

Sturgeon retired from the Air Force as a lieutenant colonel in 1967. He then worked as the chief test pilot for Raytheon until 1983. Sturgeon lives in eastern Massachusetts with his wife and travels around the western U.S. every two or three years.[35]

James Hagerstrom

Hagerstrom saw more aerial combat than any pilot in this study with the exception of Robinson Risner. In addition to shooting down six Japanese planes in World War II and 8.5 MiGs in Korea, Hagerstrom flew thirty combat missions in Vietnam with the Seventh Air Force. Despite these distinctions and the medals that came with them (including a Silver Star and a Distinguished Flying Cross with five oak leaf clusters), Hagerstrom never made it to general. Unlike Brown, whom Hagerstrom once referred to as one "of the best damned fighter pilots I ever met," Hagerstrom was unable to temper his flight suit attitude and make the transition from fighter pilot to Air Force bureaucrat. Up until his very last day in the service, Hagerstrom never hesitated to let his opinion be known even if it meant ruining his chances of promotion. As he put it, "I had the ability to spar with four generals and admirals due to the fact that I shot down more than five aircraft in two wars and most of them had never even seen an enemy aircraft."[36]

When he returned from Korea, Hagerstrom was promoted to lieutenant colonel and placed in charge of a group of F-86s and later F-100s at Foster AFB at Victoria, Texas. In 1956 he became chief of the fighter branch at Far East Air Forces in Fu Chu, Japan. One year later, Tiger Wong, head of the Taiwanese Air Force, invited him to Taiwan to teach the Nationalist Chinese pilots how to shoot down MiGs.

From Taiwan, Hagerstrom went to Hawaii, was promoted to full colonel, and was asked to evaluate the air forces of U.S. allies in the Pacific for Pacific Air Forces (PACAF). He also set up a program to evaluate the new Sidewinder air-to-air missile, and became one of the early advocates for keeping guns on fighter aircraft. This position placed him at odds with top Air Force and Navy leadership who favored equipping fighters such as the F-4 with missiles only. During the Vietnam War, Hagerstrom's position on guns was confirmed: after several aircraft losses, the Air Force reluctantly began to equip its top-of-the-line F-4 with guns in addition to the missiles.

Hagerstrom left PACAF in 1960 and joined the Office of the Inspector General at Norton AFB, California. At Norton, he headed up the "Fly-safe" program for fighters and enrolled in law school at Loyola University in Los Angeles. In 1962 he attended the Industrial College of the Armed Services and finished his law degree at Georgetown. Hagerstrom then served as vice wing commander for an F-4 wing at George AFB before heading to Vietnam in 1965. In Vietnam, he became the director of the combat operations control center for the Seventh Air Force at Tan Son Nhut. While in this position, Hagerstrom became embroiled with General William Westmoreland over Air Force roles and missions. Hagerstrom believed that more air assets should be devoted to bombing strategic targets such as Hanoi. Westmoreland, on the other hand, wanted more air power for close air support. Hagerstrom complained that "we used to bomb suspected VC this and that and it was sheer bullshit. No one knew where the hell the targets were. How can you count bodies from the air?" [37] Unfortunately for Hagerstrom, MiGs might have gotten him promoted to full colonel, but they did not help him in this argument, and Westmoreland ended up ordering Hagerstrom out of the theater.

After spending Christmas of 1965 with his wife in San Francisco, Hagerstrom ended up back in Udorn in 1966. Brigadier General John Murphy met Hagerstrom on the flight line at three in the morning and said, "Goddamn Jim. We need you." Hagerstrom set up an interdiction operation in four days and helped run the covert air war in Laos.

While in Laos, Hagerstrom also attempted to rescue fellow Korean War ace Robinson Risner, who was shot down in 1965. Through a Filipino friend named Tony Aquino, the uncle of politician Corazon

Aquino, Hagerstrom discovered that Risner still was alive in 1967. He then called another friend, Walter Cronkite of CBS News, and asked him to head up a fund-raiser to bail Risner out. James Donovan, the lawyer who got U-2 pilot Francis Powers out of the Soviet Union, was enlisted as the go-between. At this point, the State Department phoned Hagerstrom and told him to back off. For Hagerstrom, this was the final straw: "I got disgusted with the whole thing and resigned," he explained. "Vietnam was wrong, we shouldn't have been there." [38]

The first thing he did upon retirement was build a sailboat and sail around the Pacific. He then practiced law in Guam and served as an adviser to the island's leaders.

In 1992, Hagerstrom spoke of purchasing an ultralight airplane and "flying 500 feet from the ground chasing buzzards, hawks, and eagles with the wind blowing in your face." Flying used to be "fun" for Hagerstrom, but as his career progressed, it became more controlled and bureaucratic: "People don't have much fun flying anymore. They aren't allowed to have fun. Everything is modeled and pre-planned.[39] Hagerstrom died of cancer in July 1994 and was buried with full military honors at Arlington National Cemetery.

Clearly, as these vignettes illustrate, the pilots in this study overwhelmingly chose to continue flying in the Air Force after Korea. As a consequence, they also attended service schools, received Air Force-sponsored schooling through AFIT or Bootstrap, worked in other military jobs besides flying, and rose within the Air Force bureaucracy. The Air Force enabled most to develop marketable skills outside of piloting—skills they could eventually parlay into jobs in the civilian sector. Turner, for example, developed an expertise in civilian aviation and eventually landed a position with the NTSB; Pomeroy became a skilled administrator and eventually found work in charitable foundations; Berke became a security policy specialist; Bailey secured a position in airfield management; Hagerstrom earned a law degree while in the Air Force and eventually became a successful attorney; and Crockett worked in the area of equal opportunity.

Despite diversification, maturation, and education, most managed to maintain their flight suit attitude even if it meant losing a promotion or two. Most hit a "glass ceiling" at the rank of colonel. However, as Hagerstrom once remarked, it is at that stage where "MiGs start to matter less and power politics take over." Unfortunately for Hagerstrom and many others, their "wild-ass" times in Korea did not prepare them for this "game."

Once retired from the military, however, many pilots found excellent outlets for flight suit panache. Crockett plays tennis, Turner skis, Berke flies planes with the Confederate Air Force and the Civil Air Patrol, Tomlinson travels to exotic lands with Rockwell International, Sturgeon travels the West, Bailey hunts game, Pomeroy cruises the East Coast in his powerboat, and Hagerstrom planned to purchase an ultralight before he died.

Far and away the most important outlet for flight suit attitude, though, are the annual reunions these men have with fellow pilots. These reunions are organized around units (the 58th Fighter-Bomber Association), aircraft type (the F-86 Sabre Association), and even by Aviation Cadet class (Class 52H). Some pilots also arrange informal reunions with close friends. On Sturgeon's trailer trips, he often stops to visit old friends in the Air Force, and Pomeroy recently went to England to visit friends he met during his RAF tours. Through these reunions, pilots attempt to relive their glory days, and catch up with old friends. Interestingly enough, reunions are always flight suit affairs where status is based upon having flown together, not upon a pilot's rank at retirement or civilian status. The F-86 Sabre Pilots Association states in its recruitment literature that "it is a 'Jock's Club' so we make no effort to cater to the elite among us [including seventy retired generals, two senators, one congressman, and two astronauts]. We acknowledge and congratulate them on their achievements but retain the camaraderie shared by airmen."[40] This camaraderie, in turn, stems from the collective flight suit belief that "the best damn pilots who ever stepped into a cockpit belong to the F-86 Sabre Association."[41]

Epilogue

Most of the pilots interviewed for this book lament the end of the flight suit era. The Air Force of today, argue pilots such as Hagerstrom and Berke, is too big, too bureaucratic, and no longer encourages initiative and independence in its pilots. Instead, all mission planning is done in the Pentagon, and missions themselves are closely controlled and monitored by Airborne Early Warning Planes (AWACS). The pilot who is too aggressive and pursues a plane into unauthorized air space is summarily court-martialed. Similarly, the pilot who displays his flight suit attitude at a pilot's convention is immediately given an Article 15. After all, there are plenty of other pilots who want to fly F-15s and are willing to behave themselves for the privilege: the Air Force, in short, no longer has to tolerate flight suit excesses. Veteran flight suit types, not surprisingly, argue that this is a travesty. "We need to encourage this type of behavior," claims pilot Jerry Minton, "because in combat, this is what motivates the pilot to fight and fly." The experiences of the Air Force in the Korean War would tend to confirm Minton's point of view. However, there were definite liabilities that came with flight suit attitude.

One such liability was alcohol abuse. While officers in the 1950s were less well informed about the dangers of drinking and operating aircraft than we are today, most understood that hangovers did not enhance combat effectiveness. Hagerstrom never drank because he wanted to be at 100 percent when he went up to face the MiGs. Alcohol was also banned from many dayrooms, and commanding officers warned junior birdmen that "Korea was the easiest place in the world to become an alcoholic." Nevertheless, pilots did fly drunk, and some left the theater as alcoholics. One pilot in the study claimed that the saddest point of his post-Korea career was running into Jim Lowe, a famous Korean War ace who became an alcoholic.[1] "He was a lost soul," remembered the pilot. "There was simply no place for this yahoo in the modern Air Force."

Another result of flight suit attitude in the Korean War was that it encouraged officers to visit prostitutes. Not only did such practices set a bad example for enlisted men and facilitate the spread of venereal disease, but they also created tensions for married officers. M. J. Bailey looked down upon the officers in Japan who solicited prostitutes. Turner, on the other hand, "thoroughly enjoyed himself in Japan," and rationalized prostitution as a basic fact of life for the warrior. To reconcile his guilt over sleeping with prostitutes, he even brought his wife to Japan after the war to meet the famous ladies of the Sabre Dancer establishment. Perrin Gower, likewise, had nothing but fond memories of Myoshi's Bordello in Tokyo. "I'll never forget my first night there," he exclaimed. "One pilot went from room to room, breaking through screen walls as he went."

Clearly, such behavior would have been unacceptable for an officer in the Continental United States (CONUS). Yet flight suit attitude continued through the Vietnam War; in fact, America's first ace in that war, Randy Cunningham, was turned down several times for a regular commission because of "immaturity."[2] During the Cold War, the Air Force hierarchy viewed flight suit attitude as a necessary evil. The Paul Turners of the service were too useful to discard. If one got out of hand, he was transferred to a flight suit outpost such as Wheelus Air Force Base in Libya, Osan in Korea, Zaragoza in Spain, or RAF Bensonhurst in England. Once removed from CONUS, these men were less threatening to the Air Force and its reputation. Furthermore, they provided the service with a well-spring of talent for future wars. It is worth remembering that many of the pilots in this book served admirably in Vietnam, and that Miramar and Nellis, the fighter schools that created the top pilots of the Vietnam conflict, were staffed with Korean War veterans.

The flight suit officer proved to be so valuable in war because he was willing to perform almost any mission. Even when their less spirited wingmen chose to remain behind, Hagerstrom and Turner never hesitated to cross the Yalu in search of MiGs. Bailey or Heiner never shied away from a heavily guarded bridge, and Pomeroy flew his unarmed T-6 over North Korean trenches on a daily basis. Twenty years later in Vietnam, many of these flight suit officers would continue to perform the most dangerous missions: note that Risner, Brown, and Tomlinson were shot down for their overzealousness in Southeast Asia.

More significantly, flight suit attitude instilled pilots with a sense of purpose and combat motivation that was sorely needed in the individualistic world of fighter warfare. While on leave in Japan, M. J. Bailey knew implicitly that his chances of survival were not good; but rather than request a desk assignment or succumb to the fear of flying, he returned to Korea to continue flying dangerous and often futile interdiction missions. Likewise, Hagerstrom could easily have left Korea with seven and a half kills, but he chose to violate regulations and fly one last mission against the MiGs. Flight suit attitude, in short, motivated pilots to fight in much the same way that group dynamics motivate the ordinary infantryman.

At the beginning of the Korean War, the Air Force had only 411,277 military personnel; by 1953, that number had increased to 977,593.[3] During this period of war and rapid growth, the Air Force gave flight suit officers a long leash. As long as they continued to down MiGs and bridges in impressive numbers, these officers could do as they pleased during their off-hours. When the war ended, however, so too did the "wild-ass days." Flight suit officers would have to scale down their antics in the United States. Those who wanted to rise in the Air Force would have to turn in their flight suits for Class B uniforms and learn how to become good staff officers. Fortunately for the most recalcitrant, flight suit assignments did exist during the Cold War at overseas bases: George Berke, for example, doubted he would have been able to survive in the post-Korea Air Force if it had not been for a series of assignments at RAF Bensonhurst. Furthermore, as many of these men reached the field grade ranks, the Vietnam War once again provided them with an outlet for their aggression and a route to future promotions. It is doubtful that either Frederick Blesse, Robinson Risner, or Earl Brown would have become flag officers without the Vietnam War. These men did not possess the educational pedigree to move up through staff assignments: what spared these pilots and others like them from obscurity were good stick and rudder skills, ample courage, and a healthy dose of flight suit attitude. As Virgil put it, "Fortune favors the bold."[4]

● ● Appendix 1 ● ●

Air Interdiction in Korea: An Operational Overview

In the years following World War II, Air Chiefs of Staff Carl Spaatz and Hoyt Vandenberg encouraged their service to focus most of its attention upon developing a credible strike force of intercontinental bombers. These men believed that the next war would be a full-fledged nuclear war with the Soviet Union, and their great hope was that air power would single-handedly win that conflict. Much to their dismay, America's next war would be a limited war in an agricultural region, against a lesser developed nation. The Korean War was the ultimate paradox for postwar American air power, for it was a struggle where a World War II-style strategic bombing campaign was not feasible. As an agricultural nation, North Korea possessed very few cities and large industries, and China, its primary source for manufactured goods, was off-limits to American bombing. Hence, the Air Force had to abandon its strategic bombing doctrine and develop new missions for this limited war.

Close air support of ground troops was one mission which the Air Force could perform, though it did not particularly relish this type of bombing. After fighting hard in the late forties to gain independence from the Army, the last thing the air leadership wanted to do was to provide secondary support for the Army in the form of airborne artillery. Consequently, the air leadership looked to air interdiction as the primary air power mission of the war. In his instructions to General Stratemeyer, the 1950 Far East Air Forces (FEAF) commander, Vandenberg stressed "the vital necessity of destruction of North Korean objectives north of the 38th parallel" even though the Supreme U.N. commander, General Douglas MacArthur, explicitly forbade such non-battlefield support operations during this period. According to Vandenberg, "It [was] axiomatic that tactical operations on the battlefield cannot be fully effective unless there is simultaneous interdiction and destruction of sources behind the battlefield."[1] In short, the stage was set for a single-service, air interdiction solution to the Korean War. In the end, over 47.8 percent of all U.S. combat air sorties (USAF, USN, USMC) would be devoted to interdiction missions. By comparison, only 0.2 percent were dedicated to strategic bombing, 18.5 percent to close air support, 18.6 percent to counterair, 13.1 percent to reconnaissance, and 1.8 percent to antisubmarine patrol.[2]

Air Interdiction during the Early Stages of the War, June 1950–November 1950

Initially, air interdiction was employed as a means of blunting the advance of the North Korean People's Army (NKPA) toward Pusan. The NKPA possessed over 180,000 soldiers and 300 Soviet manufactured T-34 tanks. Opposing this force was the 82,000-man Republic of Korea Army (ROKA): essentially a large militia with poorly trained troops, no tanks, and very few pieces of heavy equipment. To reinforce this rabble, the U.S. sent the 24th Division to Korea, but one division was hardly enough to turn the tide of the battle. What saved the U.N. forces from a Dunkirk-type evacuation at Pusan was the combination of tenacious fighting by the ground forces and the skillful employment of air power.

This air power, overall, consisted mainly of single-engine, tactical fighter planes such as the jet-powered F-80C and propeller driven F-51 fighter-bombers.[3] Originally designed as an interceptor, the F-80 was initially handicapped by its short range and lack of bombing racks, but it eventually became a workable fighter-bomber after certain modifications were made. For example, with the addition of standard wing tanks, its operational radius jumped from 100 miles to 225, and by the end of the campaign, the range was increased to 350 miles with enlarged tanks built in Misawa, Japan.[4] The bomb rack problem did not improve during the Pusan fight, but what the F-80 lacked as a bomber, it made up for as a strafer. Jet propulsion eliminated propeller torque and made this plane's guns far more accurate than the F-51's.[5] The F-80 could also carry up to sixteen high-velocity aerial rockets (HVAR). A single 5-inch HVAR could disable a T-34 if aimed at the tank's treads, but "most pilots got the best results when they fired a salvo or ripple of all four of their rockets." But because the HVAR was not always successful against the front armor of a T-34, FEAF began using the more powerful antitank aerial rockets (ATAR) by the end of July.[6] Later in the war, the F-80 was modified to carry two 500-pound bombs; but for the Pusan fight, the primary bomb deliverer was the F-51.[7]

Although vulnerable to ground fire because of its water-cooled engine, the F-51 proved to be an effective ground support aircraft because it could operate close to the front lines from improvised, dirt air strips and carry up to six 150-gallon napalm bombs. Napalm proved ideal against tanks. Not only did it easily ignite the rubber in a T-34's treads, it also did not require a direct hit to destroy a target: one 150-gallon bomb could incinerate a 275-foot-long by 100-foot-wide pear-shaped foot-print.[8]

In a method which later became known as "battlefield air interdiction," fighters and B-26 medium bombers attempted to wear down the NKPA by striking reinforcements, supplies, and other second-echelon targets moving toward the battlefield along various supply routes. Tanks and other targets were located by means of armed reconnaissance. According to one pilot, you were "allotted a stretch of road to patrol for a given period of time, with instructions to shoot up anything that moved upon it."[9] Surprisingly, this approach produced excellent results. The rough terrain in South Korea compelled the NKPA to launch their tank thrusts along the few roads that existed, making these vehicles very easy to locate by air. The NKPA also generally moved their convoys by day and rarely assigned anti-aircraft units to protect them. When convoys did travel at night, lights were carelessly left on. Once discovered, troop and tank convoys were generally poorly defended. As a result, the effects of interdiction often proved devastating. On 10 July, for example, a flight of F-80s discovered a large convoy "backed up bumper to bumper behind a destroyed bridge" at Pyongtaek, and by the end of the day, these pilots, along with reinforcements, managed to destroy 117 trucks, seven half-tracks, and thirty-eight tanks.[10]

By 23 September 1950, the Fifth Air Force had flown "21,979 sorties, of which 5224, or 24%, were devoted to interdiction."[11] It, along with the FEAF Bomber Command and Navy units, claimed to have destroyed 875 vehicles, 1,314 rail cars, 280 locomotives, 140 bridges, and "maintained 47 rail cuts."[12] So vital was this air campaign to the defense of Pusan that General Walton Walker, the commander of the U.S. Eighth Army in Korea, made the following statement to the USAF Evaluation Board in November 1950: "I will gladly lay my cards right on the table and state that if it had not been for the air support that we received from the Fifth Air Force we would not have been able to stay in Korea."[13] During a time of acute interservice rivalry between the Army and the Air Force, such praise was unusual but not unfounded. In September and October of 1950, after MacArthur's Inchon invasion had pushed the NKPA back across the 38th Parallel, U.N. research teams surveyed the main axes of the NKPA attack. These teams located 180 destroyed NKPA tanks and determined that 102 of them had been destroyed by air action, 39 by tank fire, and another 39 by artillery and bazooka fire. In short, a clear majority of the tanks had been incapacitated by air power.[14]

Tank kills alone, though, did not stop the NKPA advance on Pusan. Interdiction strained the NKPA supply system near the breaking point. The records of a typical NKPA division reveal that from 25 June to 15 July, it received 18 tons of food, 12 tons of POL (petroleum, oil, and lubricants), and 166 tons of ordnance; by contrast, the same division only received 2.5 tons of food, 2 tons of POL, and 17 tons of ordnance in the period from 16 August to 20 September. In individual terms, this meant that the average food ration dropped from 800 grams of rice, dried fish, meat, and vegetables at the beginning of the campaign to 400 grams of straight rice by the end.[15] So acute was this food shortage problem that the captured chief of staff of the NKPA's 13th Infantry Division reported that "50 percent of the personnel had lost the stamina necessary to fight in mountainous terrain." The same officer also complained that his division was down to 200–250 shells and only a "very small amount of gasoline" on 21 September 1950, the day he was captured.[16]

Clearly, interdiction had destroyed a large number of NKPA "capital" weapons and was having noticeable effects on NKPA performance by the end of September 1950. However, it should be emphasized that the Battle of the Pusan Perimeter was hardly a single-service effort. What ended the Pusan battle was not strategic interdiction per se, but the destruction of the NKPA advance at the Naktong River between 31 August and 23 September by the Eighth Army and by MacArthur's Inchon invasion of 15 September. It was these actions that finally compelled the NKPA, weakened significantly by air power, to institute a general withdrawal from South Korea.

Later Interdiction Campaigns, December 1950–May 1952

During MacArthur's drive to the Yalu, FEAF continued to engage in close air support and battlefield air interdiction missions. However, after the Chinese intervention on 26 November 1950, FEAF began to shift its focus from second-echelon targets close to the main battle line to supply targets well to the North Korean rear. The basic plan, which eventually became known as "STRANGLE" and later "SATURATE," called for air power to isolate completely the Communist front-line force from its supplies, and compel Communist negotiators at Panmunjom to acquiesce quickly to the U.N. demands for an armistice. These demands were as follows:

1. The establishment of a cease-fire along the militarily defensible line of contact between the armies.

2. A joint commission to supervise the truce.

3. The exclusion of all political questions not directly related to the proposed cease-fire.[17]

Unfortunately for FEAF planners, STRANGLE/SATURATE failed to live up to its high expectations. Lack of coordination with ground troops, inadequate technology, highly effective Communist countermeasures, and the low Communist supply requirements hindered the campaign from day 1.

The first concerted attempt by FEAF to single-handedly isolate the battlefield was Interdiction Plan 4 (5 December 1950–30 May 1952), which had divided North Korea into a series of eleven prioritized interdiction zones. It called for FEAF B-29s to attack the most important zones first: the rail bridges at Sinuiju, the choke point at Manpojin, and the rail yards at Pyongyang. The problem with this zone system was that it enabled the Communist logisticians to move forces through lower priority zones while the high priority ones were being attacked. It also enabled them to concentrate their air defenses in the higher priority zones—a difficult challenge, as FEAF found out on 12 April 1952. On this day, "big" day for the campaign, a strike force of forty-eight B-29s attacking the transportation center of Sinuiju encountered between seventy-two and eighty-four MiGs, and lost three Superfortresses in the ensuing melee. After this encounter, FEAF commander George Stratemeyer canceled further Bomber Command attacks against these vital bridges.[18] By May, with B-29 losses up to eight for the month, Stratemeyer threw in his cards for good and redirected his B-29s against airfield targets. For the remainder of the war, interdiction missions would be performed primarily by the fighter-bombers of the Fifth Air Force, the tactical aviation component of FEAF.[19]

The Fifth Air Force's approach to interdiction was different than Bomber Command's yet equally problematic. Since February 1951, it had been concentrating its efforts against supply trucks, roads, and highway bridges between railheads near the 39th parallel and the Communist front line. By hitting the vehicular supply system in a zone which fell 50 miles behind the Communist front line, Fifth Air Force planners believed they had the best interdiction formula for winning the war. What they failed to recognize was the devastating consequences that countermeasures could have on minimizing the effectiveness of such a strategy, especially as the battle line became increasingly static in May 1951 (the date the campaign was formally designated as STRANGLE I).[20]

Flak traps wreaked havoc on slow-flying F-51s and B-26s. Supply bunkers, protected with anti-aircraft artillery (AAA), proved almost invulnerable to the 150-gallon napalm bombs carried by most F-51s. Finally, road repair crews, stationed every 3 kilometers along main routes, repaired roads, detoured trucks around damaged bridges, and removed unexploded cluster bombs "by detonating them with rifle fire or dragging rope across the stretch of road affected."[21] The Communist forces also stepped up their use of secondary roads and pack animals for transporting supplies. So successful were the Communists in thwarting STRANGLE I that by early July, the U.N. Command calculated that these forces were stockpiling over 800 tons of supplies per day.[22] Hence, in August 1951, FEAF shifted the focus of interdiction to the railways but maintained objectives identical to those of STRANGLE I. This new effort was appropriately code-named STRANGLE II.

Despite the problems encountered with Interdiction Plan 4, FEAF returned to rail bombing in the STRANGLE II effort for several reasons: there were very few rail lines, they were easy to identify by air, and they required heavy equipment to repair.[23] The system also transported the bulk of the Communist supplies: the 3,000 tons required by the front-line Communist forces each day could be transported with only 120 boxcars; by comparison, it took 6,000 trucks to accomplish the same task — 18.2 percent of the entire Soviet and Chinese monthly production of 2-ton trucks.[24] Furthermore, FEAF calculated that by transferring from rail to trucks, the Communist forces would lose 5,000 trucks a month from mechanical failure and air attack — 15 percent of the esti-mated Chinese and Russian truck production.[25] This figure, FEAF be-lieved, was much higher than the Chinese or Soviets were willing to bear.[26]

The specific goal of the campaign was to reduce dramatically the capacity of the railroads in ninety days and completely shut them down in six months.[27] B-29s, with heavy 2,000-pound bombs, were assigned to demolish the rail bridges at Pyongyang, Sonchon, Sunchon, Sinanju, and Huichon.[28] More accurate fighter-bombers with smaller 500-pound bombs were charged with cutting the main north-south lines between Sonchon and Sariwon, Huichon and Kunu-ri, and Kunu-ri and Son-chon.[29] The Navy air units allotted to STRANGLE II agreed to cut the

!ateral rail line between Samdong-ni and Kowon, and the main north-south line between Kilchu and Pyonggang. The Seventh Fleet also agreed to keep twenty-seven previously destroyed highway and rail bridges out of action should the Communist forces attempt to repair them. Finally, B-26 Night Intruders and Navy F4U-5N Night Corsairs were ordered to maintain pressure on the road system by attacking vehicle convoys at night.[30]

Initially, STRANGLE II appeared to be working well. After the first month of the campaign, 40 percent of the rail line from Pyongyang to Sariwon, 70 percent of the line between Sinuiju and Sinanju, and 90 percent from Sinanju to Pyongyang was reduced to one track.[31] However, as the campaign developed, so too did enemy flak and countermeasures. During August, flak destroyed 30 Fifth Air Force aircraft and damaged another 24; by October, this figure jumped to 33 and 239, respectively. As a consequence, the Fifth Air Force, as of October, was devoting 20 percent of its sorties to flak suppression.[32]

Even worse, the MiG situation was also becoming more serious. New drop tanks installed in October enabled the MiG-15 to fly as far south as Pyongyang. "Trains" of between sixty and eighty MiGs would stream across the border hoping to evade the F-86 MiG patrols, the so-called MIGCAPs. As trains encountered U.N. Sabres, flights would break off and battle the F-86s while the main train kept heading south in search of fighter-bombers or bombers. In September, MiGs compelled the Fifth Air Force to halt fighter-bomber operations north of the Chongchon River; in late October, the loss of five B-29s in three days convinced the FEAF Bomber Command to halt all daylight bombing raids with B-29s, a feat which even the German Luftwaffe had never been able to accomplish.[33]

Given the increasingly hostile combat environment, FEAF decided to experiment with what became known as "saturation" tactics in January 1952 to accelerate the collapse of the North Korean rail system. The rationale of saturation tactics was that by concentrating a bombing effort against a rather small area of the rail system, FEAF could prevent all repairs from being accomplished, thereby completely denying the enemy the use of that area. This tactic was first employed in January against "narrow defiles" where the main lateral railways crossed a major north-south roadway at Wadong.[34] Known as the Wadong choke point, this area was bombed round-the-clock by B-29s and B-26s for forty-four days, with roughly four thousand 500-pound bombs.[35] The results of this operation, though, were meager. The rail line was closed for only one week.[36]

Although the Wadong effort was less than satisfactory, FEAF nevertheless implemented saturation tactics on a broader scale on 3 March 1952. This plan, code-named "SATURATE," focused Fifth Air Force and Navy fighter bomber attacks on short sections of the track to prevent those sections from being repaired. Additionally, night bombers were ordered to attack the same targets to achieve a round-the-clock effort.[37] Despite the intensive efforts of FEAF, however, SATURATE failed to achieve significant results: the Communist forces simply diverted supplies around choke points using porters and trucks.

By May 1952, two thousand military aircraft had flown over 87,552 interdiction missions during the STRANGLE II/SATURATE campaign. FEAF claimed it had destroyed 34,211 road vehicles, 276 locomotives, 3,820 railcars, and two-thirds of all rail bridges spanning over 300 feet.[38] FEAF also claimed that 19,000 rail cuts were made, and 90 percent of the Communist supplies and 95 percent of the prewar rail traffic north of the 39th parallel were stopped.[39]

Even if these figures are true, which is doubtful given the poor bomb damage assessment capability of FEAF, STRANGLE II/SATURATE had mixed results. During STRANGLE II/SATURATE, the Communists were never able to launch an all-out assault on the U.N. Indirectly, interdiction also compelled the Communist forces to endure innumerable hardships. Troops coming from China had to march the entire distance from the Yalu River to the 38th parallel. Troops marched 17.5 to 20 miles per night, carried 75- to 90-pound backpacks, and were forced to take isolated paths through very mountainous areas. Lunch was often skipped during these marches, and days were spent huddled in hastily dug foxholes.[40] According to one Korean prisoner of war, "We sweated so much that our thick quilted clothes were drenched with sweat and therefore many of us had colds and caught disease." Another POW claimed that "about 10 percent were left behind with frost bite and heavy colds."[41] In short, in order to minimize the danger of air attack, the Communist forces subjected themselves to long and arduous night marches through very difficult terrain.

Despite these hardships the Communist forces were able to stockpile thirty to sixty days' worth of supplies along the front, build elaborate fortifications, and even launch limited attacks during the campaign. Furthermore, the North Korean and Chinese units were firing 100,000 artillery rounds in May 1952, compared to only 8,000 when STRANGLE II/SATURATE began.[42] In short, STRANGLE II/SATURATE never weakened the Communist front to the point where it was ready to collapse—the primary goal of the campaign. In fact, the Communist forces actually increased their offensive potential during the campaign.

More significantly, STRANGLE II/SATURATE had almost no effect on the armistice negotiations. Not only did it fail to compel the Communists into accepting the armistice on U.N. terms, but it also failed to persuade them to soften their demands. U.N. negotiators, in the meantime, offered "concession after concession until the U.N. could give little more than peace with honor."[43] These concessions ranged from abandoning their claim to the disputed village of Kaesong, to agreeing to cease all offensive ground operations larger than a battalion in size.[44] So frustrating was this failure of air power to influence the peace proceedings at Kaesong and later at Panmunjom that FEAF completely altered its bombing strategy in June of 1952. General Otto Weyland, the commanding officer of FEAF, ordered FEAF, and asked the Navy, to engage in strategic bombing missions against the few strategic targets left in North Korea, namely hydroelectric plants and irrigation dams.

According to the Operations Analysis Office of the Fifth Air Force, interdiction in Korea was severely hampered for the following reasons:

   a) The enemy relied almost exclusively upon night movement of men and supplies and FEAF only possessed a limited number of dedicated night attack planes (its 100 B-26 Night Intruders).
   b) His needs are simple and limited. One Communist division of 10,000, for example, could subsist on 50 tons of supplies per day; an American division of 16,000, by comparison, required over 500 tons.

c) He relies upon manpower, to a large extent, both for transportation and in front-line combat.

d) The rugged character of much of the terrain provides unusual opportunities for cover which the enemy cleverly exploits.[45]

Not mentioned in this report, but equally important, was the impressive ability of the Communists to repair and defend their lines of communication. The North Korean Military Highway Administration and Railway Recovery Bureau pre-positioned fifty repair troops at every major rail station, and ten at posts every four miles along the 600 miles of North Korean track. These crews repaired minor cuts in two to six hours, bridges in two to four days, and "saturation" efforts in four to seven days.[46] Along roads, repair crews were positioned at 2.5- to 3-kilometer intervals and repaired roads using simple tools such as "shovels, picks, axes, and wire cutters."[47]

For the fighter pilots of the Fifth Air Force, however, the primary menace was the Communist air defense system. By the end of STRANGLE II/SATURATE, over 50 percent of Communist AAA resources were guarding rail lines and bridges, "a threat estimated at 132 heavy guns (such as 85-mm and 76-mm artillery) and upwards of 700 automatic weapons (ranging from 37-mm artillery down to 12-mm and 7.62-mm machine guns)."[48] Placed along most rail lines, these guns, combined with MiG sorties, downed over 243 fighter bombers of the Fifth Air Force and damaged another 290.[49] In fact, Communist active countermeasures were destroying aircraft faster than the U.N. could replace them: the diminutive Fifth Air Force was so small that it could not even absorb losses of between twenty and thirty planes a month.[50]

Appendix 2

Korean Conflict Aerial
Victory Credits

(The following is an excerpt from the report by Dr. Daniel L. Haulman and Colonel William C. Stancik, USAFR, "Air Force Victory Credits: World War I, World War II, Korea, and Vietnam," United States Air Force Historical Research Center, 1988)

Headquarters Far East Air Forces (HQ FEAF), the organization responsible for awarding victory credits during the Korean Conflict, required proof of the destruction of enemy aircraft before issuing general orders to confirm claims. This proof usually consisted of witness statements, gun camera film, or the sighting of aircraft wreckage.

Criteria for awarding credit for victories in the Korean Conflict were originally more liberal than the criteria employed in World War II. Far East Air Forces at first awarded credit for destruction of enemy airplanes on the ground. It also awarded credit to members of other services even if they did not belong to Air Force units. These credits have been deleted from the current list, which counts only United States Air Force members who achieved aerial victories. For an accounting of the personnel originally awarded victory credits by HQ FEAF, consult USAF Historical Study No. 81.

Aerial victory credits were denied to gunners aboard bombardment aircraft during World War II because the bombers flew in such large formations that it was impossible to tell with certainty which gunners deserved credit. Official credits were awarded to gunners aboard B-29 aircraft in the Korean conflict because a typical bomber formation consisted of only four aircraft and their claims could be verified.

Following the policy used for apportioning victory credits in World War II, FEAF divided into fractions each credit awarded to more than one flyer. For example, if two fighter pilots fired on and destroyed one enemy plane, each received one-half credit. Korean victory credits, however, were never divided among more than two men.

(To conserve space, the alphabetical list in table 2 only contains the name of the pilot and the numbers of credits to his name. Those interested in the rank of the pilot, his serial number, his unit designation, the type of aircraft flown, the type of aircraft destroyed, the date of each kill, and the FEAF general order number for each credit should consult the source listed above or contact the Air Force Historical Support Agency, Bolling Air Force Base, Washington, DC 20332, telephone 202–767–0412)

TABLE 2
Korean Conflict—Alphabetical Listing

Name	Kills	Name	Kills
Adams, Donald E.	6.5	Beck, Garold R.	.5
Akin, Robert W.	1	Becker, Richard S.	5
Aldrin, Edwin E.	2	Berdoy, Ronald A.1	.5
Amell, Zane S.	3	Bertram, William E.	1
Anderson, Roscoe E.	1	Best, Jack R.	1
Anderson, Sabin L.	2.5	Bettinger, Stephen L.	5
Anderson, Simon K.	2	Blakeney, Lewis L.	.5
Angle, William D.	.5	Blesse, Frederick C.	10
Arbuckle, Frank H. M.	1	Borders, William S.	1.5
Arnold, James E.	.5	Bouchard, Alvin R.	2
Ashby, Ralph H.	1	Bowman, William R.	2
Asla, Felix Jr.	4	Box, Norman L.	3
Atkinson, Gordon W.	.5	Brietenstein, Alan P.	.5
Austin, Coy L.	2	Brossart, Clifford F.	1.5
Ayersman, Richard L.	2	Brown, Russell J.	1
Babb, Marshall F.	.5	Brown, Stuart L. Jr.	2
Baker, Royal N.	13	Brueland, Lowell K.	2
Baldwin, Robert P	.5	Bryant, Duane K.	1
Ballinger, Edward P.	1	Bryce, Paul W.	1
Bambrick, Martin J.	1	Burke, John J.	2
Banks, Ralph E.	4	Burns, Richard J.	1
Barnes, Robert E.	1	Butler, Heber M.	1
Barrett, Fred H.	1	Butler, Joseph R.	1
Barton, Raymond O. Jr.	2	Buttelmann, Henry	7
Beach, Billy G.	2	Canady, Craig R.	.5

TABLE 2 *(continued)*

Name	Kills	Name	Kills
Caple, Joe A.	1	Erdmann, Robert H.	1
Carl, Charles G. Jr.	2	Erikson, Lester A.	1
Carley, Curtis N.	1	Evans, Douglas K.	2
Carlile, Homer J.	1	Evans, Raymond E.	1
Carr, Charles C.	1.5	Eversole, Leonard B.	1
Carter, Leland W.	1	Farris, Joe B.	.5
Carter, Robert D.	1	Fellman, Walter W. Jr.	4
Carus, Glenn A.	1.5	Fernandez, Manuel J. Jr.	14.5
Chandler, Kenneth D.	1	Fields, Joseph E. Jr.	1.5
Chandler, Van E.	3	Fincher, Deltis H.	.5
Charlton, Homer R. Jr.	1	Finnegan, William H.	1
Christison, Charles B.	2	Fischer, Harold E.	10
Clark, Francis B.	1	Fischer, Franklin L.	3
Cleveland, Charles G.	4	Fisher, Richard W.	1
Coberly, Theodore S.	2	Fithian, Ben L.	1
Colman, Philip E.	4	Flake, Alma R.	2
Condrick, Richard J.	1.5	Fletcher, Edward C.	1
Cook, William W.	.5	Fletcher, Westwood H. Jr.	1
Cooke, Robert G.	1	Forbes, Don R.	1
Cooley, Kenneth C.	.5	Fortner, Farrie D.	1
Copeland, David P.	1	Foster, Cecil G.	9
Copeland, Walter R.	1	Fox, Orrin R.	2
Cosby, William L. Jr.	3	Frailey, Richard W.	1
Cox, Al B.	1	Frazier, Frank D.	.5
Craig, William B.	1	Frazier, Henry W.	1
Craig, WilliamL.	2	Frederick, Peter J.	3
Creighton, Richard D.	5	Freeland, David B.	1
Crescibene, Henry A.	1	Friend, John C.	1
Curtin, Clyde A.	5	Gabreski, Francis S.	6.5
Davey, Calvin G.	2	Gabriel, Charles A.	2
Davidson, David T.	2	Garrison, Vermont	10
Davis, George A. Jr.	14	Garvin, Tom P.	1
Davis, James C.	1	Gately, Frank J.	1
Davis, Philip C.	1.5	Gibson, Harold C.	1
Davis, Robert L.	.5	Gibson, Ralph D.	5
Dawson, William R.	1	Gilbert, Clyde R.	1
Dennehy, Daniel J.	1	Giordano, Bruno A.	1
Dewald, Robert H.	1	Giraudo, John C.	2
Dewey, Ryland T.	2	Glessner, James L. Jr.	1
Dittmer, Karl K.	3	Golf, Merle N.	2
Dobbs, Billy B.	4	Goodnough, David H.	1
Dunlap, Elmer W.	.5	Goodridge, Robert L.	1
Dunn, George W.	2.5	Goodwill, John W.	1.5
Dupree, Forist G.	1	Gordon, Mose W. Jr.	1
Dye, Ercel S.	1	Gordon, Otis Jr.	1
Dymock, Alfred W. Jr.	2	Gray, Fred W.	.5
Eagleston, Glenn T.	2	Green, John P.Jr.	1
Eisenhut, Van C.	1	Green, Louis A.	4
Ellis, Joseph R.	1	Greene, Norman S.	1
Ely, Ivan J. Jr.	2	Griffith, Donald Q.	1
Emmert, Benjamin H. Jr.	1	Groening, Samuel A.	.5

TABLE 2 (*continued*)

Name	Kills	Name	Kills
Guidroz, Richard P.	1	Kelley, George P. III	1
Guinther, William M.	2	Kelley, Albert S.	2.5
Hagerstrom, James P.	8.5	Keyes, Ralph E.	1
Harris, Elmer W.	3	Kincheloe, Iven C. Jr.	5
Harrison, James B.	1	Kinsey, Raymond A.	1
Hartrim, Ronald W.	.5	Knoy, William C.	1
Harvey, Julian A.	.5	Koenig, Ramon L.	1
Hatzenbuehler, Edwin J. Jr.	.5	Korbel, William A.	1
Heard, John M.	2	Kozack, Thomas F.	1
Heckman, James E.	1	Kratt, Jacob Jr.	3
Heller, Edwin L.	3.5	Kulengosky, Anthony Jr.	3
Hemmer, Donald J.	1.5	Kumpf, James W.	.5
Henderson, Paul R. Jr.	3	Landry, Howard J.	1
Hepner, Edmund G.	1	Lane, Howard M.	1
Herrick, Harold J.	2	Latshaw, Robert T. Jr.	5
Hesse, Erwin A.	1	Lavene, Harry J.	1
Hewett, John M. Jr.	.5	Lee, Robert L.	1
Heyman, Richard M.	1	Lefevers, Cecil E.	.5
Hinton, Bruce H.	2	Lewis, Jere J.	2
Hockery, John J.	1	Liles, Brooks J.	4
Hodge, Robert R.	.5	Liley, Leonard W.	7
Hoelscher, William B.	1	Little, Donald E.	1
Holker, Booth T.	2	Little, James W.	1
Honaker, John W.	2	Livingston, Justin W.	2
Hooten, Donald H.	1	Love, George W.	1.5
Horowitz (Salter), James A.	1	Love, Robert J.	6
Hovde, William J.	1	Low, James F.	9
Howell, George W. Jr.	1	Loyd, Charles F.	1
Howell, Ronald B. Jr.	1	Loyd, William F.	1
Howerton, James M. Jr.	1	Ludwig, John H.	.5
Hroch, Merlyn E.	.5	Lyle, Vernon J.	2
Hudson, William G.	1	Lyvere, Gerald E.	1
Humphreys, Francis A.	3	Mahurin, Walker M.	3.5
Inferrera, John A.	2	Mailloux, William P.	1
Jabara, James	15	Malone, Cleve P.	1
Jensen, George W.	1	Mamerow, Frederick E. W.	1
Johns, Richard S.	1	Mann, Howard P.	2
Johnson, James K.	10	Markham, Theon E.	1.5
Johnson, Samuel R.	1	Marsh, Roy W.	1
Johnson, William O.	1	Marshall, Winton W.	6.5
Jolley, Clifford D.	7	Martin, James F.	1
Jones, George L.	6.5	Martin, Maurice L.	1
Jones, Harry A. Jr.	1.5	Martin, Richard R.	1
Jones, John H.	1	Martocchia, Michael R.	2
Jones, Paul E.	2	Marvin, John M.	1
Juhlin, Lloyd D.	2	Mass, Jack E.	4
Kanop, Earl A.	1	Mathews, Freeland K.	2
Kasler, James H.	6	Matthews, George D.	1
Kauttu, Paul A.	2.5	Mattson, Conrad E.	4
Kees, Elwood A.	1	Maxwell, Earle P.	1
Keller, Frank O.	1	McAllister, William W.	1

TABLE 2 (*continued*)

Name	Kills	Name	Kills
McBride, Robert W.	1	Pena, Alphonso R.	1
McCarthy, Arthur H.	2	Perdue, Robert E.	.5
McConnell, Joseph M. Jr.	16	Perkins, Leon B. Jr.	1
McCulley, James A.	3	Pesacreta, Samuel	1
McElroy, Carroll B.	2	Phillips, John R.	1
McHale, Robert V.	1	Pierce, Jimmie	1
McIntosh, Robert H.	1	Pincoski, Richard A.	1.5
McKee, John L.	1.5	Pittman, Biffle O.	1
McKee, Robert D.	1	Pogreba, Dean A.	1
McKittrick, Robert W.	1	Porter, Ira M.	3
McLain, Roy W.	.5	Powell, Edgar N.	.5
McLean, Donald A.	.5	Powers, Lewis W.	2
McQuade, Thomas H.	2	Powers, William E.	.5
Metten, John L.	1	Preston, Benjamin S. Jr.	4
Meyer, John C.	2	Price, Howard I.	1.5
Miller, Alfred M.	1	Raebel, James B.	3
Miller, Russell H.	1	Ragland, Dayton W.	1
Mitchell, John W.	4	Ransbottom, Richard O.	1
Mitchell, Paul C.	1	Rapp, Kenneth H.	1
Mitson, Claude C.	2	Redpath, Philip A.	1
Moore, John H.	2	Reeder, Samuel J.	1
Moore, Lonnie R.	10	Reeves, Theil M.	1
Moore, Robert H.	5	Reynolds, Henry S.	.5
Moorman, Alvin R.	2.5	Ricker, Merton E.	3
Moran, Charles B.	1	Riester, Charles O. Jr.	1
Morton, Duncan M.	1	Risner, Robinson	8
Moulton, Aubrey C. Jr.	1	Roach, Paul E.	2.5
Moyle, Richard B.	1	Roberts, James O.	1
Mullins, Arnold	1	Robinson, Jack A.	1
Nelson, Milton E.	4	Robison, Frank P.	1
Neubert, Ernest F.	.5	Roesler, Lawrence	2
Nichols, James G.	2	Rogge, Gene F.	1
Nott, Thomas E.	1	Rohrer, Samuel T.	.5
Novak, Michael J.	1	Ronca, Robert F.	1
Nutt, Waymond C.	1	Ruch, Harry E.	1
Nystrum, Conrad P.	1	Ruddell, George I.	8
Ober, George W.	1	Russell, Len C.	1
Ochs, Robert C.	1	Ryan, William J.	2
O'Connor, Arthur L.	2	Salze, Floyd W.	2
Odiorne, John M.	1	Sandlin, Harry T.	1
Ohlinger, Orren H.	1	Sands, Robert L.	3
Ola, George J.	1	Saunders, Jesse L.	2
Oligher, Arthur E.	.5	Saunders, Percy L.	.5
Opfer, Gus C.	2	Savage, Walter G.	1.5
Overton, Dolphin D. III	5	Schillereff, Raymond E.	1
Owens, Charles D.	2	Schinz, Albert W.	.5
Palmer, Kenneth L.	1	Schmidt, Harold B.	.5
Parker, Jerald D.	1	Schoeneman, Richard H.	3
Parr, Ralph S. Jr.	10	Schrimsher, William E.	.5
Patterson, Lyle R.	1	Schwab, Jack C.	1
Payne, Earl S.	1	Setters, Harold M.	1

TABLE 2 (*continued*)

Name	Kills	Name	Kills
Seuffert, Thomas W.	1	Thresher, Robert D.	1
Sheaffer, William F.	3	Thyng, Harrison R.	5
Shealy, Kenneth A.	1	Tilton, James E.	1
Shofner, William C.	1	Tuel, Houston N.	3
Simmons, Alfred C.	1	Underwood, Harry L.	.5
Skeen, Kenneth L.	1	Van Etten, Chester L.	1
Slaughter, William W.	1	Van Sickle, Philip H.	1
Smiley, Albert B.	3	Vandeventer, Kirk	2
Smiley, Dale W.	2	Veatch, Royal A.	1
Smith, Bobbie L.	1	Vetort, Francis J.	1
Smith, Foster L.	4.5	Visscher, Herman W.	1
Smith, Richard B. Jr.	1	Wade, Clyde L.	1
Smith, Robert E.	1	Watson, Cleve B.	1
Smith, Robert W.	2	Wayne, Robert E.	2
Sommerich, Eugene M.	.5	Webb, Jerry M.	1
Spalding, John R.	1	Weber, Herbert	1
Spataro, George J.	2	Webster, Edward H.	1
Spath, Charles R.	.5	Wescott, William H.	5
Spitzer, Herschel D.	1	Whisner, William T. Jr.	5.5
Spivey, Fred R.	1	White, Thomas R.	1
Stacy, Vincent E.	1.5	Whitehead, Asa S.	1.5
Stange, Laverne G.	1	Whitehurst, Elbert W.	1
Staudte, Raymond W.	1	Wilcox, Stanton G.	1
Steinbis, Raymond E.	.5	Willard, Garry A. Jr.	1
Stime, David R.	1	Williams, Francis A.	3
Stogdill, Maynard E.	1	Wilson, Nelton R.	2
Stone, Stephen A. Jr.	1	Windoffer, Robert A.	1
Straub, Robert L.	2	Winslow, Murray A.	4
Strozier, Robert L.	1.5	Winslow, Robert A.	1
Summers, Charles W.	1	Winters, John D.	1
Swift, Kenneth L.	1	Wood, George J.	1
Tankersley, Leeman M.	1	Woodworth, Gene H.	.5
Taylor, John E. Jr.	2.5	Wright, Vernon L.	1
Thomas, John B.	1	Wurster, Charles A.	2
Thomas, William K.	1	Yancey, William B. Jr.	1.5
Thompson, James L.	2	Young, Sam P.	1
Thompson, Lloyd J.	1	Zistte, Walter G.	1

Far East Air Forces Table of Equipment and Sorties by Aircraft Type, 1952

Tables 3 and 4 illustrate the extent to which Korea was a fighter war. At no point during the period 1951–1952 did the Far East Air Forces deploy more bombers than fighters (see table 3). However, the true extent of the fighter effort is revealed in table 4. On average, there were four fighter sorties to every bomber sortie during this period.[1]

Another significant trend illustrated by the tables is FEAF's increasing emphasis on the high performance F-86. In July 1951, FEAF had only 41 of these planes, and this small fleet only flew 734 sorties. By May 1952, those numbers had increased to 131 and 5,190, respectively.

TABLE 3

Far East Air Forces' Aircraft Strength for Selected Months, 1951–1952

	July 1951	September 1951	November 1951	January 1952	March 1952	May 1952
Aircraft—Total	990	1,038	1,004	1,101	1,086	1,031
Bomber—Total	198	201	186	200	211	209
B-26	103	104	97	104	106	107
B-29	95	97	89	96	105	102
Fighter—Total	380	415	381	421	398	367
F-51	95	110	96	71	60	47
F-80	136	118	98	69	81	79
F-82	5	6	6	10	—	—
F-84	103	137	125	123	88	87
F-86	41	44	56	133	133	131
F-94	—	—	—	15	36	23
Cargo—Total	244	245	242	240	245	225
C-46	55	59	61	60	65	54
C-47	52	46	46	51	51	42
C-54	59	59	58	61	62	63
C-119	78	80	77	68	67	66
C-124	—	1	—	—	—	—
Recon—Total	72	85	100	117	104	108
RB-26	17	22	22	21	22	25
RB-29	13	11	11	12	12	14
RB-45	2	2	3	3	3	3
RB-50	—	—	—	2	3	3
WB-29	14	14	15	14	12	12
RF-51	5	6	20	31	23	22
RF-80	21	30	29	33	27	25
RF-86	—	—	—	1	1	4
FAC	54	92	95	123	128	122
T-6	54	52	48	60	63	57
Miscellaneous	42	44	47	63	65	65

TABLE 4
USAF Sorties by Aircraft Type for Selected Months, 1951–1952

	July 1951	September 1951	November 1951	January 1952	March 1952	May 1952
Sorties—Total	15,914	19,311	19,166	18,581	19,653	23,954
Bomber—						
Total	1,998	2,482	2,298	2,168	2,027	2,231
B-26	1,499	1,962	1,868	1,653	1,552	1,825
B-29	499	520	430	515	475	406
Fighter—						
Total	6,796	9,650	9,187	7,997	9,412	12,758
F-51	2,370	2,811	2,070	1,333	1,172	1,421
F-80	2,289	2,777	2,678	1,600	2,438	3,460
F-82	75	135	87	101	—	—
F-84	1,328	2,808	3,349	2,577	2,289	2,418
F-86	734	1,119	1,003	2,340	3,359	5,190
F-94	—	—	—	46	154	269
Cargo—Total	5,072	4,790	5,058	5,333	5,392	4,682
C-46	850	535	1,041	1,100	966	887
C-47	927	1,268	1,144	1,324	1,578	1,158
C-54	66	2,548	2,235	2,298	2,256	2,015
C-119	2,379	400	465	551	499	588
C-124	—	4	—	—	—	—
Recon—Total	851	1,152	1,383	1,549	1,604	2,443
RB-26	358	467	343	190	429	498
RB-29	39	56	47	30	44	62
RB-45	9	1	8	6	28	9
RB-50	—	—	—	—	—	3
WB-29	32	30	30	31	31	32
RF-51	93	98	411	775	624	988
RF-80	320	500	544	515	447	815
RF-86	—	—	—	2	1	36
FAC	833	942	945	1,009	769	1,210
T-6	833	942	945	1,009	769	1,210
Miscellaneous	12	2	—	71	54	101

Tabulation of Sorties Flown by the Air Force, Navy, Marine Corps, and Allied Air Services in Korea

TABLE 5
Korean War: Total Sorties (1,040,708)

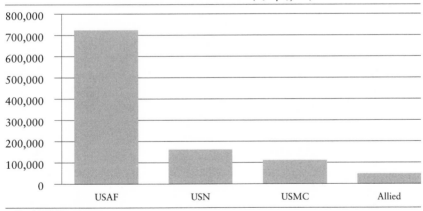

Total USAF: 720,980
Total USN: 167,552
Total USMC: 107,303
Total Allied: 44,873
SOURCE: Robert F. Futrell, *The United States Air Force in Korea, 1950–1953* (Washington, D.C.: Center for Air Force HIstory, 1987), p. 690.

● ● Appendix 5 ● ●

Air Force, Marine, and Allied
Aircraft Losses in Korea

TABLE 6

Korean War: Operational Losses

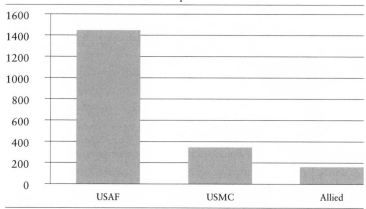

Total USAF: 1,446
Total USMC: 368
Total Allied: 152

SOURCE: Robert F. Futrell, *The United States Air Force in Korea, 1950–1953* (Washington, D.C.: Center for Air Force History, 1987), p. 691.

Notes

Notes to Chapter 1

1. Unless noted, all material from this section is from author interview, 21 May 1995.

2. Overall, some 249 Air Force personnel (mostly pilots) were captured and held as POWs by the North Koreans. See Robert F. Futrell, *The United States Air Force in Korea: 1950–1953*, rev. ed. (Washington, D.C.: Center for Air Force History, 1983), p. 692.

3. While Risner did not know the origin of the call-sign "John Red," it was popular during the Korean War for flights to be named after various alcoholic beverages. "John Red" was, in all likelihood, short for Johnnie Walker Red Label, a popular brand of scotch whiskey.

4. MiG Alley was a square sector just south of the Yalu River bordered by the towns of Sinuiju, Changju, Sinanju, and Huichon. Because of its close proximity to the large Chinese air base at Antung, most MiG kills achieved in Korea occurred in this area.

5. A pipper is a spot of light projected onto the windshield of the F-86 by the plane's computing gun sight. When the spot of light illuminates a target, the pilot can take a shot.

6. In a split-S maneuver, an aircraft makes a half-roll onto its back and then dives, either leveling off on a reversed heading after completing a half loop, or continuing the dive.

7. Risner later noted that this pilot definitely did not look Korean, but could not tell whether the pilot was Russian or Chinese. According to Futrell, *U.S. Air Force in Korea*, p. 419, approximately 150 Soviet pilots flew in the Korean War. All of these pilots operated out of Antung air base. For additional information on Soviet pilots who fought in Korea, see Jon Halliday, "A Secret War: U.S. and Soviet Air Forces Clashed Directly in Korea," *Far Eastern Economic Review,* 22 April 1993, pp. 32–36.

8. During the initial engagement with the MiGs, Risner had ordered the other two pilots in his flight to engage the 1, 2, and 3 MiGs. These pilots later reported that the MiGs evaded their pursuit.

9. To "jink" an aircraft means to jerk the aircraft about in evasive action.

10. Chodo was a South Korean-controlled island in the Yellow Sea near the 38th parallel. The USAF maintained radar facilities there, and kept SA-16 "Dumbo" rescue sea planes and helicopters.

11. The familiar psalm goes as follows: "The Lord is my shepherd. I shall not be in want. He makes me lie down in green pastures, he leads me beside quiet waters, he restores my soul. He guides me in paths of righteousness for his name's sake. Even though I walk through the valley of the shadow of death, I will fear no evil, for you are with me; your rod and your staff, they comfort me. You prepare a table before me in the presence of my enemies. You anoint my head with oil; my cup overflows. Surely goodness and love will follow me all the days of my life, and I will dwell in the house of the lord forever."

12. T. R. Milton, "Robinson Risner: The Indispensable Ingredient," in John L. Frisbee, ed., *Makers of the United States Air Force* (Washington, D.C.: Center for Air Force History, 1987), p. v.

13. During the Vietnam War, for example, Risner easily could have opted for a desk job in the Pentagon, but instead chose to fly the F-105 fighter-bomber missions against targets in the most heavily defended sections of North Vietnam. On 16 September 1965, he was shot down, and eventually spent seven and a half long years in the Hanoi Hilton. These experiences are recounted in his book, *The Passing of the Night: My Seven Years as a Prisoner of the North Vietnamese* (New York: Random House, 1973).

14. These categories are not necessarily mutually exclusive.

15. See Futrell, *U.S. Air Force in Korea*; Richard Hallion, *The Naval Air War in Korea* (Baltimore: Nautical and Aviation Publishing, 1986).

16. See Michael Sherry, *The Rise of American Air Power: The Creation of Armageddon* (New Haven, Conn.: Yale University Press, 1987); Ronald Schaffer, *Wings of Judgment: American Bombing in World War II* (New York: Oxford University Press, 1986).

17. Sources on the exact number of North Korean civilians killed by American air power are sketchy. The Air Force Historical Support Office does not maintain an official number on civilian casualties. Mark Clodfelter, in *Warfare and Armed Conflicts: A Statistical Reference to Casualty and Other Figures, 1618–1991*, vol. 2 (Jefferson, N.C.: McFarland, 1992), pp. 1215–1216, estimates from Department of Defense sources that over one million North Korean civilians were killed during the course of the conflict, but does not indicate how many of those deaths were caused by air power. Finally, Bruce Cumings, in *War and Television* (New York: Verso, 1991), p. 158, claims that the Air Force killed two million civilians.

18. Cumings, *War and Television*, p. 158. Cumings's assertions are supported by Air Force General Curtis LeMay. According to LeMay, "We went over there and fought the war and eventually burned down every town in North Korea anyway, some way or another, and some in South Korea too. We even burned down Pusan—an accident, but we burned it down anyway. . . . Over a period of three years, we killed off—what—twenty percent of the population of

Korea as direct casualties of war, or from starvation and exposure?" See Curtis E. LeMay, Richard H. Kohn, and Joseph Harahan, *Strategic Air Warfare: An Interview with Generals Curtis E. LeMay, Leon W. Johnson, David A. Burchinal, and Jack J. Catton* (Washington, D.C.: Center for Air Force History, 1988), p. 88.

19. The phrase "emancipation of American air power" was popularized by the air power theorist Alexander De Seversky in his book, *Air Power: The Key to Survival* (London: Jenkins, 1952).

20. Operations Statistics Division, Department of Statistical Service, Office of the Comptroller, "United States Air Force Statistical Digest: Fiscal Year 1952," (Washington, D.C., 1952), table 18: "FEAF—Aircraft in Committed Units Possessed and Combat Ready," p. 34.

21. Some historians may question the "social history" label that I attach to this book. How can a study of pilots be considered social history? By conventional definitions of the field, social historians should be concerned with examining the history of underrepresented groups, namely African Americans, workers, and women. In this study, I will expand the traditional boundaries of social history by exploring an all-male, predominately white, warrior culture. What will make this study social history is its emphasis on the social background, individual experiences, and mentalité of pilots. My reliance upon unofficial sources such as oral history and memoirs also places this study squarely in the category of social history.

22. For more on the life of James Salter, see William Dowie, "James Salter," in Patrick Meanor, ed., *American Short-Story Writers since World War II* (Detroit: Gale Research, 1993), pp. 282–287.

23. Ann Evory and Linda Metzger, *Contemporary Authors,* New Revision Series, vol. 10 (Detroit: Gale Research, 1983), p. 415.

Notes to Chapter 2

1. Vance Mitchell, "The First Generation: A Personnel Policy History of the Air Force Officer Corps, 1944–1974" (unpublished manuscript, Center for Air Force History, Washington, D.C., 1992), p. 97.

2. Ibid., p. 96.

3. Ibid., p. 99.

4. Ibid., p. 103.

5. This academic deficiency was so serious that the Air Force launched several educational programs designed to remedy the situation. In 1946, it opened the Air Force Institute of Technology (AFIT), a program which literally paid officers to obtain college and graduate degrees in designated technical fields. Officers enrolled in AFIT received full academic scholarships (all tuition, books,

and fees) and were paid their entire Air Force salary while attending school on a full-time basis. The program started out with 189 students and grew to 1,200 by 1951.

Besides AFIT, the Air Force also instituted a program called "Bootstrap." Bootstrap was designed to raise the general educational level of the Air Force by providing some financial support for tuition expenses related to off-duty college and graduate school education. It also brought college courses directly to the airman through "on-base campuses." Schools which contributed faculty members to this program included UCLA, the University of Maryland, the State University of Washington, and the University of Alabama. An additional incentive program, appropriately called "Operation Midnight Oil," paid for warrant officers and commissioned officers below the rank of lieutenant colonel to go on temporary duty as full-time students during the final semester of their Bootstrap baccalaureate program. In return, the officers had to agree to serve on active duty for two years after completion of their degrees.

By the spring of 1950, AFIT, Bootstrap, Midnight Oil, the GI Bill, and correspondence courses had enticed over 20 percent of Air Force personnel to seek a college degree. This number, though, dropped precipitously once the Korean War began, and new, undereducated recruits once again began to fill the Air Force ranks. See Mitchell, "First Generation," pp. 99–111; *Air Force Officer's Guide,* 5th ed. (Harrisburg, Pa.: Military Service Publishing Co., 1952), p. 298; Irving Casey, "Social Origins and Career Patterns of United States Air Force Generals and Colonels" (Ph.D. diss, American University, 1967), p. 132; and *Air Force Times,* 1 April 1950, p. 1.

6. Morris Janowitz, *The Professional Soldier: A Social and Political Portrait* (Glencoe, Ill.: Free Press, 1960), p. 106.

7. George Cullum, *Biographical Register of the Officers and Graduates of the United States Military Academy,* Supplement, vol. 9, ed. Charles Branham (West Point, N.Y.: Association of Graduates, U.S. Military Academy, 1950), pp. 1498–1598; Julian Olejniczak, ed., *1992 Register of Graduates and Former Cadets: United States Military Academy* (West Point, N.Y.: Association of Graduates, U.S. Military Academy, 1992), pp. 400–475; Mitchell, "First Generation," pp. 114–118. Overall, classes 47–54 of West Point graduated 3,527 cadets, of which 1,015 accepted USAF commissions.

8. Janowitz, *Professional Soldier,* p. 127.

9. Stephen Ambrose, *Duty, Honor, Country: A History of West Point* (Baltimore: Johns Hopkins University Press, 1966), pp. xiii-xiv.

10. Casey, "Social Origins," p. 77.

11. Janowitz, *Professional Soldier,* pp. 19, 100.

12. The sources for this section on Risner are as follows: author interview, 21 May 1995; Mark C. Cleary, "Interview of Brigadier General Robinson

Risner," Austin, Texas, 1–2 March 1983, United States Air Force Oral History Program, Center for Air Force History, Washington, D.C.; and Robinson Risner, *The Passing of the Night: My Seven Years as a Prisoner of the North Vietnamese* (New York: Random House, 1973).

13. The Army stationed several squadrons of fighters in Panama during the war to guard the Panama Canal.

14. Risner, *Passing of the Night,* p. 36.

15. The sources for this section on Brown are as follows: William Earl Brown, interview by author, tape recording, Center for Air Force History, Washington, D.C., 7 April 1993; William Earl Brown, "A Fighter Pilot's Story," Charles A. Lindbergh Memorial Lecture, 21 May 1992, National Air and Space Museum Occasional Paper Series, no. 4.

16. The source for this section on Crockett is Woodrow Crockett, interview with author, tape recording, Center for Air Force History, Washington, D.C., 31 March 1993.

17. "History of the 349th Field Artillery," Headquarters: 349th Field Artillery, Fort Sill, Okla., 1942.

18. Charles Boyle, General Orders No. 3, Headquarters: 349th Field Artillery, Fort Sill, Okla., 8 January 1942.

19. The source of this section on Tomlinson is Frank Tomlinson, interview with author, tape recording, Center for Air Force History, Washington, D.C., 9 December 1992.

20. The source of this section on Pomeroy is Robert Pomeroy, interview with author, tape recording, Center for Air Force History, Washington, D.C., 2 February 1993.

21. For a good description of military academy life, see Joseph Ellis, *School for Soldiers: West Point and the Profession of Arms* (New York: Oxford University Press, 1974), and Stephen Ambrose, *Duty, Honor, Country: A History of West Point* (Baltimore: Johns Hopkins University Press, 1966).

22. The source for the section on Turner is Paul Turner, interview with author, tape recording, Center for Air Force History, Washington, D.C., 3 March 1993.

23. Interestingly enough, the character of the pilot in the movie is loosely modeled after Turner.

24. The source for this section on Bailey is M. J. Bailey, interview with author, telephone interview, Washington, D.C., 9 September 1994.

25. The source for this section on Berke is George Berke, interview with author, tape recording, Center for Air Force History, Washington, D.C., 22 March 1993.

26. All three degrees were paid for by the military: the B.A. through the GI bill, and the M.A. and Ph.D. through AFIT.

27. The source for this section on Heiner is Howard Heiner, interview with author, tape recording, Washington, D.C., 14 December 1992.

28. The source for this section on Sturgeon is Raymond Sturgeon, interview with author, tape recording, Bedford, Mass., 21 June 1994.

29. The source for this section on Hagerstrom is James Hagerstrom, interview with author, tape recording, Center for Air Force History, Washington, D.C., 3 February 1993.

30. C. Wright Mills, *The Power Elite* (New York: Oxford University Press, 1956), p. 47.

31. Berke's degree was paid for by the GI bill, and Pomeroy's by the U.S. Military Academy.

32. Michael Sherry, *The Rise of American Air Power: The Creation of Armageddon* (New Haven, Conn.: Yale University Press, 1987), p. 217.

Notes to Chapter 3

1. During the Korean War, Nellis AFB was the home of the Air Force's advanced single-engine fighter and aerial gunnery schools. In short, it was the final stop in the fighter pilot training cycle—the place where the Air Force transformed pilots into MiG killers. For more on the early history of Nellis, see Thomas A. Manning, *History of Air Training Command, 1943–1993* (Randolph AFB, Texas: Office of History and Research, Headquarters, Air Education and Training Command, 1993), pp. 18, 19, 26, 31, 32, 39, 43, 46, 47, 63.

2. Vance Mitchell, "The First Generation: A Personal Policy History of the Air Force Officer Corps, 1944–1974" (unpublished manuscript, Center for Air Force History, Washington, D.C., 1992), p. 736, pp. 183–184, p. 767.

3. Historical Division, Flying Training Air Force, "History of the Flying Training Air Force," 1 January-30 June 1953, vol. 1, Waco, Texas, 10 September 1953, Center for Air Force History, Washington, D.C., p. 83.

4. Mitchell, "First Generation," p. 733.

5. Civilian contractors were trained as flight instructors at Craig Air Force Base. See "History of the Flying Training Air Force," 1 July-31 December 1952, vol. 1, pp. 80–85.

6. Pomeroy interview.

7. Ibid.

8. Mitchell, "First Generation," pp. 731–732.

9. Ibid., p. 733.

10. Mitchell, pp. 733–734.

11. "History of the Flying Training Air Force," 1 July-31 December 1952, vol. 1, p. 41; Mitchell, "First Generation," p. 203.

12. "History of the Flying Training Air Force," 1 July-31 December 1952, vol. 1, p. 65.

13. Mitchell, "First Generation," p. 205.

14. Ibid.

15. Ibid., pp. 205–206.

16. Ibid., p. 208.

17. Alan Gropman, *The Air Force Integrates 1945–1964* (Washington, D.C.: Center for Air Force History, 1985), p. 121. The percentage of blacks in the general population in 1949 was approximately 10 percent.

18. Mitchell, "First Generation," p. 784.

19. Personal Papers of George Berke, Reston, Virginia. Berke completed this analysis with the help of *Hondo Final,* 53-E and *Contrails,* 53E, Williams AFB, Arizona (his class yearbooks).

20. Director of Statistical Services, *United States Air Force Statistical Digest* (Washington, D.C.: Office of Statistical Services, 1947), tables 8, 11.

21. Statistical Services, *United States Air Force Statistical Digest* (Washington, D.C.: Office of Statistical Services, January 1949-June 1950), tables 20, 21, 23.

22. See Gropman, *Air Force Integrates,* Appendix 1, table 2, p. 223.

23. Ibid., p. 132.

24. Ibid., p. 132.

25. Ibid., pp. 135–136.

26. "History of the Air Training Command," 1 July to 31 December 1949, pp. 29–31, as cited in ibid., p. 136.

27. These schools were located at the following bases: Bainbridge, Bartow, Columbus, Goodfellow, Greenville, Hondo, Malden, Marana, Spence, and Stallings. See "Flying Training Air Force Statistical Digest," 31 July 1952, in Records of the Flying Training Air Force, Center for Air Force History, Washington, D.C.

28. "History of the Flying Training Air Force," 1 July-31 December 1952, vol. 1, pp 49–57, and vol. 2, pp. 484–549.

29. "History of the Flying Training Air Force," 1 July-31 December 1952, vol. 1, p. 61.

30. Turner interview.

31. They included Bainbridge, Bartow, Columbus, Greenville, Hondo, Malden, Marana, Spence, and Stallings. Only the Primary school at Goodfellow AFB was staffed by military instructors. "History of the Flying Training Air Force," 1 July-31 December 1952, vol. 2, p. 670.

32. "History of the Flying Training Air Force," 1 July-31 December 1952, vol. 2, pp. 45–46.

33. "Report of Conference, Primary Training, Headquarters Flying Training

Air Force, Roosevelt Hotel, Waco, Texas, 4–5 December 1952," in "The History of the Flying Training Air Force," 1 July-31 December 1952, vol. 2, p. 579.

34. It was assumed that ROTC, West Point, and Annapolis graduates were already familiar with military ways and did not need this additional training. When these officers joined the Aviation Cadets in Primary, they lived apart from the Aviation Cadets and participated only in flight training and ground school with them.

35. In October 1947, the Aviation Cadet Examining Board at Randolph AFB, Texas, recommended a one-to-five month preflight training program, and the Flying Division of the Air Training Command recommended a twelve-week program in December 1948. "The History of the Flying Training Air Force," 1 July-31 December 1952, vol. 1, p. 46.

36. This segment was later increased to twelve weeks in October 1952. "History of the Flying Training Air Force," 1 January-30 June 1953, vol. 1, p. 38.

37. Ibid., vol. 2, pp. 375–400.

38. Ibid., pp. 375–400.

39. According to George Berke, military academy graduates took the code much less seriously than the Aviation Cadets. Although Pomeroy vehemently disagrees with this claim, Berke remembered seeing West Point graduates passing test answers back and forth. "The motto of these guys was cooperate and graduate," Berke claimed. "To them the Honor Code was like the tax code—you look for loopholes." Berke interview; Pomeroy interview.

40. "History of the Flying Training Air Force," 1 January-30 June 1953, vol. 1, p. 38; "History of the Flying Training Air Force," 1 July-31 December 1952, vol. 1, pp. 46–47.

41. Tomlinson interview.

42. "History of Flying Training Air Force," 1 January-30 June 1953, vol. 1, p. 40.

43. Pomeroy interview.

44. Pomeroy interview.

45. Mitchell, "First Generation," p. 206.

46. Berke interview.

47. Tomlinson interview.

48. Crockett interview.

49. Gropman, *Air Force Integrates,* p. 156.

50. Crockett interview.

51. Gropman, *Air Force Integrates,* p. 135.

52. Ibid.

53. Turner interview.

54. Berke interview.

55. Brown, "A Fighter Pilot's Story," p. 5.

56. Tomlinson interview.

57. Brown, "A Fighter Pilot's Story," pp. 5–6.

58. Brown interview.

59. Pomeroy interview.

60. Pomeroy interview.

61. "History of the Flying Training Air Force," 1 July-31 December 1952, vol. 2, p. 670.

62. Mitchell, "First Generation," p. 733.

63. Rebecca Hancock Cameron, "To Fly: Military Flight Training, 1907–1945" (draft, historical manuscript, Center for Air Force History, Washington, D.C., 1993), p. 449.

64. Tomlinson interview.

65. Cameron, "To Fly," pp. 446–447.

66. A chandelle is an abrupt and steep climbing turn made in an airplane, in which the airplane's momentum provides additional acceleration for the climb. The purpose of the candela is to change the direction of flight and change altitude at the same time.

67. Cameron, "To Fly," p. 450.

68. "History of the Flying Training Air Force," 1 July-31 December 1952, vol. 1, p. 84.

69. Tomlinson interview.

70. Cameron, "To Fly," pp. 446, 454.

71. Such was not the case at the segregated World War II Tuskegee field. Due to the lack of other black AAF facilities, many washouts were made privates and stationed at Tuskegee, "depressing morale." See Stanley Sandler, *Segregated Skies: All-Black Combat Squadrons of WW II* (Washington, D.C.: Smithsonian Institution Press, 1992), p. 32.

72. Tomlinson interview.

73. Cameron, "To Fly," p. 453.

74. The plane used for this training was the Piper PA-18. "History of the Flying Training Air Force," 1 January-30 June 1953, vol. 1, p. 83.

75. "History of the Flying Training Air Force," 1 July-31 December 1952, vol. 1, p. 78.

76. Pomeroy, in general, was very sensitive to any critical remarks about the U.S. Military Academy. "West Pointers," he claimed, "wanted their wings just as much as the next guy; one of my classmates washed out and he was not a happy camper—he knew his military career was over with, and just marked time until he could get out." Pomeroy interview.

77. "History of the Flying Training Air Force," 1 July-31 December 1952, vol. 1, p. 78.

78. Ibid., p. 77.

79. Pomeroy interview.

80. "History of the Flying Training Air Force," 1 January-10 June 1952, vol. 2, pp. 600–660.

81. Timothy Strongin, "A Historical Review of the Fear of Flying among Aircrewmen," *Aviation, Space, and Environmental Medicine,* vol. 58, no. 2 (1987), p. 264.

82. Ibid., p. 265.

83. Ibid., p. 264.

84. Ibid., pp. 264–265.

85. Lucio Gatto, "Understanding the 'Fear of Flying' Syndrome," *U.S. Armed Forces Medical Journal,* vol. 5, no. 8 (1954), p. 1100.

86. Even today, the condition is poorly understood. In "Flying and Danger, Joy and Fear," *Aviation, Space, and Environmental Medicine,* vol. 57, no. 9 (February 1986), pp. 131–136, Dr. David Jones of the Neuropsychiatric Branch of the USAF School of Aerospace Medicine, Brooks AFB, Texas, defined FOF as a "complex phenomenon, mixing elements of mental health and neurotic roots, childhood dreams and fears, real dangers and imaginary threats, and all the varieties of life experiences which may befall a flier as he or she ages." In short, FOF could be almost anything: all that is clear from this definition is that it is a complex psychiatric condition.

87. Lucio Gatto, "Understanding the 'Fear of Flying' Syndrome," *U.S. Armed Forces Medical Journal,* vol. 5, no. 8 (1954), p. 1100. Timothy Strongin, a researcher at the Neuropsychiatry Branch of the USAF School of Aerospace Medicine, offered the following symptomatic definition of FOF in a 1987 historical review of FOF in *Aviation, Space, and Environmental Medicine:*

> Its clearest manifestation is the frank refusal to fly or fear of the plane or the possible consequences of flying. More subtle is the case of a flier who says he would be willing to fly, if only he were able to concentrate, relax, get some sleep, or overcome some other manifestation of inner turmoil. Depending on the fliers personality, one observes that dissociative symptoms (sleepwalking, amnesia), restlessness, substances abuse (drugs, food, and alcohol), emotional regression, somatization (ulcers, gastritis, colitis, headaches, dermatitis), or conversion (hearing loss, back pain, weakness) may also indicate underlying anxiety.

Clearly, agreement between these specialists not only exists with respect to the primary symptom of FOF, a refusal to fly, but also with other symptoms, including anxiety and a range of psychosomatic conditions. Furthermore, Gatto's and Strongin's symptomatic descriptions are nearly equivalent: the jargon is somewhat different but the basic symptoms are the same. See Strongin, "Historical Review," p. 264.

88. Jones suggests that many cases of FOF could have been cured through basic therapy. See Jones, "Flying and Danger," pp. 131–136.

89. Mitchell, "First Generation," p. 185.

90. Ibid., pp. 190–191.

91. Ibid., pp. 191–192.

92. Ibid., p. 193.

93. Ibid., p. 193.

94. Ibid., p. 192.

95. Ibid.

96. Ibid., p. 186.

97. Ibid., pp. 187–188.

98. Ibid., p. 189.

99. Lucio Gatto, "Understanding the 'Fear of Flying' Syndrome, II: Psychosomatic Aspects and Treatment," *U.S. Armed Forces Medical Journal*, vol. 5, no. 9 (1954), p. 1285.

100. Strongin, "Historical Review," p. 265.

101. An analysis of classes 52-E, F, and G, reveals that an average of 7.5 percent of those eliminated were washed out due to fear of flying. "History of the Flying Training Air Force," 1 January-30 June 1952, vol. 2, pp. 627–670.

102. Report of the Conference, Primary Pilot Training, Headquarters Flying Training Air Force, Roosevelt Hotel, Waco, Texas, in "History of the Flying Training Air Force," 1 July-31 December 1952, vol. 1, pp. 578–585.

103. A more recent study by the Naval Aviation Medical Institute in 1964 suggests that aviation students afflicted with FOF do not want to fly "not so much because of a fear of death but because of their inability to deal with conflicts precipitated by the more mundane aspects of learning to fly (e.g., frequent tests, and relationships with instructors). These students often expressed their FOF overtly through motion sickness. Strongin, "Historical Review," p. 266.

104. "History of the Flying Training Air Force," 1 July-31 December 1952, vol. 1, p. 63; "History of the Flying Training Air Force," 1 January-30 June 1953, vol. 1, p. 83.

105. "History of the Flying Training Air Force," 1 July-31 December 1952, vol. 1, p. 98.

106. Headquarters Flying Training Air Force, "Statistical Digest," 30 September 1952, p. 16 in "History of the Flying Training Air Force," 1 July-31 December 1952, vol. 2, p. 765.

107. Berke interview.

108. Brown, "A Fighter Pilot's Story," p. 8.

109. Ibid.

110. Ibid., p. 9; Berke interview.

111. Brown, "A Fighter Pilot's Story," p. 10.

112. Ibid., p. 11.

113. Ibid.

114. Although this accident actually occurred at Brown's Advanced training at Nellis, I included it here because it is a good example of how G forces can kill a novice pilot. Brown interview; Brown, "A Fighter Pilot's Story," p. 16.

115. Berke interview.

116. Turner interview.

117. Berke papers, "Williams Analysis"; Berke interview.

118. Charles Watry, *Washout: The Aviation Cadet Story* (Carlsbad: California Aero Press, 1983), p. 118.

119. Dixon was later killed in a plane crash at Rametelli in Italy. Crockett interview.

120. Crockett interview.

121. "History of the Flying Training Air Force," 1 July-31 December 1952, vol. 1, p. 99; "History of the Flying Training Air Force," 1 January-30 June 1952, vol. 1, p. 62.

122. Berke interview.

123. "History of the Flying Training Air Force," 1 January-30 June 1952, vol. 2, p. 634.

124. Thirteen French, three Dutch, and two British; Berke papers.

125. Brown interview.

126. Interestingly, this same cadet later became the head of the Danish FAA. Turner interview.

127. Brown, "A Fighter Pilot's Story," pp. 6–7.

128. Management Analysis Division, Air Force Training Command, "Analysis of Class 52-E," in "The History of the Flying Training Air Force," 1 January-30 June 1952, vol. 2, p. 629.

129. Everett Dodd, "The Tale of 'Tiger,' " *Air Force Magazine,* July 1953, p. 72.

130. Wayne Thompson, "The Air War in Korea," in Bernard Nalty, ed., "History of the United States Air Force 1907–1982" (unpublished manuscript, Center for Air Force History, Washington, D.C., 1992), p. 279.

131. Berke interview.

132. Ibid.

133. Brown, "A Fighter Pilot's Story," p. 14.

134. Ibid.

135. Mike Spick, *The Ace Factor: Air Combat and the Role of Situational Awareness* (Annapolis, Md.: Naval Institute Press, 1988), p. 128.

136. Brown, "A Fighter Pilot's Story," p. 14.

137. Spick, "Ace Factor," p. 128.

138. Tomlinson interview.

139. Berke interview.

140. Tomlinson interview.

141. J. G. Potter, "Sarge Looks at Today's Cadet," *Air Force Times,* 16 September 1950, p. 16.

142. Dodd, "Tale of 'Tiger,' " pp. 72–79; Potter, "Sarge," p. 16.

143. Ibid.

144. Tomlinson Interview.

145. "History of the Flying Training Air Force," 1 July–31 December 1952, vol. 1, pp. 74–75.

146. Dodd, "Tale of 'Tiger,' " p. 75.

147. "History of the Flying Training Air Force," 1 July–31 December 1952, vol. 1, p. 75.

148. Dodd, "Tale of 'Tiger,' " p. 76.

149. "History of the Flying Training Air Force," 1 July–31 December 1952, vol. 1, p. 76.

150. Dodd, "Tale of 'Tiger,' " p. 75.

151. "History of the Flying Training Air Force," 1 July–31 December 1952, vol. 1, pp. 75–76.

152. Dodd, "Tale of 'Tiger,' " p. 75.

153. Berke interview.

154. Ibid.

155. Mitchell, "First Generation," pp. 728–730.

Notes to Chapter 4

1. Kills are split in half when shots on a downed aircraft are registered by the gun cameras of both the shooter and his wingman.

2. S. L. A. Marshall, *Men against Fire: The Problem of Battle Command in Future War* (New York: William Morrow, 1947), p. 154. It should be mentioned that in 1988, historian Roger Spiller attempted to verify, by reviewing the documentation for *Men against Fire,* Marshall's claim that no more than 15 percent of all U.S. infantrymen in World War II ever fired their weapon. Much to the dismay of John Keegan, Russell Weigley, and other military historians who have relied on Marshall's numbers to support their claims, Spiller found no evidence that Marshall had done the five hundred-company level interviews as he had claimed in his book. Marshall's surviving field notebooks also show no signs of statistical calculations that suggest a 15 to 1 ratio of fire. Despite these rather disturbing findings, the primary group theory has yet to be dismantled in military circles. Works that adhere to the theory, such as John Keegan's *The Face of Battle* (New York: Viking, 1976), continue to be assigned at the military

academies and war colleges, and infantry concepts derived from the theory, such as the fire team concept, are still a part of modern U.S. Army doctrine. For more on the controversies surrounding *Men against Fire,* see Fredric Smoler, "The Secret of the Soldiers Who Didn't Shoot," *American Heritage,* March 1989, pp. 5, 35–45.

3. Breaking radio silence was considered a very serious breach of discipline. In one particular incident, pilot Frank Baker "raised more than eyebrows" when he accidentally broke radio silence and sang "Daddy's Little Girl" in a deep Southern baritone over the radio net. According to another pilot who was flying that day, "It was absolutely hairy." See "Baker Breaks Silence with Cradle Song," *Air Force Times,* 1 September 1951, p. 14.

4. Walker Mahurin, *Honest John* (New York: Putnam, 1962), p. 50.

5. Ibid., p. 30.

6. James Salter, *The Hunters* (New York: Bantam, 1956), p. 152.

7. George Berke, "Greenfields" (unpublished manuscript, Reston, Virginia, 1992), p. 42.

8. The term "peak experience" was coined by the psychologist Abraham Maslow and refers to the transcendent experiences which one occasionally feels during intense lovemaking, moments of religious ecstasy, or even while viewing a natural wonder such as a sunset on a clear evening. See Abraham Maslow, *Religions, Values, and Peak Experiences* (Columbus: Ohio State University Press, 1964).

9. Robinson Risner, *The Passing of the Night: My Seven Years as a Prisoner of the North Vietnamese* (New York: Random House, 1973), p. 53.

10. John Sherwood, "Air Interdiction during the Korean War: An American Solution to War in the Developing World" (Master's thesis, Columbia University, 1991), p. 6.

11. Mike Spick, *The Ace Factor: Air Combat and the Role of Situational Awareness* (Annapolis, Md.: Naval Institute Press), p. 29.

12. Richard Hallion, *The Naval Air War in Korea* (Baltimore: Nautical and Aviation Publishing, 1986), pp. 28–29.

13. Robert Futrell, *The United States Air Force in Korea, 1950–1953* (Washington, D.C.: Center for Air Force History, 1983), p. 98.

14. Ibid., p. 102.

15. Ibid., pp. 219, 244.

16. Thomas Jarnette, "4th Fighter-Interceptor Group Operations in MiG Alley," 17 June 1953, Records of the Fourth Fighter Wing, Center for Air Force History, Washington D.C., pp. 13–14. Hereafter, "Operations in MiG Alley."

17. Hallion, *Naval Air War in Korea,* p. 151.

18. Ibid.

19. Mahurin, *Honest John,* p. 177.

20. Ibid., p. 33.

21. Ibid.

22. Hallion, *Naval Air War in Korea*, p. 151.

23. "Operations in MiG Alley," p. 3.

24. Futrell, *U.S. Air Force in Korea*, p. 419.

25. Jon Halliday, "A Secret War: U.S. and Soviet Air Forces Clashed Directly in Korea," *Far Easter Economic Review,* 22 April 1993, pp. 32–36.

26. It was suspected that these "honchos" were mostly Soviet veterans of World War II; Brown interview.

27. Futrell, *U.S. Air Force in Korea*, p. 414–415; Hagerstrom interview.

28. Fifth Air Force, "Intelligence Summary," 28 December 1951, as cited by Eduard Mark, "Aerial Interdiction: Air Power and the Land Battle in Three American Wars" (unpublished manuscript, Center for Air Force History, Washington, D.C., 1992), pp. 313–314.

29. Futrell, *U.S. Air Force in Korea*, pp. 411, 414.

30. Ibid., pp. 608–609.

31. In one particular instance, a flight of MiGs even strafed a comrade who had bailed out over the Yellow Sea in an effort to keep his identity a secret. See Hallion, *Naval Air War in Korea*, pp. 152–153.

32. A leading edge is the edge of an airfoil, as of a wing, propeller, or stabilizer, which first meets or bites the air.

33. Marcelle Size Knaack, *Post-World War II Fighters: 1945–1973* (Washington, D.C.: Center for Air Force History, 1986), pp. 61, 80–81; Futrell, *U.S. Air Force in Korea*, p. 512.

34. Spick, *The Ace Factor,* pp. 28–29.

35. Author interview with Blake Morrison, editor, *USAF Fighter Weapons Review* (57TSS/TSM), 4269 Tyndall Avenue, Suite 104, Nellis AFB, Nevada 89191–6074, 19 June 1995. Mr. Morrison is one of the leading Air Force experts in fighter tactics.

36. Spick, *The Ace Factor,* p. 129.

37. Frederick C. Blesse, "No Guts—No Glory," as reprinted in Spick, *The Ace Factor,* pp. 177–202.

38. Brown interview.

39. Tomlinson interview.

40. Robin Olds as cited by Spick, *The Ace Factor,* p. 150.

41. Frederick Blesse, *Check Six: A Fighter Pilot Looks Back* (Mesa, Ariz.: Champlin Fighter Museum Press), pp. 63–64.

42. Randall Cunningham as cited by Spick, *The Ace Factor,* p. 152.

43. Tomlinson interview.

44. "Operations in MiG Alley," p. 31.

45. Mahurin, *Honest John,* pp. 34–35.

46. "Operations in MiG Alley," p. 18.

47. Brown interview; "Operations in MiG Alley," p. 18.

48. Mahurin, *Honest John,* p. 34.

49. Hagerstrom interview.

50. The subject of pilot alcoholism will be examined in greater detail in chapter 5.

51. Brown interview.

52. Ibid.; Tomlinson interview.

53. Brown interview.

54. Ibid.

55. "Operations in MiG Alley," p. 18.

56. Ibid.

57. Manuel "Pete" Fernandez, Jr., Foreword, "Operations in MiG Alley," p. iii.

58. "Operations in MiG Alley," pp. 5–6; Risner, *Passing of the Night,* p. 50.

59. Mahurin, *Honest John,* p. 35.

60. Hagerstrom interview.

61. "Operations in MiG Alley," p. 21.

62. Spick, *The Ace Factor,* p. 126; Hagerstrom interview.

63. Mahurin, *Honest John,* p. 31.

64. Ibid., p. 62.

65. Pomeroy interview.

66. Special Report, The Records of the 4th Fighter Wing, June 1952, Center for Air Force History, Washington, D.C.

67. After-Action Report, Records of the 4th Fighter-Interceptor Wing, October 1952, Center for Air Force History, Washington, D.C.

68. Mission Report, HQ, 4th Fighter-Interceptor Group, 4 November 1951, Records of the 4th Fighter-Interceptor Group.

69. This maneuver is a series of turn reversals performed in an effort to achieve an offensive position after an attacker has been forced into a flight path overshoot.

70. Mark C. Cleary, "Interview of Brigadier General Robinson Risner," Austin, Texas, 1–2 March 1983, United States Air Force Oral History Program, Center for Air Force History, Washington, D.C., pp. 33–35.

71. "No Guts, No Glory" as cited by Spick, *The Ace Factor,* p. 191.

72. Salter, *The Hunters,* p. 26.

73. Mahurin, *Honest John,* p. 31.

74. During the Korean War, it was not unusual for pilots from other U.N. nations to be integrated into a wing or even a squadron. Marines also occasionally served in temporary additional duty (TAD) slots with such wings as the Fourth.

75. Hagerstrom interview.

76. Hagerstrom interview.

77. Turner interview.

78. Salter, *The Hunter,* pp. 152–153.

79. Turner interview.

80. Ibid.

81. Hagerstrom interview.

82. Jon Halliday, "A Secret War: U.S. and Soviet Air Forces Clashed Directly over Korea," *Far Eastern Econ. Rev.,* 22 April 1993.

83. Blesse, *Check Six,* p. 67.

84. Hagerstrom interview.

85. Blesse, *Check Six,* p. 71.

86. Hagerstrom interview.

87. Ibid.

88. A previous kill of Hagerstrom's was later confirmed, bringing his overall total to 8.5; Hagerstrom interview.

89. Risner, *Passing of the Night,* p. 53.

90. Blesse, *Check Six,* p. 65.

91. Hagerstrom interview.

92. Ibid.

93. Mahurin, *Honest John,* p. 125.

94. Ibid., p. 126.

95. Blesse, *Check Six,* p. 65.

96. "Cultural studies," claims historian Emily Rosenberg, "is not a methodology but an approach, based upon interrelationships and context, that is concerned with rethinking categories of knowledge and examining forms of power. . . . The boundaries of such conventional binaries may be bridged by the concept of 'discourse,' which deals with interrelationships between the construction of institutions that embody power and the symbolic codes that constitute 'truth' or 'naturalness.' Discursive analysis can highlight connections between seemingly unrelated categories of experience"; see " 'Foreign Affairs' after World War II," *Diplomatic History,* vol. 18, no. 1 (Winter 1994), p. 60.

97. Hagerstrom interview.

98. Berke, "Greenfields," p. 140.

99. Ibid., p. 87.

100. Salter, *The Hunters,* p. 173.

101. Ibid.

102. Blesse, *Check Six,* p. 69.

103. Salter, *The Hunters,* p. 57.

104. Ibid.

105. Ibid., p. 55.

106. Ibid., p. 66.

107. Ibid.

108. Hagerstrom interview.

109. James Brooks, interview with John Dick, Jr., 5 February 1977, United States Air Force Oral History Collection, Center for Air Force History, Washington D.C.

110. Blesse, *Check Six,* p. 71.

Notes to Chapter 5

1. James Salter, *The Hunters* (New York: Bantam, 1956), p. 128.

2. Ibid., p. 154.

3. Ibid., p. 47.

4. Ibid., p. 109.

5. Ibid., pp. 183–184.

6. Like Salter (a pilot with the 4th Wing), Walt Sheldon had extensive firsthand experience with fighter pilots. As a combat journalist in Korea, not only did he live with pilots, but he even flew missions in a T-6 forward air controller.

7. Forward air control duty involved traveling in a jeep near the front line and calling in air strikes as they were needed. Jets were too fast and carried too little fuel to search out targets for themselves. Thus, they needed FACs to identify targets and guide them to them.

8. Walt Sheldon, *Troubling of a Star* (Chicago: Sears Book Club, 1953), p. 70.

9. Ibid., p. 33.

10. Robert F. Futrell, *The United States Air Force in Korea, 1950–1953* (Washington, D.C.: Center for Air Force History, 1983), p. 692.

11. Sturgeon interview.

12. Heiner interview; M. J. Bailey, diary for 1952, original with author, Diamond Bar, Calif.

13. Historical Report of the 51st Fighter-Interceptor Group assigned to the 51st Fighter-Interceptor Wing for October 1951, p. 3.

14. FEAF Command Report, vol. 1, August 1951, Records of the United Nations Far Eastern Command, Record Group 407, National Archives, Suitland Annex, Washington, D.C., p. 4.

15. Perrin Gower, interview with author, 3 February 1993, Center for Air Force History, Washington, D.C.

16. Bailey, 22 June 1952.

17. Heiner interview.

18. FEAF Command Report, vol. 1, February 1951, Tab B.

19. Heiner interview; Summary of Aircraft Loss (Forbes), 18th Fighter Bomber Wing, 5th Air Force, Far East Air Forces, Historical Report, January-June 1953, Records of the 18th Fighter Bomber Wing, Center for Air Force History, Washington, D.C.

20. Heiner interview; Summary of Aircraft Loss (Forbes).

21. Heiner interview.

22. Bailey, 23 April 1952.

23. Bailey, 25 April 1952.

24. Sturgeon interview.

25. Bailey, 12 April 52.

26. E. R. James, taped dictation for author, St. Louis, MO, 22 April 1993.

27. Bailey diary, 20 May 1952.

28. Gower interview.

29. Douglas Evans, *Sabre Jets over Korea: A Firsthand Account* (Blue Ridge Summit, Pa.: Tab Books, 1984), pp. 84–85. This book is based on the diary Evans kept as a Sabre pilot in Korea.

30. Bailey, 11 February 52.

31. Heiner interview.

32. Bailey, 14 May 52.

33. Bailey, 30 June 52.

34. Operations Analysis Office Memorandum No. 43, p. 67.

35. Operations Analysis Office Memorandum No. 43, p. 68.

36. Sheldon, *Troubling of a Star,* p. 42. Ironically, Bailey met Sheldon during the war and took him up in a two-seat T-33 to record a battle between F-86s and MiGs. Sheldon got some "good stuff, but broke one of his eardrums letting down at K-2." Bailey "sure felt badly about it but couldn't let down any other way." Bailey, 23 June 1952.

37. Jerry Minton, taped dictation, Fort Worth, Texas, 1 May 1995.

38. Ibid.

39. Sheldon, *Troubling of a Star,* p. 28.

40. Operations Analysis Office Memorandum No. 43, pp. 42–44.

41. Sturgeon interview.

42. Ibid.

43. Ibid.

44. William Elder, interview with James Hasdorff, 13 September 1984, United States Air Force Oral History Collection, Center for Air Force History, Washington, D.C., p. 93.

45. Sturgeon interview.

46. Berke interview.

47. Pomeroy interview.

48. Bailey, 14 April 52.

49. Minton dictation.

50. Lucio Gatto, "Understanding the 'Fear of Flying' Syndrome, II," *U.S. Armed Forces Medical Journal,* vol. 5, no. 9 (1954), p. 1285.

51. H. A. Schultz, "Fear of Flying," *USAF Medical Service Digest,* November 1952, pp. 29–31.

52. Gatto, "Understanding the 'Fear of Flying' Syndrome, II," p. 1285.

53. Lucio E. Gatto, "Understanding the 'Fear of Flying' Syndrome," *U.S. Armed Forces Medical Journal,* vol. 5, no. 8 (1954), p. 1110.

54. Ibid., p. 1114.

55. Robert Lifton, "Psychotherapy with Combat Fliers," *U.S. Armed Forces Medical Journal,* vol. 4, no. 4 (April 1953), p. 529.

56. Ibid., p. 530.

57. James dictation.

58. Dean Price, letter to 80th Squadron Association, as reprinted in "80th Squadron Headhunters Squadron History" (80th Squadron Association, 16 May 1995).

59. Evans, *Sabre Jets over Korea,* p. 140.

60. Late in the war, the Air Force did deploy an F-84 variant with swept wings; the vast majority of F-84s in Korea were the straight-wing variety. Evans, *Sabre Jets over Korea,* p. 138.

61. Minton interview.

62. Kenneth Koon, interview with author, tape recording, Danvers, Mass., 7 January 1993.

63. Sheldon, *Troubling of a Star,* p. 144.

64. "80th Fighter Squadron Headhunters Squadron History," p. 6.

65. Sturgeon interview.

66. Ibid. The Silver Star was granted for gallantry to persons serving in any capacity with the Air Force when an action did not warrant the Medal of Honor or the Distinguished Service Cross. For more on Air Force medals during this period, see Air Force Regulation AFR-35–50, *Service Medals.*

67. History of the 51st Fighter Interceptor Wing, 1 January-30 June 1953.

68. *The Truckbuster,* vol. 1, no. 20 (15 April 1952), 18th Fighter-Bomber Wing, Dogpatch, Korea, Records of the 18th Fighter-Bomber Wing, Center for Air Force History, Washington, D.C., p. 3.

69. Ibid.

70. Ibid.

71. Ibid.

72. Ibid.

73. Sturgeon interview.

74. Heiner interview.

75. Berke interview.

Notes to Chapter 6

1. Nancy Shea, *The Air Force Wife* (New York: Harper, 1951), pp. 4–5.

2. Robert Futrell, *The United States Air Force in Korea, 1950–1953* (Washington, D.C.: Center for Air Force History, 1983), pp. 62–63.

3. Ibid., p. 63.

4. Ibid., p. 66.

5. Sturgeon interview.

6. Berke interview.

7. Dean Hess, *Battle Hymn* (New York: McGraw-Hill, 1956), p. 148.

8. Turner interview.

9. Berke interview.

10. Hess, *Battle Hymn*, pp. 80–81.

11. Futrell, *U.S. Air Force in Korea*, p. 233.

12. Hess, *Battle Hymn*, p. 93–94.

13. Sturgeon interview.

14. Futrell, *U.S. Air Force in Korea*, p. 65.

15. Ibid., p. 110.

16. Ibid., p. 394.

17. Ibid., pp. 112, 399–400.

18. Ranald Adams, interview with author, tape recording, Alexandria, Virginia, 21 October 1993.

19. Hess, *Battle Hymn*, p. 94.

20. Futrell, *U.S. Air Force in Korea*, p. 395.

21. Tomlinson interview.

22. Turner interview.

23. Tomlinson interview.

24. James Salter, *The Hunters* (New York: Bantam, 1956), p. 34.

25. Heiner interview.

26. Douglas Evans, *Sabre Jets over Korea* (Blue Ridge Summit, Pa.: Tab Books, 1984), p. 120.

27. Don Parker as cited in Dermot Moore and Peter Bagshawe, *South Africa's Flying Cheetahs in Korea* (Johannesburg: Ashanti Publishing, 1991), pp. 237–238.

28. Don Parker as cited in ibid., pp. 237–238.

29. Ibid.

30. Brian Martin as cited in ibid., p. 250.

31. Evans, *Sabre Jets over Korea*, p. 86.

32. Ibid., p. 65.
33. Tomlinson interview.
34. Historical Report of the 51st Fighter Interceptor Wing, Twentieth Air Force, Far East Air Forces for December 1951.
35. Sturgeon interview.
36. Koon interview.
37. Heiner interview.
38. History of the 4th Fighter Interceptor Wing, 1 July-31 December 1951.
39. Tomlinson interview.
40. History of the 4th Fighter Interceptor Wing, 1 July-31 December 1952.
41. Brown interview.
42. Blesse, *Check Six,* p. 61.
43. Evans, *Sabre Jets over Korea,* p. 141.
44. History of the 4th Fighter Interceptor Wing, October 1952.
45. Historical Report of the 51st Fighter Interceptor Wing, Twentieth Air Force, Far East Air Forces for December 1951.
46. Evans, *Sabre Jets over Korea,* p. 141.
47. Koon interview.
48. Ibid.
49. Letter from Dean Price to the 80th Squadron Association, "80th Squadron Headhunter Squadron History," p. 28.
50. Tomlinson interview.
51. Walt Sheldon, *Troubling of a Star* (Chicago: Sears Book Club, 1953), p. 64.
52. Crockett interview.
53. Koon interview.
54. Ibid.
55. Hagerstrom interview.
56. Brown, who often got sick during training, never drank before flying.
57. Brown interview.
58. Sturgeon interview.
59. Koon interview.
60. Robert Scott Shaw as cited in Moore and Bagshawe, *Flying Cheetahs,* pp. 87–88.
61. Moore and Bagshawe, *Flying Cheetahs,* p. 88.
62. Gower interview.
63. History of the 4th Fighter Interceptor Wing, 1 July-31 December 1952.
64. Evans, *Sabre Jets over Korea,* p. 199.
65. Ibid., p. 19.
66. Brown interview.
67. Shea, *Air Force Wife,* p. 67.

68. Ibid., pp. 191–192.

69. Ibid.

70. Salter, *The Hunters*, p. 17.

71. Heiner interview.

72. "Round eyes" is a derogatory term used by U.S. serviceman to refer to Western women in Asia.

73. "Clubmobile Service," statement prepared by American Red Cross on its Overseas Experience in World War II for use of the Assembly Committee on Service to the Armed Forces, Gift Collection Records of the American Red Cross, 1947–1964, 900.616 AT (FEA) SRAO, 1952–57, Box 1858, Record Group 200, National Archives, Suitland Annex. For more information on Red Cross activities during World War II, see Oscar Whitelaw Rexford, *Battlestars and Doughnuts: World War II Clubmobile Experiences of Mary Metcalfe Rexford* (St. Louis: Patrice Press, 1989).

74. "General Summary Report American Red Cross Club Program—Korea, November 1950-June 1952," 900.11/616 Recreation FETO—Korea, Records of the American Red Cross, 1947–1964, Box 2020.

75. Brief Summary of the Supplemental Recreational Activities Overseas, American Red Cross Clubmobile Service in Korea, October 1953-October 1954, Gift Collection Records of the American Red Cross, 1947–1964, 900.616 AT (FEA) SRAO, 1952–57, Box 1858.

76. Marie-Louise Van Vechten, "Narrative Report: K-9 Canteen, Pusan, Korea," 30 April 1951, 900.11/616 Club and Recreation Program Establishment in 1950 and History to 31 March 1952, Records of the American Red Cross, 1947–1964, Box 2020.

77. Ibid.

78. "The 80th Fighter Squadron Headhunter Squadron History," p. 28.

79. Letter from Robert C. Lewis, Red Cross Vice President, to Major General James Richardson, Deputy Chief of Staff for Personnel, Department of the Army, 13 April 1960, 900.11/91 FETO—Criticisms and Controversial Subjects, Records of the American Red Cross, 1947–1964, NARA Suitland, RG200, Box 2021; Recruitment Flyer, 900.616 AT (FEA) SRAO 1952–57, Records of the American Red Cross, 1947–1964, Box 1858.

80. Memorandum to Robert C. Lewis from Robert Wilson, 11 April 1960, 900.11/91 FETO—Criticisms and Controversial Subjects, Records of the American Red Cross, 1947–1964, Box 2021.

81. G. B. Kuebler to Basil O'Connor, 14 January 1948, 900.11/91 FETO—Criticisms and Controversial Subjects, Records of the American Red Cross, 1947–1964, Box 2021.

82. Letter from Frank Cleverly, Administrator for Foreign Operations, American Red Cross, to Robert Lewis, Commissioner, American Red Cross, 3

March 1948, 900.11/91 FETO—Criticisms and Controversial Subjects, Records of the American Red Cross, 1947–1964, Box 2021.

83. Jessica Hunter, "A Day with the Red Cross Clubmobile Girls in Korea," 900.11/616 Club and Recreation Program Establishment in 1950 and History to 31 March 1952, Records of the American Red Cross, 1947–1964, Box 2020.

84. "General Summary Report, American Red Cross Club Program—Korea, November 1950-June 1952," 900.11/616 Recreation FETO—Korea, Records of the American Red Cross, 1947–1964, Box 2020.

85. Turner interview.

86. History of the 4th Fighter Interceptor Wing, 1 July-31 February 1952.

87. History of the 4th Fighter Interceptor Wing, October 1952, February 1953.

88. When he developed the pictures, Satterlee had considered making Rooney eight-by-ten glossy photos, but decided on five-by-sevens because he thought they would be easier to carry. Francis Satterlee, interview with author, tape recording, Washington, D.C., 19 February 1993.

89. Moore and Bagshawe, *Flying Cheetahs,* pp. 221–222.

90. Ibid.

91. Turner interview.

92. Historical Report of the 51st Fighter Interceptor Wing, Twentieth Air Force, Far East Air Forces for May 1951.

93. Historical Report of the 51st Fighter Interceptor Wing, Twentieth Air Force, Far East Air Forces for February 1952.

94. Berke interview.

95. Turner interview.

96. 18th Fighter Bomber Wing, Fifth Air Force, Far East Air Forces, Historical Report, January-June 1953.

97. John Minturn Verdi, "First Hundred: A Memoir of the Korean War, 1952–1953" (unpublished manuscript, Northport, Ala., 1988), p. 40.

98. Ibid., p. 40; Tomlinson interview.

99. Turner interview.

100. Ibid.

101. Verdi, "First Hundred," p. 41.

102. Berke, "Greenfields," p. 88.

103. Ibid.

104. Gower interview.

105. Sheldon, *Troubling of a Star,* p. 240–241; Salter, *The Hunters,* pp. 108–109.

106. History of the 4th Fighter Interceptor Wing, October 1951.

107. *The Truckbuster,* vol. 1, no. 18 (17 March 52).

108. 18th Fighter Bomber Wing, Fifth Air Force, Far East Air Forces, Historical Report, January-June 1953.

109. Berke interview.

110. Bailey diary, 19 April 1951.

111. Bailey diary, 17 April 1952.

112. Heiner interview.

113. Jock Lello as cited in Moore and Bagshawe, *Flying Cheetahs,* pp. 240–241.

114. Sturgeon interview.

115. James dictation.

116. Brown interview.

117. Evans, *Sabre Jets over Korea,* p. 10.

118. Moore and Bagshawe, *Flying Cheetahs,* p. 11.

119. History of the 4th Fighter Interceptor Wing, January 1953.

120. *The Truckbuster,* vol. 1, no. 22 (16 May 52).

121. History of the 4th Fighter Interceptor Wing, 1 July–31 December 1952.

122. Ibid.

123. Tomlinson interview; James dictation; Lottinger interview.

124. Roy Lottinger, interview with author, tape recording, 7 January 1993, Amherst, N.H.

125. Historical Report of the 51st Fighter Interceptor Wing for May 1951.

126. History of the 4th Fighter Interceptor Wing, October 1951.

127. 18th Fighter Bomber Wing, Fifth Air Force, Far East Air Forces, Historical Report, January–June 1953.

128. Berke interview.

129. Ibid.

130. Dick Clifton as cited in Moore and Bagshawe, *Flying Cheetahs,* pp. 213–214.

131. Berke interview.

132. Turner interview.

133. Tomlinson interview.

134. Crockett interview.

135. Evans, *Sabre Jets over Korea,* p. 228.

136. Turner interview.

137. Berke interview.

138. Hess, *Battle Hymn,* p. 159.

139. Ibid.

140. Ibid.

141. Adams interview.

142. Tomlinson interview; Heiner interview; Brown interview; Gower interview.

143. Blesse, *Check Six,* p. 61.

144. Tomlinson interview.

145. Gower interview.

146. Tomlinson interview.

147. William Wallrich, "Bedcheck Charlie Flies Again," *Air Force,* vol. 36, no. 9 (September 1953), pp. 108–113.

148. Futrell, *U.S. Air Force in Korea,* p. 664.

149. Wallrich, "Bedcheck Charlie," pp. 108–113; Futrell, *U.S. Air Force in Korea,* p. 665.

150. Futrell, *U.S. Air Force in Korea,* pp. 310–312, 662–666.

151. Bailey diary, 16 June 1952.

152. Futrell, *U.S. Air Force in Korea,* pp. 662–664.

153. History of the 4th Fighter Interceptor Wing, 1 July–31 January 1952.

154. Tomlinson interview.

155. Ibid.

156. Gower interview.

157. Futrell, *U.S. Air Force in Korea,* pp. 665–666.

Notes to Chapter 7

1. Tomlinson interview.

2. Ibid.

3. The sources for this section are as follows: Risner interview, 21 May 1995; Mark C. Cleary, "Interview of Brigadier General Robinson Risner," Austin, Texas, 1–2 March 1983, United States Air Force Oral History Program, Center for Air Force History, Washington, D.C.; T. R. Milton, "Robinson Risner: The Indispensable Ingredient," in John L. Frisbee, ed., *The Makers of the United States Air Force* (Washington, D.C.: Center for Air Force History, 1987); and Robinson Risner, *The Passing of the Night: My Seven Years as a Prisoner of the North Vietnamese* (New York: Random House, 1973).

4. Brown interview.

5. William Earl Brown, "A Fighter Pilot's Story," Charles A. Lindbergh Memorial Lecture, 21 May 1992, National Air and Space Museum Occasional Paper Series no. 4, pp. 35–36.

6. Ibid.

7. Brown interview.

8. Ibid.

9. Marcelle Size Knaack, *Post-World War II Fighters: 1945–1973* (Washington, D.C.: Center for Air Force History, 1986), p. 207.

10. Crockett interview.

11. Tomlinson interview.

12. Ibid.

13. Ibid.

14. Pomeroy interview.

15. Ibid.

16. "Little Switch" was the swap of sick and wounded POWs that occurred between 20 April and 3 May 1953. The U.N. turned over a total of 6,670 Communist POWs, and in return received 684 POWs. See Clay Blair, *The Forgotten War: America in Korea, 1950–1953* (New York: Anchor Books, 1987), p. 972.

17. Turner interview.

18. Ibid.

19. Ibid.

20. Ibid.

21. Bailey interview.

22. Ibid.

23. Berke interview.

24. Ibid.

25. Ibid.

26. Ibid.

27. Ibid.

28. Ibid.

29. Berke interview; 201 File for George Berke and "Work History," personal papers of George Berke, Reston, Virginia.

30. Heiner interview.

31. Ibid.

32. Ibid.

33. Risner, *Passing of the Night,* p. 5.

34. Sturgeon interview.

35. Ibid.

36. Hagerstrom interview.

37. Ibid.

38. Ibid.

39. Ibid.

40. Dee Harper, F-86 Sabre Pilots Association recruitment letter, 13 September 1994.

41. Ibid.

Notes to Chapter 8

1. The name of the pilot is withheld at the pilot's request.

2. Robert Wilcox, *Scream of Eagles: The Creation of Top Gun and the U.S. Air Victory in Vietnam* (New York: John Wiley and Sons, 1990), pp. 212, 288.

3. Department of Defense, *Selected Manpower Statistics: Fiscal Year 1994*

(Washington, D.C.: Directorate for Information, Operations, and Reports, 1994), p. 15.

4. Erasmus, *Adagia,* 1588. This saying was adopted by the 80th Fighter Squadron after the Korean War and placed, in Latin, under the Headhunter patch.

Notes to Appendix 1

1. Hoyt Vandenberg as cited in Robert Futrell, *U.S. Air Force in Korea, 1950–1953* (Washington, D.C.: Center for Air Force History, 1983), pp. 46–47.

2. Richard Hallion, *The Naval Air War in Korea* (Baltimore: Nautical and Aviation Publishing, 1983), p. 205.

3. As of 28 June 1950, the FEAF order of battle stood as follows: "Two fighter-bomber wings and one interceptor wing (all with F-80C Shooting Stars), two all-weather fighter squadrons (F-82 Twin Mustangs), and an understrength light bombardment wing of B-26 Invaders. . . . It also had one group of B-29 Superfortresses, which by 1950 were classified as medium bombers. FEAF also had an additional F-80 wing, and one F-82 squadron, but these 20th Air Force units were reserved for the defense of Okinawa and the Marianas." Eduard Mark, "Aerial Interdiction" (unpublished manuscript, Center for Air Force History, Washington, D.C., 1982), p. 316.

4. Mark, "Aerial Interdiction," p. 272.

5. Ibid., p. 271.

6. Futrell, *U.S. Air Force in Korea,* pp. 88–89; Hallion, *Naval Air War in Korea,* p. 49.

7. Historical Report of the 51st Fighter-Interceptor Wing, Twentieth Air Force (Attached to Fifth Air Force) for September 1951, Records of the 51st Wing, Center for Air Force History, Washington, D.C., p. 6.

8. In all, napalm destroyed 71 percent of the observed aerial tank kills while rockets destroyed only 21 percent. Air University Far East Research Group, 2d Logistical Command, APO 59, Interdiction Bombing Experiences of Selected CCF and North Korean Army Units, Report No. 3, North Korean 10th Division, 6 May 1951, based on eighteen POW replies to AUFERG Questionnaire 2b, planned by Project RAND in collaboration with Operations Analysis, 5th Air Force, and Air University Far East Research Group by Alexander George, "Project RAND," Headquarters USAF, Records of the 5th Air Force, Center for Air Force History, Washington, D.C.; Hallion, *Naval Air War in Korea,* p. 49; Office of the Secretary of Defense, "Air War in Korea," *Air University Quarterly Review,* vol. 4, no. 2 (1953), p. 23.

9. Max Hastings, *The Korean War* (New York: Simon and Schuster, 1987), p. 257.

10. Mark, "Aerial Interdiction," pp. 273, 278; Edmund Dews and Felix Kozaczka, "Lessons from Past Campaigns," RAND #N-1743 (Santa Monica: RAND, 1980), p. 62; Robert Jackson, *The Air War over Korea* (New York: Charles Scribner's Sons, 1973, p. 23.

11. Mark, "Aerial Interdiction," p. 279.

12. Ibid., pp. 279–280.

13. Dews and Kozaczka, "Lessons from Past Campaigns," p. 61.

14. Ibid., p. 60.

15. Mark, "Aerial Interdiction," p. 281.

16. Interrogation Report, HQ 8th U.S. Army, Korea, Senior Colonel Lee Hak Ku, 21 September 1950, as cited by Mark, "Aerial Interdiction," p. 281.

17. David Rees, *Korea: The Limited War* (New York: St. Martin's Press, 1964), p. 291.

18. FEAF Bomber Command, "Heavyweights over Korea," as reprinted in James Stewart, ed., *Airpower: The Decisive Force in Korea* (New York: Arno, 1980), pp. 82–85.

19. Mark, "Aerial Interdiction," p. 299.

20. Mark Clodfelter, *The Limits of Air Power: The American Bombing of North Vietnam* (New York: Free Press, 1989), p. 17.

21. Mark, "Aerial Interdiction," p. 307.

22. Ibid.

23. Futrell, *U.S. Air Force in Korea*, pp. 437–442.

24. Gregory Carter, "Some Historical Notes on Air Interdiction in Korea," RAND #P3452 (Santa Monica: RAND, 1966), p. 2; Felix Kozaczka, "Air War in Korea: VI. Enemy Bridging Techniques," *Air University Quarterly Review*, vol. 5, no. 4 (1954), p. 50; M. J. Armitage and R. A. Mason, *Air Power in the Nuclear Age*, 2d ed. (Chicago: University of Chicago Press, 1985), p. 38.

25. Operations Analysis Office Memorandum No. 49, 19 November 1951, "An Evaluation of the Interdiction Program in Korea," Donald Schiller, Analyst, RG342, Box 3518, National Archives, Suitland Annex, pp. 1–9.

26. Mark, "Aerial Interdiction," p. 309.

27. Futrell, *U.S. Air Force in Korea*, p. 439.

28. Hallion, *Naval Air War in Korea*, p. 92; Futrell, *U.S. Air Force in Korea*, p. 440.

29. Futrell, *U.S. Air Force in Korea*, p. 408.

30. Ibid., pp. 439–441.

31. Mark, "Aerial Interdiction," p. 312

32. Ibid., p. 313.

33. Ibid., pp. 313–314.

34. Jackson, *Air War over Korea*, p. 136.

35. Ibid.

36. Ibid.

37. Ibid., p. 138; Futrell, *U.S. Air Force in Korea,* pp. 447–453.

38. Futrell, *U.S. Air Force in Korea,* pp. 471–474; Kozaczka, "Enemy Bridging Techniques," p. 50.

39. Futrell, *U.S. Air Force in Korea,* pp. 471–474.

40. Headquarters, 5th Air Force, Operations Analysis Office, APO 970, Operations Analysis Office Memorandum No. 43, 21 May 1951, Physical and Psychological Effects of Interdiction Air Attacks as Determined from POW Interrogations, Analyst, Alexander George (TDY from RAND Corporation), Records of the Fifth Air Force, Center for Air Force History, Washington, D.C., pp. 81–82. Hereafter, Operations Analysis Office Memorandum No. 43.

41. Air University Far East Research Group, 2d Logistical Command, APO 59, Interdiction Bombing Experiences of Selected CCF and North Korean Army Units, Report No. 1, 12 April 1951, based on eighteen POW replies to AUFERG Questionnaire 2b, planned by Project RAND in collaboration with Operations Analysis, Fifth Air Force, and Air University Far East Research Group, Records of the Fifth Air Force, Center for Air Force History, Washington, D.C., pp. 13–16.

42. Dews and Kozaczka, "Lessons from Past Campaigns," p. 57.

43. Futrell, *U.S. Air Force in Korea,* pp.471–474.

44. David Rees, *Korea: The Limited War* (New York: St. Martin's Press, 1964), pp. 298–300.

45. Operations Analysis Office Memorandum No. 43, p. 2; General Headquarters, United Nations Command, Far East Command, May 1951, Records of the United Nations Far East Command, Record Group 407, National Archives, Suitland Annex, p. 28.

46. Futrell, *U.S. Air Force in Korea,* p. 473.

47. Carter, "Some Historical Notes on Interdiction," p. 14.

48. Hallion, *Naval Air War in Korea,* p. 105.

49. Although these figures cover the period between the beginning of the war and March 1952, most of the losses were incurred during the rail campaign starting in August 1952. See Jackson, *Air War over Korea,* p. 138 and Futrell, *U.S. Air Force in Korea,* p. 446.

50. Mark, "Aerial Interdiction," p. 317.

Note to Appendix 3

1. The source of both tables is Operations Statistics Division, Directorate of Statistical Services, United States Air Force, "Air Force Statistical Digest 1951" (Washington, D.C., 1952).

Bibliography

I. Unpublished Sources

After-Action Report. Records of the 4th Fighter-Interceptor Wing. October 1952. Center for Air Force History, Washington, D.C.

Air University Far East Research Group. 2d Logistical Command, APO 59. Interdiction Bombing Experiences of Selected CCF and North Korean Army Units. Report No. 1. 12 April 1951. Based on eighteen POW replies to AUFERG Questionnaire 2b. Planned by Project RAND in collaboration with Operations Analysis, Fifth Air Force and Air University Far East Research Group. Records of the Fifth Air Force. Center for Air Force History, Washington, D.C.

———. Interdiction Bombing Experiences of Selected CCF and North Korean Army Units. Report No. 3. North Korean 10th Division. 6 May 1951. Based on eighteen POW replies to AUFERG Questionnaire 2b. Planned by Project RAND in collaboration with Operations Analysis, Fifth Air Force, and Air University Far East Research Group by Alexander George. Headquarters USAF. Records of the Fifth Air Force. Center for Air Force History, Washington, D.C.

Bailey, M. J. Diary for 1952. Diamond Bar, Calif.

Berke, George. "Greenfields." Unpublished manuscript. 1992. Reston, Va.

———. Personal papers. Reston, Va.

Boyle, Charles. General Orders No. 3. Headquarters: 349th Field Artillery. 8 January 1942. Fort Sill, Okla.

Brown, William Earl. "A Fighter Pilot's Story." Charles A. Lindbergh Memorial Lecture. 21 May 1992. National Air and Space Museum Occasional Paper Series No. 4.

Caddell, Joseph William. "Orphan of Unification: The Development of United States Air Force Tactical Air Power Doctrine, 1945–1947." Ph.D. diss., Duke University, 1984.

Cameron, Rebecca Hancock. "To Fly: Military Flight Training, 1907–1945." Draft, historical manuscript. 1993. Center for Air Force History, Washington, D.C.

Carter, Gregory. "Some Historical Notes on Air Interdiction in Korea." RAND #P3452. Santa Monica: RAND, 1966.

Casey, Irving. "Social Origins and Career Patterns of United States Air Force Generals and Colonels." Ph.D. diss., American University, 1967.

Dews, Edmund, and Felix Kozaczka. "Lessons from Past Campaigns." RAND #N1743. Santa Monica: RAND, 1980.

18th Fighter Bomber Wing. Fifth Air Force. Far East Air Forces. Historical Report, January to June 1953. Center for Air Force History, Washington, D.C.

80th Fighter Bomber Association. "The 80th Fighter Squadron Headhunters Squadron History." Personal papers of Jerry Minton. Fort Worth, Texas.

FEAF Command Report. Volume I. August 1951. Records of the United Nations Far Eastern Command. Record Group 407. National Archives, Suitland Annex, Washington, D.C.

"Flying Training Air Force Statistical Digest." 31 July 1952. Records of the Flying Training Air Force. Center for Air Force History, Washington, D.C.

Harper, Dee. F-86 Sabre Pilots Association recruitment letter. 13 September 1994.

Headquarters, Fifth Air Force. Operations Analysis Office. APO 970. Operations Analysis Office Memorandum No. 43. 21 May 1951. "Physical and Psychological Effects of Interdiction Air Attacks as Determined from POW Interrogations." Analyst, Alexander George (TDY from RAND Corporation). Records of the Fifth Air Force. Center for Air Force History, Washington, D.C.

Historical Division, Flying Training Air Force. "History of the Flying Training Air Force," 1 January–30 June 1952, vols. 1 and 2; 1 July–31 December 1952, vols. 1 and 2; 1 January–30 June 1953, vols. 1 and 2. Waco, Texas. Center for Air Force History, Washington, D.C.

Historical Report of the 51st Fighter-Interceptor Wing. Twentieth Air Force (attached to Fifth Air Force). May, September, October, December 1951, and February 1952. Records of the 51st Wing. Center for Air Force History, Washington, D.C.

History of the 51st Fighter Interceptor Wing. 1 January 1953 to 30 June 1953.

History of the 4th Fighter-Interceptor Wing. 1 July-31 December 1951; October 1952; 1 July-31 December 1952; January, February, and October 1953. Center for Air Force History, Washington, D.C.

"History of the 349th Field Artillery." Headquarters: 349th Field Artillery. 1942. Fort Sill, Okla.

James, E. R. Taped dictation for author. St. Louis, Mo. 22 April 1993.

Jarnette, Thomas. "4th Fighter-Interceptor Group Operations in MiG Alley." 17 June 1953. Records of the 4th Fighter Wing. Center for Air Force History, Washington D.C.

Mark, Eduard. "Aerial Interdiction: Air Power and the Land Battle in Three American Wars." Unpublished manuscript, 1992. Center for Air Force History, Washington, D.C.

Mission Report. Headquarters: 4th Fighter-Interceptor Group. 4 November 1951. Records of the 4th Fighter-Interceptor Group. November 1951. Center for Air Force History, Washington, D.C.

Mitchell, Vance. "The First Generation: A Personnel Policy History of the Air Force Officer Corps, 1944–1974." Unpublished manuscript. 1992. Center for Air Force History, Washington, D.C.

Nalty, Bernard, ed. "History of the United States Air Force, 1907–1982." Unpublished manuscript. 1992. Center for Air Force History, Washington, D.C.

Operations Analysis Office Memorandum No. 43. General Headquarters. United Nations Command. Far East Command. May 1951. Records of the United Nations Far East Command. Record Group 407. National Archives, Suitland Annex, Washington, D.C.

Operations Analysis Office Memorandum No. 49. 19 November 1951. An Evaluation of the Interdiction Program in Korea. Donald Schiller, Analyst. RG342, Box 3518. National Archives, Suitland Annex., Washington, D.C.

Records of the American Red Cross, 1947–1964. 900.616 AT (FEA) SRAO, 1952–57. Boxes 1858, 2020, 2021. Record Group 200. National Archives, Suitland Annex, Washington, D.C.

Sherwood, John. "Air Interdiction during the Korean War: An American Solution to War in the Developing World." Master's thesis, Columbia University, 1991.

Special Report. The Records of the 4th Fighter Wing. June 1952. Center for Air Force History, Washington, D.C.

Summary of Aircraft Loss (Forbes). 18th Fighter Bomber Wing. Fifth Air Force. Far East Air Forces. Historical Report. January-June 1953. Records of the 18th Fighter Bomber Wing. Center for Air Force History, Washington, D.C.

"The Truckbuster." Vol. 1, no. 20 (15 April 1952); vol. 1, no. 18 (17 March 1952); vol. 1, no. 22 (16 May 1952). 18th Fighter-Bomber Wing. Dogpatch, Korea. Records of the 18th Fighter-Bomber Wing. Center for Air Force History, Washington, D.C.

Verdi, John Minturn. "First Hundred: A Memoir of the Korean War, 1952–1953." Unpublished manuscript. 1988. Northport, Ala.

II. Author Interviews and Oral Histories

Adams, Ranald. Interview with author. Tape recording. 21 October 1993. Alexandria, Virginia.

Bailey, M. J. Interview with author. Telephone interview. 9 September 1994. Washington, D.C.

Berke, George. Interview with author. Tape recording. 22 March 93. Center for Air Force History, Washington, D.C.

Brooks, James. Interview with John Dick, Jr. 5 February 1977. United States Air Force Oral History Collection. Center for Air Force History, Washington D.C.

Brown, William Earl. Interview with author. Tape recording. 7 April 1993. Center For Air Force History, Washington, D.C.

Crockett, Woodrow. Interview with author. Tape recording. 31 March 1993. Center for Air Force History, Washington, D.C.

Elder, William. Interview with James Hasdorff. 13 September 1984. United States Air Force Oral History Collection. Center for Air Force History, Washington, D.C.

Gower, Perrin. Interview with author. Tape recording. 21 October 1993. Alexandria, Virginia.

Hagerstrom, James. Interview with author. Tape recording. 3 February 1993. Center for Air Force History, Washington, D.C.

Heiner, Howard. Interview with author. Tape recording. 14 December 1992. Washington, D.C.

Koon, Kenneth. Interview with author. Tape recording. 7 January 1993. Danvers, Mass.

Lottinger, Roy. Interview with author. Tape recording. 7 January 1993. Amherst, N.H.

Minton, Jerry. Tape dictation. 16 May 1995. Fort Worth, Texas.

Pomeroy, Robert. Interview with author. Tape recording. 2 February 1993. Center for Air Force History, Washington, D.C.

Risner, Robinson. Interview with author. Tape recording. 21 May 1995. Washington, D.C.

———. Interview with Mark Cleary. 1–2 March 1983, Austin, Texas. Center for Air Force History, Washington, D.C.

Satterlee, Francis. Interview with author. Tape recording. 19 February 1993. Washington, D.C.

Sturgeon, Raymond. Interview with author. Tape recording. 21 June 1994. Bedford, Mass.

Tomlinson, Frank. Interview with author. Tape recording. 9 December 1992. Center for Air Force History. Washington, D.C.

Turner, Paul. Interview with author. Tape recording. 3 March 1993. Center for Air Force History, Washington, D.C.

III. Newspaper and Journal Articles

Air Force Times. 1 April 1950.

"Baker Breaks Silence with Cradle Song." *Air Force Times,* 1 September 1951.

Dodd, Everett. "The Tale of 'Tiger.' " *Air Force Magazine,* July 1953.

Gatto, Lucio. "Understanding the 'Fear of Flying' Syndrome." *U.S. Armed Forces Medical Journal,* vol. 5, no. 8 (1954).

———. "Understanding the 'Fear of Flying' Syndrome, II: Psychosomatic Aspects and Treatment." U.S. *Armed Forces Medical Journal,* vol. 5, no. 9 (1954).

Halliday, Jon. "A Secret War: U.S. and Soviet Air Forces Clashed Directly in Korea." *Far Eastern Economic Review,* 22 April 1993.

Jones, David. "Flying and Danger, Joy and Fear." *Aviation, Space, and Environmental Medicine,* vol. 57, no. 2 (February 1986).

Kozaczka, Felix. "Air War in Korea: VI. Enemy Bridging Techniques." *Air University Quarterly Review,* vol. 5, no. 4 (1954).

Lifton, Robert. "Psychotherapy with Combat Fliers." *U.S. Armed Forces Medical Journal,* vol. 4, no. 4 (April 1953).

Office of the Secretary of Defense. "Air War in Korea." *Air University Quarterly Review,* vol. 4, no. 2 (1953).

Potter, J. G. "Serge Looks at Today's Cadet." *Air Force Times,* 16 September 1950.

Proceedings of the symposium on "The History of War as Part of General History." Institute for Advanced Study. Princeton, N.J. *The Journal of Military History,* vol. 57, no. 5 (October 1993).

Rosenberg, Emily. " 'Foreign Affairs' after World War II." *Diplomatic History,* vol. 18, no. 1 (Winter 1994).

Schultz, H. A. "Fear of Flying." *USAF Medical Service Digest,* November 1952.

Strongin, Timothy. "A Historical Review of the Fear of Flying among Aircrewmen." *Aviation, Space, and Environmental Medicine,* vol. 58, no. 2 (1987).

Wallrich, William. "Bedcheck Charlie Flies Again." *Air Force,* vol. 36, no. 9 (September 1953).

IV. Books

Air Force Officer's Guide. 5th ed. Harrisburg, Pa.: Military Service Publishing Co., 1952.

Ambrose, Stephen. *Duty, Honor, Country: A History of West Point.* Baltimore: Johns Hopkins University Press, 1966.

Armitage, M. J., and R. A. Mason. *Air Power in the Nuclear Age.* 2d ed. Chicago: University of Chicago Press, 1985.

Blesse, Frederick. *Check Six: A Fighter Pilot Looks Back.* Mesa, Ariz.: Champlin Fighter Museum Press.

Clodfelter, Mark. *The Limits of Air Power: The American Bombing of North Vietnam.* New York: Free Press, 1989.

Cullum, George. *Biographical Register of the Officers and Graduates of the United States Military Academy.* Supplement, vol. 9, ed., Charles Branham. West Point, N.Y.: Association of Graduates, U.S. Military Academy, 1950.

Cumings, Bruce. *War and Television.* New York: Verso, 1991.

Cunliffe, Marcus. *Soldiers and Civilians: The Martial Spirit in America, 1775–1865.* London: Gregg Revivals, 1973.

Ellis, Joseph. *School for Soldiers: West Point and the Profession of Arms.* New York: Oxford University Press, 1974.

Evans, Douglas. *Sabre Jets over Korea: A Firsthand Account.* Blue Ridge Summit, Pa.: Tab Books, 1984.

Frisbee, John L., ed. *The Makers of the United States Air Force.* Washington, D.C.: Center for Air Force History, 1987.

Futrell, Robert F. *The United States Air Force in Korea, 1950–1953.* Rev. ed. Washington, D.C.: Center for Air Force History, 1983.

Gabreski, Francis, and Carl Molesworth. *Gabby: A Fighter Pilot's Life.* New York: Orion Books, 1991.

Gropman, Alan. *The Air Force Integrates, 1945–1964.* Washington, D.C.: Center for Air Force History, 1985.

Gross, Charles Joseph. *Prelude to the Total Force: The Air National Guard, 1943–1969.* Washington, D.C.: Center for Air Force History, 1985.

Hallion, Richard. *The Naval Air War in Korea.* Baltimore: Nautical and Aviation Publishing, 1986.

———. *Storm over Iraq.* Washington, D.C.: Smithsonian Institution Press, 1992.

Hastings, Max. *The Korean War.* New York: Simon and Schuster, 1987.

Hess, Dean. *Battle Hymn.* New York: McGraw-Hill, 1956.

Huntington, Samuel. *The Soldier and the State: The Theory and Politics of Civil-Military Relations.* Cambridge, Mass.: Belknap Press, 1957.

Jackson, Robert. *The Air War over Korea.* New York: Charles Scribner's Sons, 1973.

Janowitz, Morris. *The Professional Soldier: A Social and Political Portrait.* Glencoe, Ill.: Free Press, 1960.

Karsten, Peter. *The Naval Aristocracy: The Golden Age of Annapolis and the Emergence of Modern American Navalism.* New York: Free Press, 1972.

Knaack, Marcelle Size. *Post-World War II Fighters: 1945–1973.* Washington, D.C.: Center for Air Force History, 1986.

Linderman, Gerald. *The Mirror of War.* Ann Arbor: University of Michigan Press, 1974.

Mahurin, Walker. *Honest John.* New York: Putnam, 1962.

Marshall, S. L. A. *Men against Fire: The Problem of Battle Command in Future War.* New York: William Morrow, 1947.

Maslow, Abraham. *Religions, Values, and Peak Experiences.* Columbus: Ohio State University Press, 1964.

Mills, C. Wright. *The Power Elite.* New York: Oxford University Press, 1956.

Moore, Dermot, and Peter Bagshawe. *South Africa's Flying Cheetahs in Korea.* Johannesburg: Ashanti Publishing, 1991.

Nye, Roger. *The Patton Mind: The Professional Development of an Extraordinary Leader.* Garden City Park, N.Y.: Avery, 1993.

Olejniczak, Julian, ed. *1992 Register of Graduates and Former Cadets: United States Military Academy.* West Point, N.Y.: Association of Graduates, U.S. Military Academy, 1992.

Parkman, Francis. *Montcalm and Wolfe.* Vol. I. Boston: Little, Brown, 1924.

Perret, Geoffrey. *Winged Victory: The Army Air Forces in World War II.* New York: Random House, 1993.

Rees, David. *Korea: The Limited War.* New York: St. Martin's Press, 1964.

Rexford, Oscar Whitelaw. *Battlestars and Doughnuts: World War II Clubmobile Experiences of Mary Metcalfe Rexford.* St. Louis: Patrice Press, 1989.

Ribuffo, Leo. *Right Center Left.* New Brunswick, N.J.: Rutgers University Press, 1992.

Risner, Robinson. *The Passing of the Night: My Seven Years as a Prisoner of the North Vietnamese.* New York: Random House, 1973.

Salter, James. *The Hunters.* New York: Bantam, 1956.

Sandler, Stanley. *Segregated Skies: All-Black Combat Squadrons of WW II.* Washington, D.C.: Smithsonian Institution Press, 1992.

Schaffer, Ronald. *Wings of Judgment: American Bombing in World War II.* New York: Oxford University Press, 1986.

Shea, Nancy. *The Air Force Wife.* New York: Harper, 1951.

Sheldon, Walt. *Troubling of a Star.* Chicago: Sears Book Club, 1953.

Sherry, Michael. *The Rise of American Air Power: The Creation of Armageddon.* New Haven, Conn.: Yale University Press, 1987.

Spick, Mike. *The Ace Factor: Air Combat and the Role of Situational Awareness.* Annapolis, Md.: Naval Institute Press, 1988.

Stewart, James, ed. *Airpower: The Decisive Force in Korea.* New York: Arno, 1980.

Watry, Charles. *Washout: The Aviation Cadet Story.* Carlsbad: California Aero Press, 1983.

Wilcox, Robert. *Scream of Eagles: The Creation of Top Gun and the U. S. Air Victory in Vietnam.* New York: John Wiley and Sons, 1990.

Index